HOME PLAN DOCTOR

HOME PLAN DOCTOR

The Essential Companion for Anyone
Buying a Home Design Plan

LARRY W. GARNETT

Storey Publishing

The mission of Storey Publishing is to serve our customers by publishing practical information that encourages personal independence in harmony with the environment.

Edited by Nancy D. Wood and Deborah Balmuth

Art direction, cover and text design by Mary Winkelman Velgos
Text layout and production by Jennifer Jepson Smith
Cover and interior house plans and elevations by Larry W. Garnett
Home interior watercolors by Sandra LaMarche/McCarthy

Indexed by Mary McClintock

Printed in the United States by Walsworth Printing Company
10 9 8 7 6 5 4 3 2 1

Library of Congress Cataloging-in-Publication Data

Garnett, Larry W.
Home plan doctor : the essential companion for anyone buying a home design plan / Larry W. Garnett.
p. cm.
Includes index.
ISBN 978-1-58017-698-9 (pbk. : alk. paper)
1. Architecture, Domestic—Designs and plans. 2. Dwellings—Planning. I. Title.
NA7115.G37 2008
728'.37—dc22

2007030803

Dedication

To my wife, Debbie,
and our three sons: Grant, Matt, and Jeff

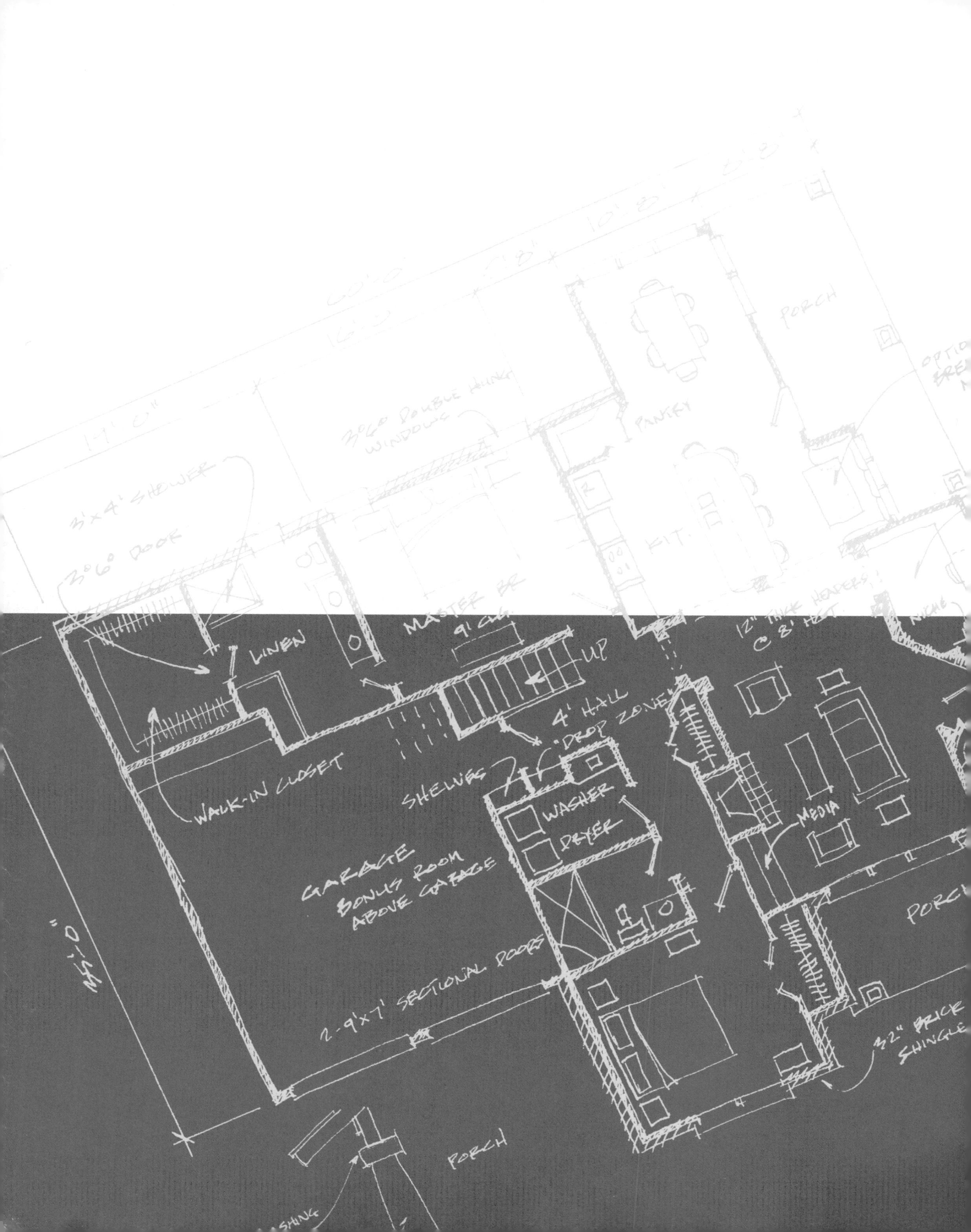

3'x4' SHOWER
3060 DOOR
3060 DOUBLE HUNG WINDOWS
PANTRY
PORCH
KIT
MASTER BR
LINEN
UP
4' HALL
DROP ZONE
12" THICK HEADERS @ 8' HGT
WALK-IN CLOSET
SHELVES
WASHER
DRYER
MEDIA
GARAGE
BONUS ROOM ABOVE GARAGE
2-9'x7' SECTIONAL DOORS
45'-0"
PORCH

Contents

Preface

As a result of spending more than thirty years helping clients design their homes, I have gained a tremendous appreciation for the challenges involved in creating and building an environment where we spend a great portion of our lives. What is it that makes a design successful? Why do some homes feel inviting and comfortable, while others seem cold and unwelcoming? This book has evolved out of a desire to help individuals understand more about the process of selecting a house plan and to offer some insights on various elements of design that can have enormous impacts on the ultimate satisfaction with the completed home.

Although housing must first be considered shelter, the environments we create play a major role in our daily lives. Not surprisingly, some of the features that ultimately contribute to a successful home design are those that might at first seem almost insignificant. Often we become so obsessed with creating an impressive exterior facade that we overlook such important concepts as storage and furniture placement. Can you imagine moving into your new home and finding that your master bedroom does not have a wall wide enough for your bed? Or that your family room with the expansive windows has a wonderful view of the lake but no place for a television? Unfortunately, these situations occur all too often.

My initial response to the publisher's suggestion that this book be called *Home Plan Doctor* was one of surprise and discomfort. However, as I spoke with the extremely talented and creative staff at Storey Publishing, I gradually became more receptive to this title. They had reviewed my material, discussed the basic premise of the book, and seemed genuinely convinced that, in essence, I was offering valuable and timely advice. In my effort to help people either create a new design or transform an existing one, I seemed to be a "doctor" for home plans. So, here I am, excited about the opportunity to help individuals and families create their perfect home plan!

— *Larry W. Garnett*

Introduction

Selecting a design for your new home should be an exciting and fulfilling experience. After all, you're about to make one of the most significant investments of your life, both financially and emotionally. Unfortunately, this enterprise all too often becomes a stressful ordeal in which overwhelming decisions must be made with surprisingly few resources to help guide you through the plan selection process.

Perhaps you've discovered an existing stock plan on the Internet. Or perhaps you're thinking about hiring a local design professional to help create your new home. Either of these paths will require you to understand construction documents and know exactly what they include. Since most stock plans will ultimately need some modifications (either the changes *you* want or those *required* by local building codes), the services of a local designer will probably still be necessary. Chapter 2 will provide important information about plan copyrights and the authorization required *before* you can make any modifications.

Whether you already have your property or are looking for the ideal site to build that plan you've been dreaming about for years, a number of critical decisions must be made. The information presented here will offer some answers and, perhaps even more important, inform you about which questions you'll need to ask your designer and builder.

Although many people begin their plan search by viewing exterior sketches, determining the right style for you is far less important than developing a house plan that takes full advantage of the building site. You'll be challenged with decisions about garage placement, window location, and the selection of various exterior materials.

While this book specifically addresses new construction, much of the information can be applied to remodeling your current home. For example, the pros and cons of various kitchen and bath designs involve the same considerations whether you're designing a new home or adding on to your present residence.

If you have difficulty understanding plans and visualizing how the home will actually look when built, you're definitely not alone! All too often those of us in the design profession assume that everyone can understand the terminology and graphic representation we provide. Unfortunately, the plans that many people believe will result in their dream home can fall far short of their expectations. While the blame may be placed on defects inherent in the design itself, more often than not the disappointment is due to the homeowner's misunderstanding of the design.

Throughout the book, tips on how to visualize and interpret a plan will be discussed. Since the information is intended to present realistic solutions, examples have been taken from readily available home designs. Thus, pointers on interior design elements such as traffic patterns and privacy will be analyzed using existing stock plans. As the "Plan Doctor," I'll indicate ways to modify these sample plans, while also providing tools and information to help improve the designs you're considering.

An in-depth discussion about square footage will provide some surprises in the way it's calculated and its relationship to the ultimate cost of your home. For instance, successful design ultimately has very little to do with square footage. In other words, merely enlarging a home rarely improves the essence of the design. In fact, rooms can become so large that they lose any sense of coziness and comfort. The introduction of open-concept floor plans a few years ago resulted in houses that seemed larger than their actual square footage. However, caution must be taken to prevent the total loss of privacy, and we'll discuss the steps necessary to do so.

The following chapters will guide you through the adventure of creating your new house plan. Some of the information will be familiar. Other information might provoke questions. I hope that the majority of the material will help you create a plan that addresses the specific needs and unique personality of your family, with the end result being a house that you will proudly call *home*.

Part One

Making Plans

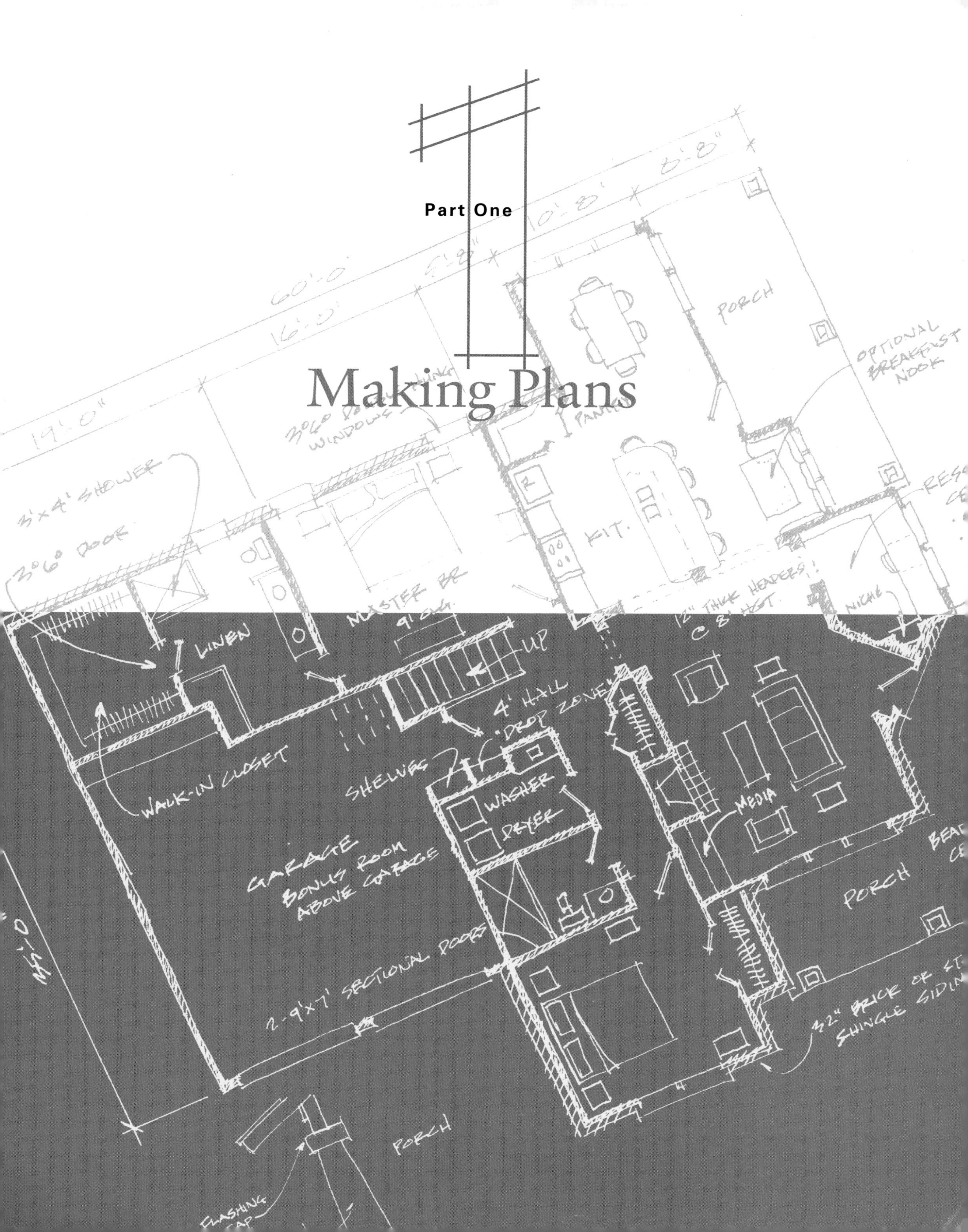

1

What Comes First?

What do you start with, the house plan or the building site? Ideally, the site comes first. With an understanding of various existing conditions — such as views, orientation towards the sun, and neighboring houses — the plan you either select or have custom-designed can take advantage of positive aspects of the property and ignore the negatives. On the other hand, if you have a plan that has been your "dream home" for years and years, you will be faced with the challenge of finding an appropriate building site for it.

Each of these situations will probably require some compromises. For example, say your dream home plan has expansive windows that your building site dictates must face west, toward the harsh afternoon sunlight. In this case you might consider revising the plan or at least adjusting the placement of the house on the lot. Or if the site slopes dramatically, you may want to revise the plan to accommodate this feature, perhaps with a walkout basement.

You Already Have the Property

If you did not receive a survey of the property at the time you purchased it, make arrangements to have one completed. The typical survey will include property boundaries and dimensions, along with such information as utility easements. You may also want to consider asking the surveyor to provide a tree location drawing so that you can place the home in a location that preserves specific trees. Be sure to specify the caliper (diameter) and species of the trees to be located. Don't make the common mistake of specifying the size only. You could call for the surveyor to note all trees 3½ inches and above and end up missing some 2-inch hardwoods that would eventually make wonderful shade trees.

If the property is located in any type of planned development or subdivision, you will also need to verify any *setback requirements*. These are the minimum (and sometimes maximum) distances your home can be located from the street and the side and rear property boundaries. In rural areas, such restrictions often do not exist. However, it's a good idea to verify this with local or county officials.

Next, you should review any *deed restrictions* that affect your property. These restrictions, outlined in the deed to your property, detail requirements regarding the construction of your home and perhaps the landscaping and future maintenance. While deed restrictions vary, one of the most common involves the overall height and square footage of the home. Such restrictions usually exist in order to maintain views throughout the development and to keep individual homes from being built that overwhelm their neighbors. Roof pitches (slopes) are another typical consideration; often both minimum and maximum pitches will be specified. And in recent years many developments have become extremely rigid regarding exterior styles they deem acceptable.

Do Your Homework

Some developments provide intricately detailed manuals specifying the type of homes they consider worthy of being built in their neighborhood. Review the pertinent information, including deed restrictions and architectural codes, very carefully. In fact, you may want to consult a real estate attorney if you have any questions. Then it's a good idea to submit a preliminary design from your architect or designer to the governing board of your development. If you're considering a stock plan or a conceptual design, show the floor plan and front rendering to the officials *before* you actually purchase the plan. In some cases you may need to make certain revisions to the plan before it will be accepted.

Some of the newest developments may require conformity for windows, doors, and exterior materials such as roofing and siding. While these restrictions might seem extreme, they're designed to protect the integrity of the neighborhood — and your personal investment.

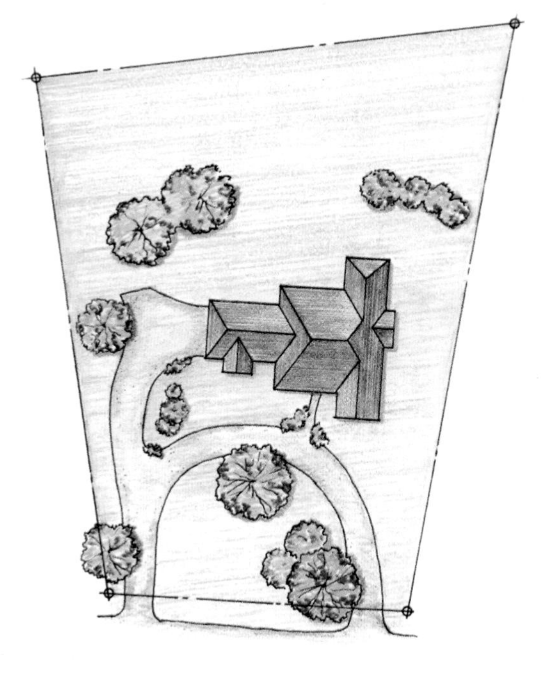

Review the site plan. Although it doesn't show the slope of the land, a site plan can give you a quick overview of how your house will be positioned on your property.

Spend some time visiting the site. Learn where the sun rises each morning and sets in the afternoon, remembering that this pattern can change rather dramatically from one season to the next. Consider various opportunities for the placement of the home, taking into account any special views that may exist. You'll probably want to save as many trees as possible, and often just a slight adjustment in the location of the house can save several trees. But don't be tempted to save a tree that will be extremely close to your home. Chances are that it will not survive the stress of construction, and removing a tree in close proximity to your house after it's built can be a dangerous and expensive task. You may want to consult with a landscape specialist to help you consider the possibilities and avoid such costly mistakes.

For property where the prime building site appears to be on a hill or elevated area, take some extra time to evaluate all the options. Many architects will suggest that you resist the urge to locate your home at the very top of the property. This is often excellent advice. Building a home at the very peak of a hill pits a man-made structure against nature. And, as we all know, nature always wins! Also, proper site selection should take into consideration not only the views *from* the home but also the views *of* the home. Placing the house at the highest point of the site often gives it a foreboding appearance. Recall some of the horror movies you've seen: the haunted house usually sits all alone at the top of the hill.

However, a general statement like this cannot apply to every situation. Each site offers unique opportunities. Your property, for example, may have a magnificent 360-degree view that exists only at the top of the hill.

The more time you're able to spend at the site, the better prepared you'll be to make the final decision regarding house placement. Always consider *all* of your options. Listen carefully to your design consultants. Review all of the information. And make your *own* final decision! As long as you make an informed choice, your decision will be the correct one for you and your family.

You Already Have the Plan

You're ready to build your dream house from a plan that's been tacked on your bulletin board for years. Now you need to find a site. Recently I was at a home and garden show where a couple approached me with a plan I had designed years ago. They enthusiastically informed me that this had been their dream home for over ten years, and now they finally were able to build. The tattered page had notes and changes they obviously had spent hours considering. After reviewing some of these revisions with them, I asked about their building site. To their credit, they had searched for over a year to find property that allowed the plan to be situated just right.

Purchasing the Plans Shown in This Book

Since my intent is to present realistic solutions to home planning challenges, all of the examples in this book have been taken from readily available home designs. The plan numbers referenced in the Conceptual Plan Index *(see page 208)* identify home plans that can be seen and purchased on the Web site www.homeplandoctor.com. As with any plans you may find in books and magazines, you can look all you want for free. However, if you decide to use a plan to build a house, you will need to buy it. (Read about copyright issues in chapter 2.)

Unfortunately, this is not always the scenario people face when they have their hearts set on a particular plan. Often they find their building site to be the wrong shape or size for their design. Sometimes the plan simply doesn't take advantage of the property's views and topography. Thankfully, adjustments usually can be made. For example, if the house is too wide, revising the garage location may provide an easy solution.

However, sometimes a plan just shouldn't be built on a particular site. The decision to dispose of your dream house design obviously is an emotional one. Here's a compromise: Show your plan to a local design professional. Spend some time discussing all the features that attracted you to the design in the first place. Chances are that the designer will be able to include these elements in a new design that also addresses the unique challenges and opportunities presented by your property.

Future Considerations

In the not-so-distant past, those fortunate enough to own a home stayed there for years. Perhaps they added on a family room or remodeled their kitchen. But most remained in this house until they retired or their work transferred them to another town. Contrast this scenario with that of the current generation of homeowners, who buy their homes at an early age and then begin the process of "flipping" the first house, making a substantial profit, and buying a bigger place.

Even though housing is essentially *shelter,* it has an immense effect on our daily lives. Only in recent times has our home been considered a financial investment that we treat like a stock. Traditionally the investment was more of an emotional one — a place to raise our family — and we hoped to pay off the mortgage before retirement.

Here's the unfortunate by-product of this change in perspective: housing, like so many other items, has become "disposable." I met with a young couple a few years ago to help them decide whether they wanted to design and build a new home or purchase a

Design Diagnosis

Adjust your plan to fit the site

If the home of your dreams is too wide for your property, you may be able to make some simple revisions instead of finding a completely new plan. Opening the garage doors to the front (A) instead of the side (B) can save at least 25 feet of lot width.

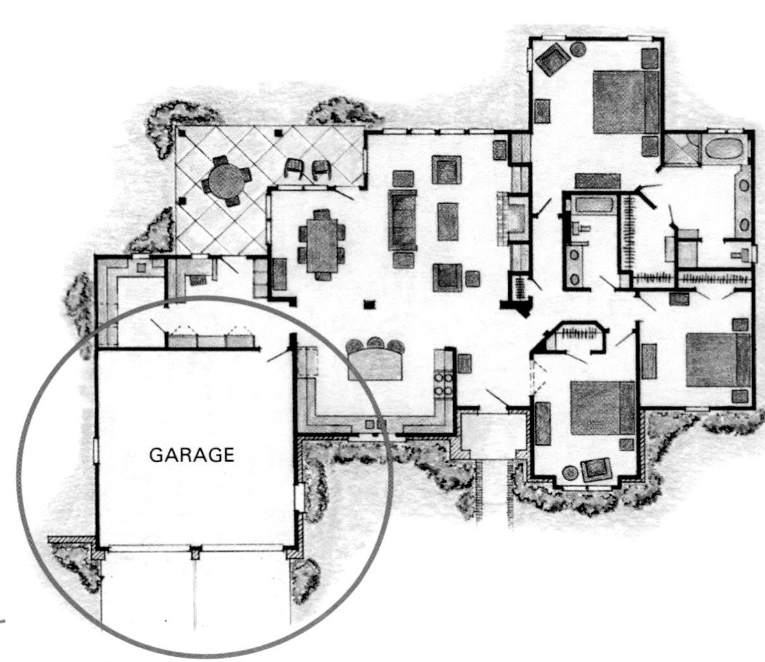

Ⓐ GARAGE DOORS OPEN TO THE FRONT

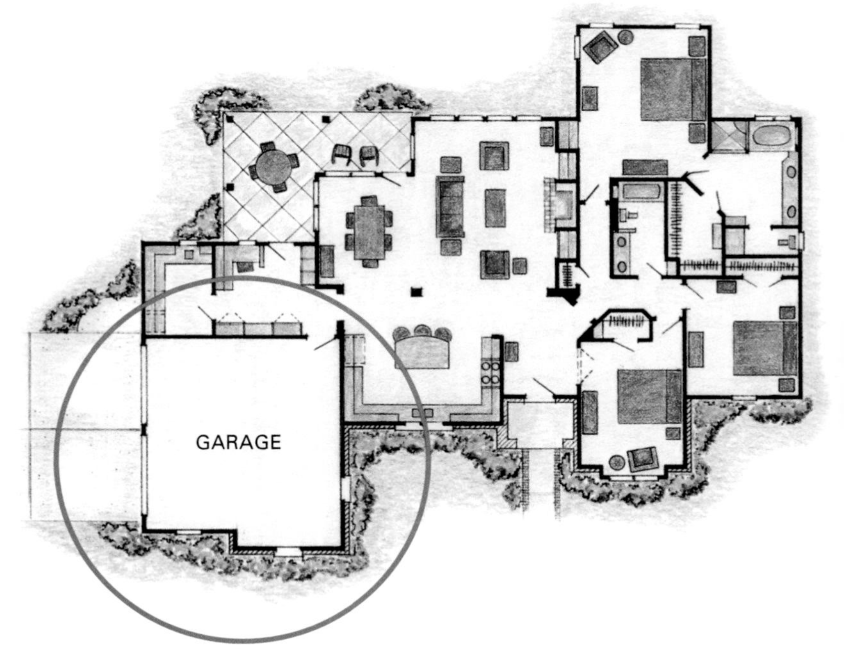

Ⓑ GARAGE DOORS OPEN TO THE SIDE

"cookie cutter" house (their description, not mine!) in a subdivision where every fourth house looks identical. Since they were seeking my opinion, I pointed out some of the inferior craftsmanship and materials of the subdivision house, explaining that the home would probably not age very well. I'll never forget the young wife's response: "Oh, that doesn't matter. We'll only be here for a couple of years. Then we'll sell, and with the profit we'll build the home we really want."

Of course there's nothing wrong with making a wise investment. But I believe this attitude of thinking of housing as disposable has been at least partially responsible for the proliferation of unattractive and substandard construction over the past few years. We've created massive numbers of sprawling developments full of houses that likely will not be worth refurbishing in years to come. Unlike many older homes, some of these new homes just simply do not have very good "bones."

Nevertheless, there's room for optimism! Pick up any newspaper or magazine and you'll find numerous articles on building green and other energy conservation concerns. Turn on the television and you'll see dozens of programs full of wonderful design ideas. Never before have so many people been so concerned about their homes. Sure, there's still a large number thinking about how they can flip their home and trade up for a larger one. But more importantly, an ever-increasing number are demanding energy efficiency and excellent design.

Green Options

For various reasons, a certain segment of the market has the inaccurate impression that the green building movement originated with baby boomer hippies who would have us all living in geodesic domes waiting for another Woodstock concert. On the contrary, this practical approach to design and building presents a sensible balance between a respect for our environment and thoughtful design principles. Using recycled materials such as glass to fabricate strikingly beautiful countertops and devising systems to collect rainwater offer a glimpse of what this movement is all about. Careful attention to the way a home sits on the site becomes as important as selecting nontoxic materials.

In a perfect situation, everyone would be morally motivated to show concern for our environment. However, the realist in me says that most will pay attention when they see cost savings and increased comfort. So, do your research, and keep an open mind. The future, in this case, is definitely already here.

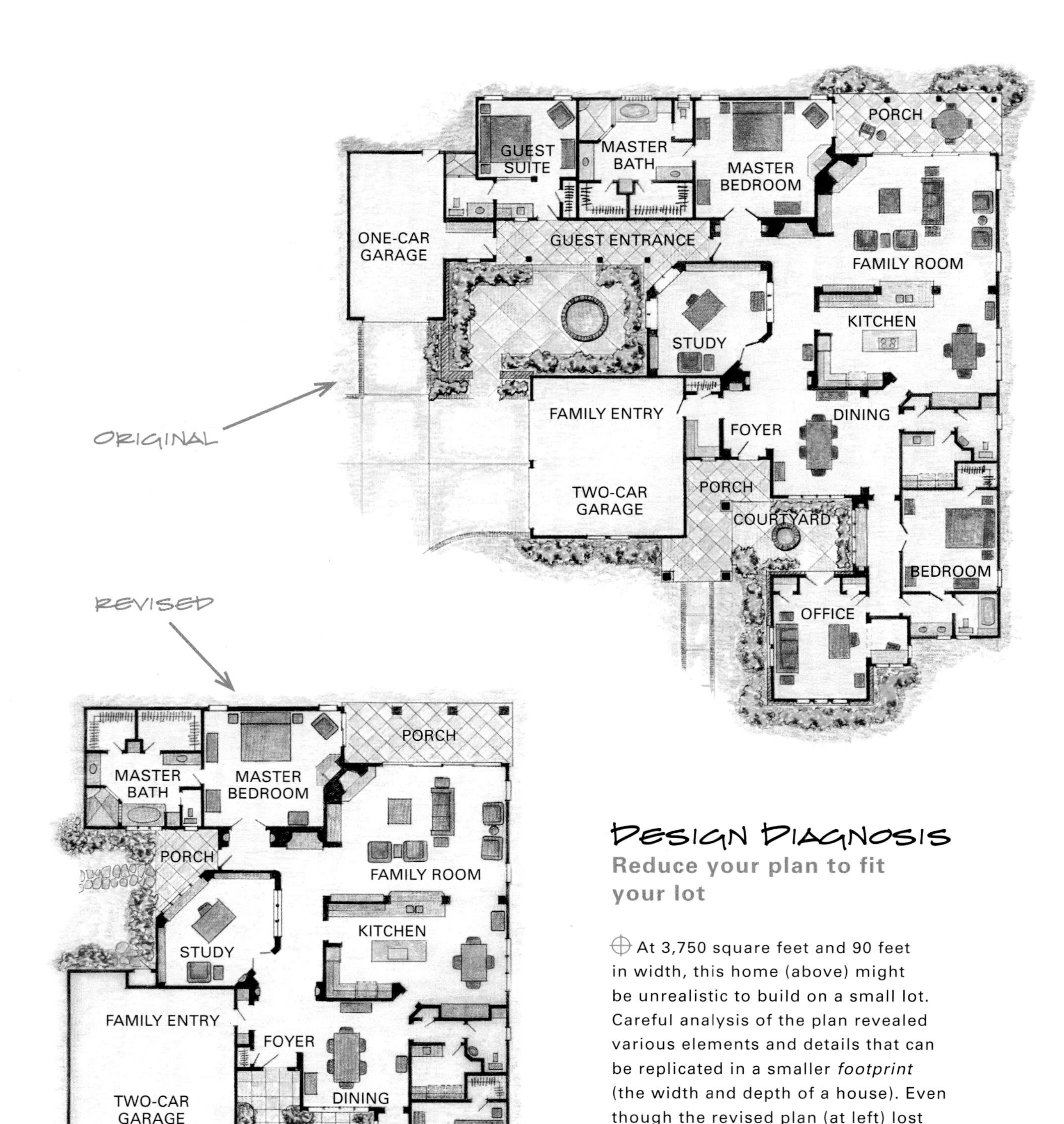

Design Diagnosis

Reduce your plan to fit your lot

At 3,750 square feet and 90 feet in width, this home (above) might be unrealistic to build on a small lot. Careful analysis of the plan revealed various elements and details that can be replicated in a smaller *footprint* (the width and depth of a house). Even though the revised plan (at left) lost 500 square feet and 30 feet in width (essentially the guest suite/entrance and the one-car garage, with a smaller family entry), the essence of the design remains intact.

Traditional Neighborhoods

Many new developments have been designed to take advantage of land-use patterns that evolved generations ago. Commonly referred to as traditional neighborhood developments (TNDs), these neighborhoods utilize patterns of development found in older sections of cities and towns throughout the country. In its most simple form, a TND might be defined as a pedestrian-friendly development where people can become less dependent on automobiles. By strategically locating residential and commercial zones within walking distance of one another, the overall pattern of the area begins to emphasize people instead of cars. Typically these areas are characterized by a diversity of housing styles and sizes, a strong neighborhood identity, and a true sense of place.

A Small Town Feel

If you've ever visited a small town with shops arranged around a downtown square, you've seen the basic inspiration for these new towns. Often even the idea of people living above their store has reemerged. Single-family and multifamily houses, along with churches and offices, can be found within a short walk of downtown.

Furthermore, the mix of housing is contrary to what we've seen recently. In most new developments the housing is segregated by price. Small starter homes are never placed anywhere close to luxurious executive mini-mansions. In fact, brick walls and gates often ensure that the residents of one area can't invade the other. (Which group is being protected from the other is a subject open to debate!) Yet if you travel through desirable older neighborhoods all across the country, you'll often find small cottages on the same street as larger, more stately homes. In many new TNDs this mix of housing once again exists. The result: an amazing neighborhood with a delightful diversity of architecture.

The sheer number of TNDs either built or in various stages of planning and construction has steadily increased over the past few years. Although most of these inspired subdivisions lack a commercial center for residents to walk to, an emphasis on pedestrian-friendly design can nonetheless be found. Narrow streets (that prevent high-speed traffic), front sidewalks, rear alleys, and front porches encourage people to interact with their neighbors. And some of these new towns have influenced the design of individual homes in many typical subdivisions.

The TND movement has inspired many design professionals to become more aware of time-tested design principles such as scale and proportion *(see chapter 3)*. While certain aspects of these design principles continue to be debated, the overall results are proving to be quite successful. Perhaps instead of the vast oceans of monotonous houses so prevalent in recent years, we'll begin to see more neighborhoods of reasonable scale and diversity.

Of course, one of the greatest challenges in any new housing solution is always transportation. An emerging concept for new developments is that of the transit-oriented development (TOD). These compact new communities are located adjacent to high-quality train systems, have a design philosophy similar to that of TNDs, and provide another alternative to suburban sprawl. They offer a walkable urban-style environment with high-density housing and less automobile traffic.

Cater to the pedestrians. Emphasize a pedestrian-friendly environment by placing the garage at the back of the house along an alley. A front porch generates the welcoming feeling of a neighborhood oriented more toward people than automobiles.

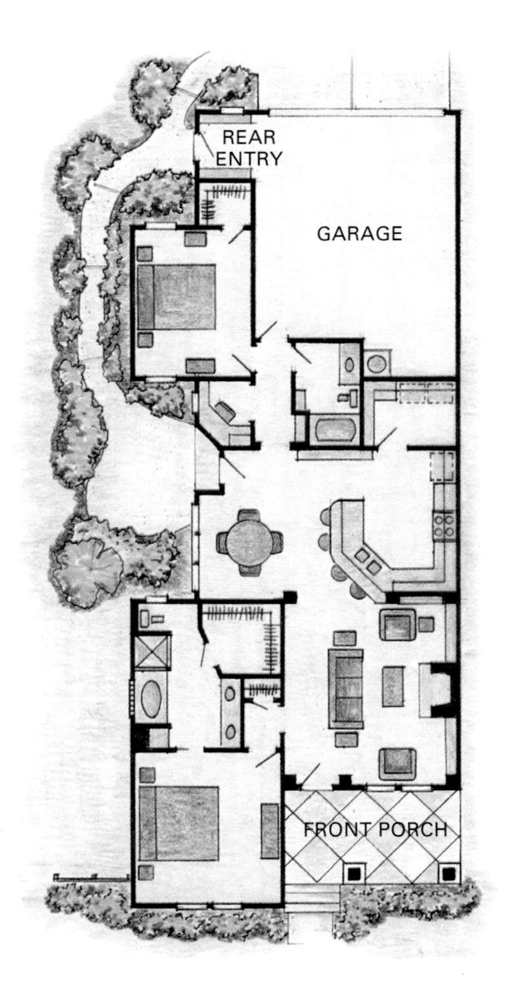

TERMS TO KNOW

Building Green. This refers to using building resources and material in a more efficient way. Also often referred to as *sustainable building*, the concept goes far beyond the selection of materials. It now encompasses more of an overall lifestyle philosophy, which includes building homes that conserve water and energy.

LEED. This is an acronym for "Leadership in Energy and Environmental Design," which is a voluntary national standard for developing green construction techniques.

Problem Solving

In general, suburban sprawl has promoted the construction of larger houses on oversized lots, with little regard for design integrity, privacy, or access to any form of transportation other than automobiles. While certain exceptions can be found, a large portion of this tremendous growth in outlying areas has resulted in developments that force us to spend an enormous amount of time in our cars with little opportunity for social interaction with our neighbors. Some segments of the media would have you believe that there's now a huge countermovement toward higher-density development and smaller homes. However, as with most rumored trends, the reality is much more complex.

In the past density related only to economics. In order to keep housing costs low, more units had to be built per acre. In recent years another benefit emerged: people discovered that well-planned, higher-density neighborhoods provide less maintenance and more convenience. In fact, when designed properly, many higher-density developments offer more privacy than the standard subdivision. Higher-density living, especially when in close proximity to entertainment and the workplace, has become extremely desirable. Due to ever-increasing energy costs this trend is likely to continue growing.

A certain number of homebuyers seem intrigued with the idea of *downsizing* their next home, perhaps because their children have left home or because they simply desire less square footage to maintain. Quite often, however, instead of downsizing, many actually end up *resizing*. In other words, the square footage of their home is not reduced by much. Rather, the overall design changes in proportion and layout. For example, a home with two bedrooms, a study, and a large combination kitchen–family–dining area might replace an existing four-bedroom home with formal living and dining rooms. The overall size, however, might not be much different.

Planning for Diversity

For some, a plan for a resized home in a planned development with such amenities as a golf course seems perfect. Others may want a similar plan but a location away from the city, perhaps on a lake or in a rural setting with several acres of land. Still others may want a completely different plan.

The diversity of our country will always dictate that no single solution to housing design and town development will satisfy everyone. Although some of these new concepts have tremendous appeal for many, they're simply not for everyone. It seems we're all prone to making design assumptions based on our personal situations and our local environment. Some of us grew up in suburbia, some in rural areas, and some in urban areas.

While many developed areas can seem almost identical due to the proliferation of common retail franchises, we still see substantial regional differences. I'm constantly reminded of this diversity when I travel. For example, the wonderful architectural heritage of the East Coast simply doesn't exist in all parts of the country. My point is this: While the design and analysis of individual houses and entire developments certainly remains critical to the well-being of our society, we must always respect the very diversity that makes this country so amazing.

As with all aspects of our lives, we must take the time to access adequate information so we can make informed choices. There's no right or wrong in regard to home design. A home plan becomes wrong only if you misunderstand an idea or concept and must live with results that don't address your personal preferences and requirements. The challenge of creating a home for your family and selecting the neighborhood or town where it will be built certainly does seem overwhelming at times. I hope that this book will offer you some assistance in this endeavor. At the very least, I trust it will inspire you to ask even more questions and ultimately find the answers you need to create the right home for you and your family.

Frequently Asked Questions

Ⓠ *Is the orientation of my lot really that important?*

Ⓐ Orientation is important. Unfortunately, lot orientation in most planned developments has more to do with the number of lots than with the ideal direction each property might face. Typically, a site that has a north–south alignment proves better than one with an east–west exposure. Obviously, not every lot can have this desired situation. But if you take the time to determine the exposure on your chosen lot, you can adapt a home plan to make the most of it. For example, you can try to find a design that has a minimum number of windows facing to the west. You probably will still want windows and doors opening to your backyard even if they face directly into the intense afternoon sun. In this case, you might consider adding or extending a covered porch to help shade the windows.

Ⓠ *What questions should I ask if my lot adjoins a golf course?*

Ⓐ If you are considering purchasing property that adjoins a golf course, you are obviously paying a significant premium to view the golf course. Nevertheless, be aware of various restrictions that may be specific to your property. For instance, will you be allowed to construct a fence? If so, it will most likely be restricted to some type of wrought iron that will not obstruct the view. However, some developments prohibit any type of fencing along the golf course. That could present a serious problem if you have pets or small children. Finally, the distinct possibility of golf balls landing in your yard and quite possibly smashing your expensive windows always exists!

Ⓠ *What should I know about property zoning where I intend to build?*

Ⓐ Zoning essentially refers to the ways in which land may be used. Some property is zoned for commercial buildings, while other parcels are restricted to residential development. Residential zoning may be further broken down into single-family and multifamily areas. Check with your local planning office and request a map that outlines designated residential, commercial, and industrial areas. Also be aware of the density allowed in residential zones. This will indicate where individual homes can be built and also where higher-density apartments and townhouses may be allowed.

Ⓠ *I'm looking at a lot in a planned development with a lot of deed restrictions. Can my development authority really dictate what color I paint my house?*

Ⓐ Absolutely! In fact, some development deed restrictions control everything from the color and type of window coverings to the flowers you can plant in your front yard. You may be required to use a certain type and color of trash receptacle, and your future NBA star's basketball hoop may not be allowed in your driveway. While such rigid restrictions have been designed to protect your property value, you certainly want to investigate the specifics before you purchase your property.

2

Finding a House Plan

Later in the book we'll discuss various ways you can analyze your family's needs and utilize certain guidelines to help you select the right design. However, let's begin by looking at the various sources available for obtaining home plans. We'll discuss three options:

- You can contact a local design professional for a custom design
- You can search for a predesigned or stock plan, either on the Internet or in magazines and books.
- You can obtain a conceptual design, a relatively new option that involves selecting a preliminary concept for a home design that you intend to modify to your specific needs and circumstances. *(See page 27.)*

Local Design Professionals

Working with a local designer or architect on a custom design can be both an exciting and a sometimes intimidating experience. For some, it offers the ultimate opportunity to create a home that addresses their needs and takes advantage of the building site. Be prepared to spend anywhere from 4 to 15 percent of the total construction cost for a custom-designed set of plans. In other words, for a $150,000 home, expect to pay from $6,000 to $22,500. While this may seem extreme, understand that the designer or architect will be developing a completely new design. He or she will spend a substantial number of hours meeting with you and preparing sketches before the actual construction drawings (blueprints) are even started. It's not unusual for the entire process to take from three months to a year.

Keep in mind that even if you decide to select a stock plan or a conceptual plan, the services of a local design professional may still be required to revise the plans so that they comply with local codes and construction techniques.

Selecting the Right Designer

You might be surprised to learn that there are three different types of design firms that create home plans: architectural, building design, and drafting services. Each offers various levels of service, expertise, and fees.

- ***Architects.*** Architects spend five to six years in college, complete three years of internship, and must successfully pass an exam in order to become licensed. To maintain this status, they must complete continuing education courses each year. Licensed architects may become members of the American Institute of Architects (AIA). While an architect must be licensed to join the AIA, membership does not necessarily mean they have more qualifications than a nonmember. The title of Fellow of the AIA (FAIA) is a highly regarded honor granted to a small number of AIA members who have made outstanding contributions to the architectural profession. *(See* Resources.*)*
- ***Building designers.*** Acquiring the status of a CPBD (Certified Professional Building Designer) requires five to six years of education and professional experience, along with the successful completion of a comprehensive exam. Continuing educational credits must be earned each year to maintain this status. Certified designers may become members of the American Institute of Building Design (AIBD). Once again, membership does not always mean a designer has more qualifications than a nonmember. An FAIBD designer has received the prestigious honor of being named a Fellow of the American Institute of Building Design. *(See* Resources.*)*
- ***Drafting services.*** These services are usually run by individuals who have practical experience in computer-aided design (CAD); many have also obtained undergraduate degrees in drafting and design.

Residential design, like various other professions, is practiced by individuals who may or may not be licensed by a recognized certification program. While having letters following his or her name does not necessarily guarantee a designer's qualifications, such certification does indicate certain levels of experience and education. A designer or architect's ability to create exceptional designs must be combined with an understanding of the construction process. Experience gained from working with builders and contractors allows a design professional to prepare drawings and details that will successfully communicate exactly how the home should be built.

Of course, deciding to work with a local designer or architect will involve a substantial commitment of time, energy, and money. Nevertheless, this might end up being the best investment you can make. After all, when you consider the magnitude of your decision to build a home, the design certainly becomes a critical element. I often remind clients of the obvious: the home they intend to build can only be as successful as the design itself!

Before You Meet with a Designer

What preparations should you make prior to meeting with a designer? For design professionals to create a plan that truly addresses the vision you have of your dream home, they must first understand your vision. It's worth emphasizing that this is, after all, *your* vision! Unfortunately, some designers and architects may see your project as a chance to express *their* creative abilities, paying little attention to what *you* want in your home. Designers should always remember that the creation of a plan for their client is truly a joint venture. Their mindset has to be focused on the idea that you will work together in the creation of your home.

During your initial interview with a designer, listen carefully to his or her responses as you explain your concerns and desires. While it may sound overly simple, the designer's use of the word "I" instead of "we" as he or she talks about the proposed design may be a cause for concern.

In an ideal world you would be able to draw the plans for your own home. Let's face it; you probably have at least a basic idea of what you want. Who better to create the design for your home? However, the fact remains that just as you would consult a doctor, an attorney, or an auto repair expert for the appropriate matters, so should you consult a design professional. Even if you possessed the training and skills to draw your own plans, you might find it extremely difficult to remain objective.

Fortunately, most designers and architects enjoy the challenge of taking a client's requirements and dreams and turning them into reality. Their creative instincts become satisfied by successfully designing a home that addresses their client's vision. I know most of my associates in the field of residential design would agree that walking through clients' completed homes — as they express heartfelt gratitude for the creation of their dream homes — never ceases to make the entire process a delightful journey.

So, how does this creative process actually work? It begins with the designer's clear understanding of your desires and, perhaps even more important, your *personal tastes.* This involves asking you to share the various pictures and ideas you've undoubtedly been

WHAT TO ASK

The selection of an individual or firm to design your home is a critical yet difficult decision. Following are several questions to ask in order to make an informed decision:

- **What experience does the firm have with residential design?** While this may seem like an absurd question, many design firms consider home design secondary to their commercial design business.
- **How much time will be devoted to preliminary design sketches?** It helps to understand the design process. The early steps in creating a new design from scratch or revising an existing plan become extremely critical. This is the point where you should see multiple solutions presented and have the chance to ask questions and make changes. Are there limitations on the number of preliminary sketches and ideas that will be studied? At what stages of the drawing process will you be able to review the plans? Generally you should at least be entitled to review the preliminary plans twice and the final construction documents once before the process is completed.
- **Are references and samples of the firm's work easily available?** Ask to see preliminary sketches and completed drawings of other projects. Also obtain a list of builders and individual clients that you can contact for references.

collecting for years. In fact, another clue that a designer may have his or her own agenda is if he or she *doesn't* want to see these items.

Organize Your Thoughts

Try to organize your information prior to your first meeting with the designer. The Design Criteria form found in the appendix might help you with this task. This form can be photocopied (or downloaded from www.homeplandoctor.com) and used as an outline for pertinent information your designer or architect will need to begin the process of designing your home.

Put together a notebook or a series of folders with sections labeled "kitchen ideas," "family rooms," and so forth. Be sure to find some exteriors that you find appealing. If a client shows me several pictures of various rooms and exteriors, invariably a common theme emerges. In other words, I can begin to understand my client's personal tastes. Three or four pictures of each area should be sufficient. Frankly, more than that might begin to confuse both you and your designer. As I always explain to my clients, creating a successful design ultimately depends on how precisely I can "read their mind" and fully understand the vision they have for their new home.

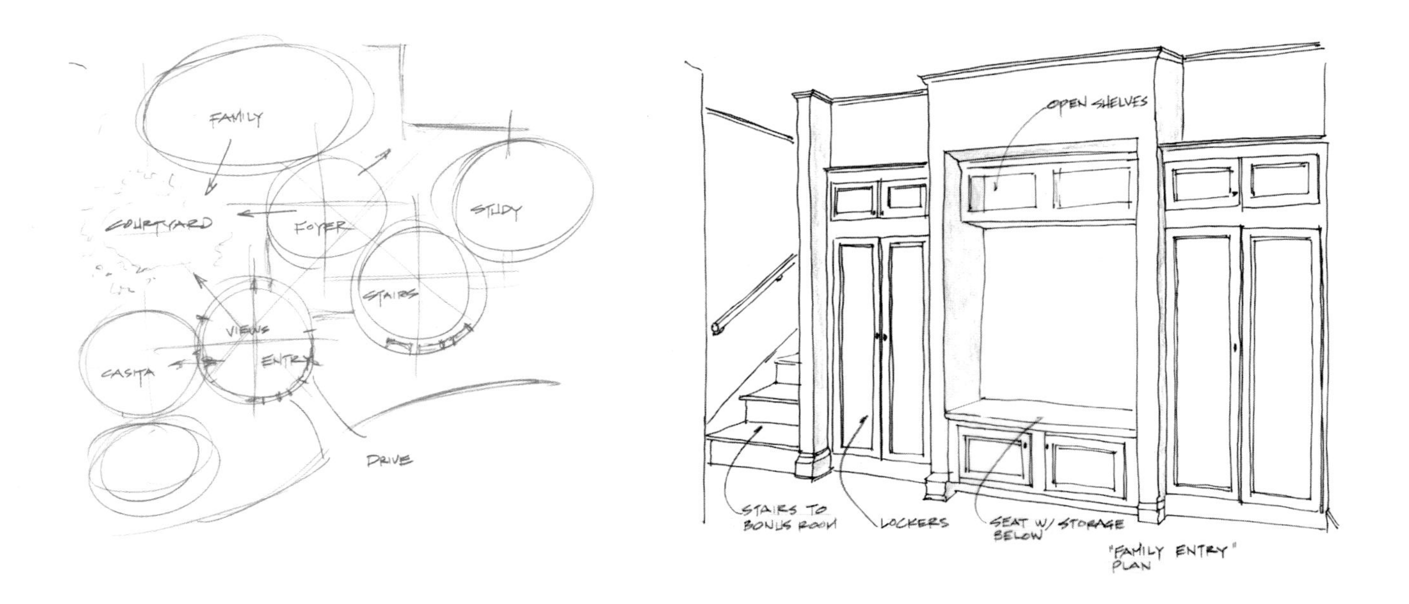

Bubble diagrams. Merely a series of circles, these diagrams show the relationship of various rooms and a general orientation on the site.

Interior sketches. During early stages your design professional may present sketches like this one to help communicate certain details of the proposed design.

Also, make notes about the most important aspects of the design. I often suggest that clients keep a notepad handy in the kitchen so they can jot down thoughts and ideas as they occur. Sometimes prioritizing this list can be valuable. Invariably budget constraints will require some items to be eliminated. It will be helpful for everyone to know from the beginning where you may be willing to make adjustments.

If you have specific ideas about such items as kitchen appliances, flooring, and lighting, go ahead and mention these in the early stages of your conferences. While there will be plenty of opportunities to make changes, this information can often be extremely helpful to your designer. Also mention any special or unique pieces of furniture you intend to use in your new home. Unfortunately, people often begin moving into their completed home only to discover there's absolutely no place for the cherished armoire that's been in the family for years. Prepare for your designer a list of each piece of furniture, including the dimensions of each; a photograph of each item with its size noted on the back works even better. While this involves some extra time and effort, the fact that you'll have a place for everything on move-in day will be the reward.

Schematics. Now you'll begin to see more definite room shapes and sizes. The placement of furniture (sketched below) will help you comprehend the actual room sizes. The exterior design begins to take shape during this stage as well.

Keep an Open Mind

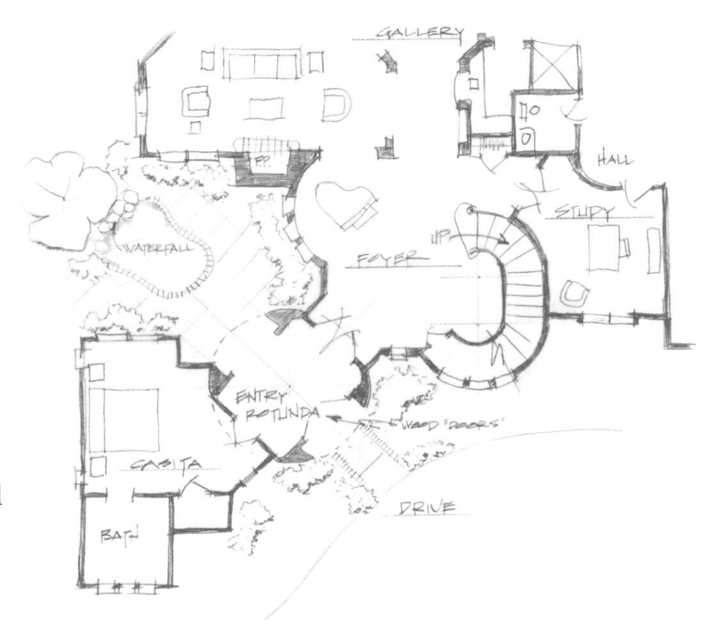

Although we've established that this is *your* home and the design must be based on *your* criteria, remember this: you should always carefully consider any feedback you receive from your designer. Since you're placing an amazing amount of trust in this individual, you must also trust his or her judgment on many design issues. I always find it best if clients do not try to sketch what they think the plan should be. If you've devoted a great deal of effort toward creating your floor plan, you'll likely have a difficult time viewing any floor plan ideas I will present to you. I think it's just human nature to react this way. You'll be more open-minded if you don't have a preconceived floor plan in the back of your mind. In my experience, the most successful home designs result from the designer paying close attention to the conversations and material the clients share and then translating that information into an exciting yet functional plan.

All designers have unique procedures they follow in their development of a home design. Essentially they will all begin with some quick sketches. These may be referred to as *schematics*, *bubble diagrams*, or *partis* (par-tees). Though these sketches may look more like scribbles to you, the thought processes behind them may consume hours, and they are an important part of the design process.

In these early stages of the design development, don't hesitate to ask questions. Design professionals may mistakenly assume that you understand all of the terminology they use and details they employ. Absolutely no question you have should be ignored.

The greatest challenge in this entire process can be the successful communication of the designer's ideas. Once again, each designer approaches this challenge in various ways. Some may use elaborate computer-generated renderings, while others will use hand-drawn sketches and verbal descriptions to help you visualize their design proposals.

In the end you will be forced to place a great deal of faith in the ability of your designer. Regardless of how elaborate or detailed the renderings or models might be, the designer remains the only person who can accurately comprehend how the completed home will appear. Certainly this is a sobering statement, and this realization often prevents people from following through with the process of custom-designing their home. If you decide to pursue this path, be prepared to invest not only the additional dollars but also the necessary amount of time. While I firmly believe the custom-designed home is the best way to approach perfection, I'm also the first to admit that this option does not work for everyone. For many people the opportunity to leisurely browse through hundreds of existing stock plans is a much more attractive option.

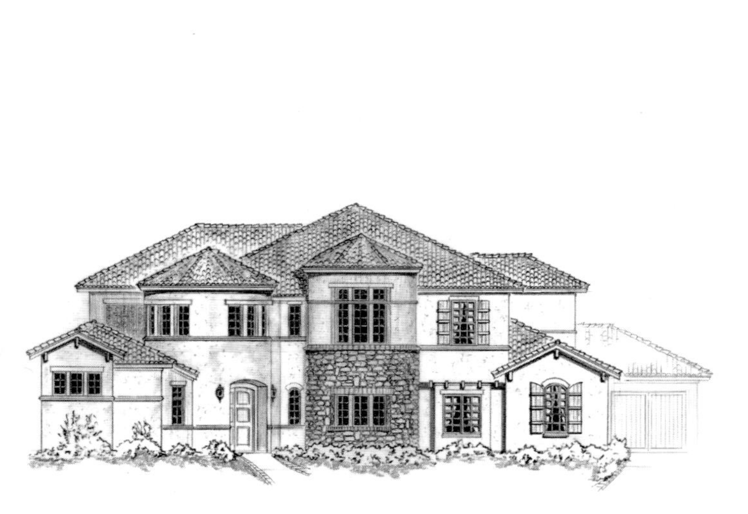

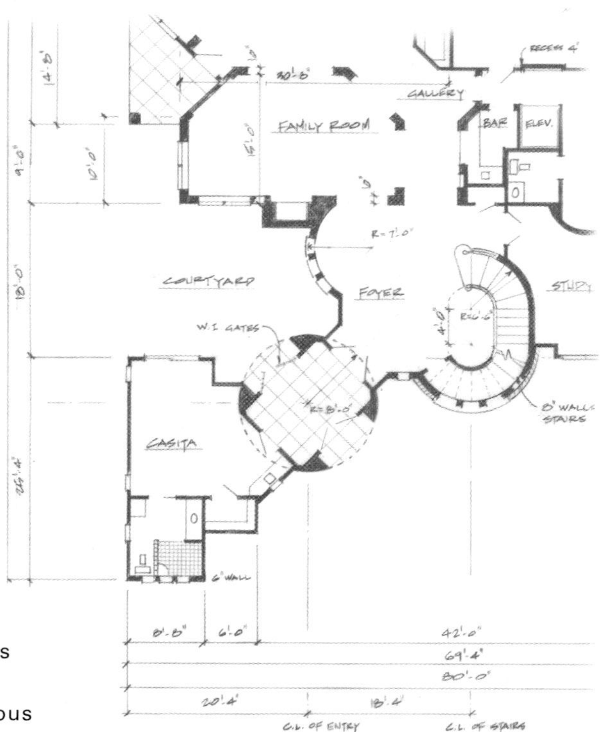

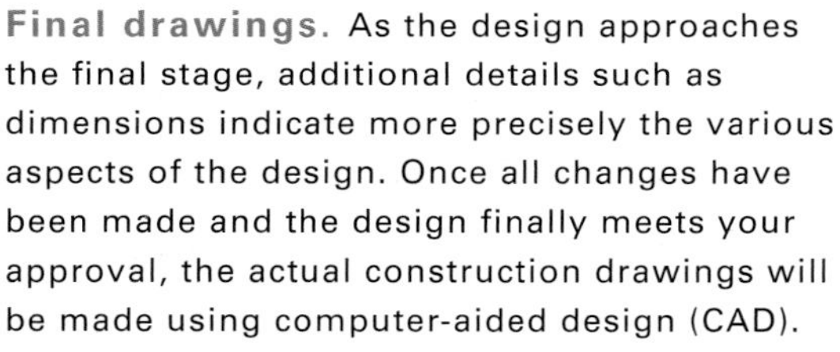

Final drawings. As the design approaches the final stage, additional details such as dimensions indicate more precisely the various aspects of the design. Once all changes have been made and the design finally meets your approval, the actual construction drawings will be made using computer-aided design (CAD).

Predesigned Stock Plans

The vast number of predesigned or stock plans now available on the Internet and at newsstands may seem overwhelming. With new plan services appearing almost daily, literally thousands of designs can now be found. The Internet has opened the doors for virtually anyone to offer house plans, regardless of his or her qualifications and experience. As in dealing with any Web-based business, you must be cautious. Nevertheless, many Internet-based companies maintain the highest level of competency, and although vast numbers of questionable house plans can be found, the ease with which plans can be published has encouraged some extremely talented design firms to offer innovative new home designs.

Predesigned house plans have been around since the 1800s. For many years pattern books offered by various magazines were a major source for home designs. Then, beginning with the Great Depression, the stock plan industry almost disappeared as residential construction dramatically declined. Throughout the 1950s and into the late 1970s, stock or mail-order plans were often considered a source only for those who were interested in an economical set of blueprints. As the home-building industry boomed toward the end of the twentieth century, some phenomenal changes occurred in the plan service business. Suddenly, highly respected designers and architects entered the field. Award-winning home plans became readily available at economical prices.

Today, several major plan services still publish plan books and magazines in addition to maintaining Web sites. These publishers represent some of the most talented architects and designers in the nation and continually search for the newest home designs. Many of the plans from the top designers and architects can be found on several different Web sites, as the various plan services often represent some of the same design firms. These firms may also have their own Web sites. While the plan content should be the same no matter where you find it, various sources may offer different services. For instance, some might offer to make changes to the plans or provide different foundation options. *(See* Resources.*)*

What's in a Plan?

Whether you're working with stock plans or with a design professional, it helps to have some background information on construction drawings. In the past duplicating original drawings involved a chemical process that produced drawings and notes in white against a dark blue background; hence the name *blueprints.* Later, as the process evolved, plans were reproduced as blue lines on a white background, called *bluelines*. Today plans are reproduced on large-format photocopiers that result in plans with black images and notes on a white background. Typically the plans are now called *construction documents* or *working drawings*, although you'll sometimes still hear the term *blueprints* used.

Plan Formats

Before you select any stock plan from the Internet or a magazine, you should understand the various formats that plan services typically offer.

- ***Prints.*** Essentially these are photocopies of the original drawings. While technically they are able to be reproduced, federal copyright laws prohibit copying them unless the original architect or designer grants authorization in writing.
- ***Reproducible plans (Mylars or vellums).*** These plans are usually printed on Mylar (a plastic film) or vellum paper (which is transparent). In the past Mylars were offered as a means to allow changes — with an electric eraser and a great deal of time and patience, information could be erased and changed. Mylars were also meant to be reproduced using a now outdated process involving special paper and chemicals. With today's printing technology and computer drafting, Mylar is seldom used to reproduce and change plans. However, you will still find plans that are generated in this format.

Some plan services require that you purchase Mylars (or vellums) as a way of charging you a higher fee that grants you permission to modify the plans. I've never been sure why they don't just charge a modification fee. Anyway, you should be aware that even though you pay for these reproducibles, your local design professional likely will advise that the plan will need to be completely redrawn with a computer. Unfortunately, unless you are able to purchase a conceptual design *(see page 27)*, you may be forced to purchase a Mylar in order to obtain the required authorization to modify the plans.

- ***CAD files.*** Computer-aided design (CAD) technology generates electronic computer files that can be easily modified and reproduced — but not by the average individual. To work with CAD files, you must have not only the appropriate computer software but also the ability to use it. Also keep in mind that there are several types of CAD software. CAD files are usually transferred on a CD-ROM or by e-mail. If you intend to have the plans modified, make sure the CAD files you purchase will be compatible with the software your builder or local drafting service is using. Although more expensive, these files are usually your best choice since modifications are much easier for your local designer to accomplish.

Plan Contents

What can you expect to be included with the plans you receive? The contents will vary depending on which design firm prepared the plans, where the firm is located, and what it considers to be a complete set of plans. Here's a list of the items typically required to obtain a building permit and begin construction:

• ***Floor plans*** indicate the location of walls, stairs, windows, and doors and include all measurements and dimensions, along with plumbing fixture locations. Most floor plans have sufficient detail to satisfy both the builder and local building code officials.

• ***Exterior elevations*** show all four exterior views (the front, both sides, and the rear), noting such important details as ceiling heights, roof pitches, and various suggested materials. Again, the typical exterior elevations usually include all necessary information to satisfy both the builder and local building code officials.

• ***Cross sections*** are cutaway views through the interior of the house showing wall heights and various structural details such as stairs, floor construction, and insulation. Imagine a huge saw cutting through the middle of your house, separating it into two halves; your view of the sawn edge of each half is a cross section. While most plans include adequate cross sections, there is a chance that some of the structural information such as beam sizes may be lacking. If so, you may need the services of a local engineer or design professional to provide this information.

• ***Framing plans*** typically show the ceiling joist layout and beam locations. They may include a roof plan, or a bird's-eye view of the rafter layout and roof pitches. Because of the often dramatic variations in structural requirements

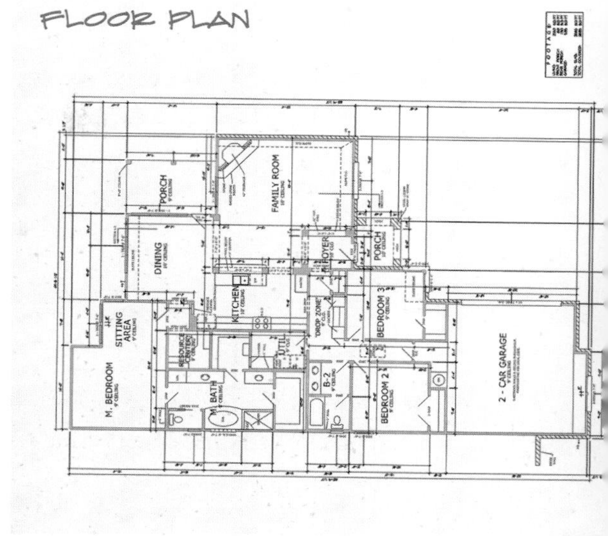

FLOOR PLAN

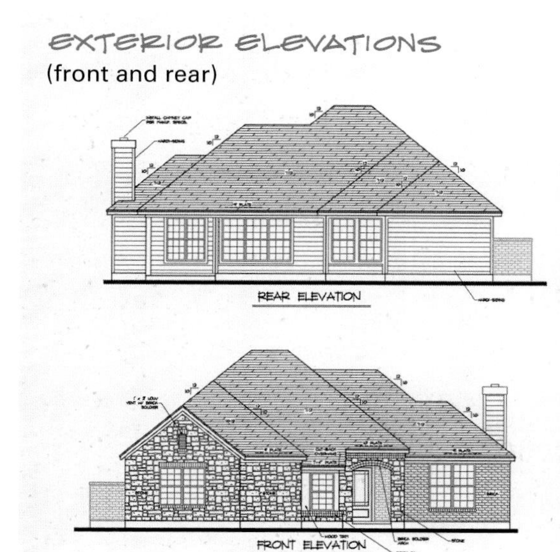

EXTERIOR ELEVATIONS
(front and rear)

EXTERIOR ELEVATIONS
(right and left sides), interior details, and cross section

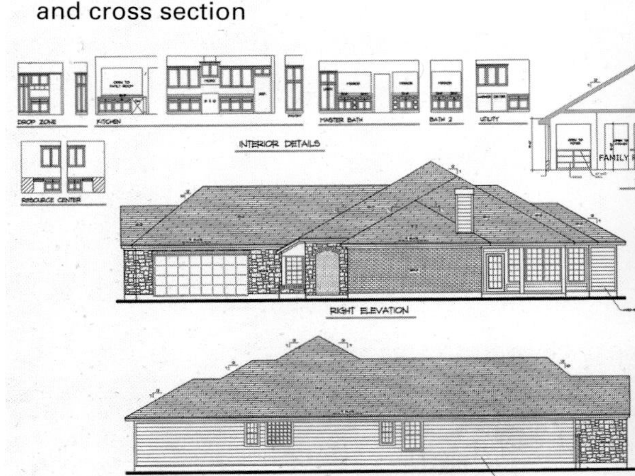

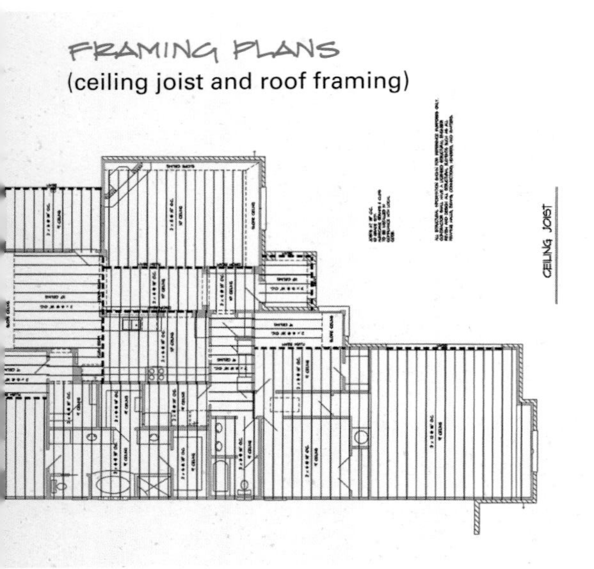

FRAMING PLANS
(ceiling joist and roof framing)

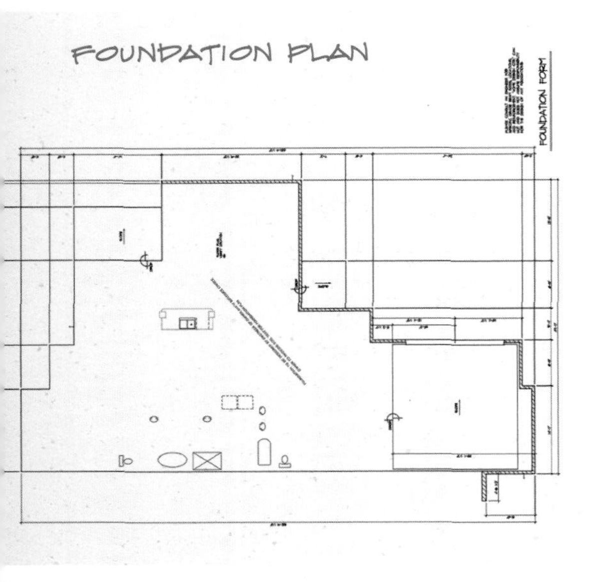

FOUNDATION PLAN

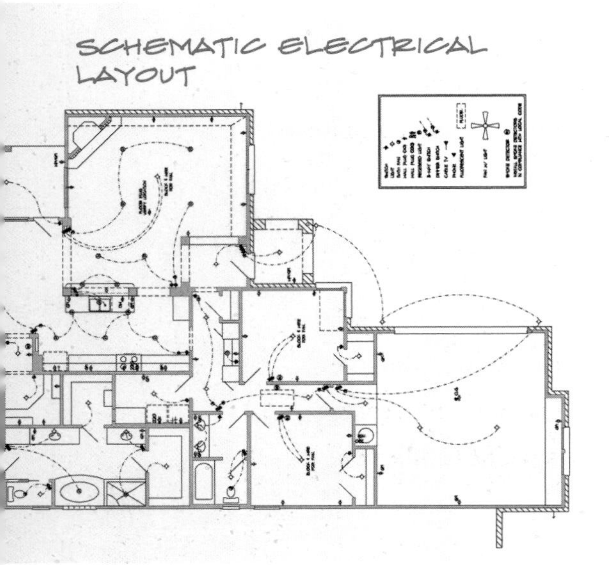

SCHEMATIC ELECTRICAL LAYOUT

from one part of the country to another, these drawings typically do not include all of the necessary information. You'll probably need some local assistance here.

- ***Interior details*** include drawings for such items as cabinets, bookcases, fireplaces, and other interior elements. Often these drawings are not necessary, as the builder's own cabinet contractor will provide them.
- ***Foundation plans*** provide a layout of the foundation with all dimensions and construction details. Basically there are three different types of foundations: basement, crawl space, and concrete slab. Due to such factors as geographical location, local construction techniques, and cost considerations, foundations can vary greatly from one area to another. Since the foundation is one of the most critical components of the entire structure, the drawings should *always* be reviewed or completely redrawn by a qualified local engineer or design professional. This is absolutely no place to economize!
- ***Schematic electrical layouts*** are essentially floor plans with all electrical outlets, lights, switches, and appliances clearly represented. Your electrical contractor will design the electrical service; as long as he or she is a licensed electrician, you shouldn't experience much difficulty here. This layout won't be your only opportunity to review the location of all switches and outlets; typically you'll have the chance to walk through the home during the framing stage and see them all.
- ***Mechanical plans*** show heating and air-conditioning details. However, such drawings are rarely required for obtaining residential building permits, and they usually are not included in stock plans because of the variations in local requirements. Should mechanical plans be required, the builder's mechanical contractor can usually provide them.

How will you know exactly which of these drawings will be included with the plans you order or have custom designed? Most plan providers indicate which drawings their plans include. However, since many plan services represent and market plans from various designers and architects, there still may be some variances. Therefore, you should ask specifically what will be included in the plans you purchase before you place the order.

Even if the plans you're considering may claim to be drawn to recognized national codes, be aware that construction techniques and requirements vary from one area to another. A plan that was created in Colorado will have been prepared with considerations for snow loads, while a design that originated on the Florida coast will include details for handling hurricane-force winds. Some plan services choose to delete such specific details from the plans they send to other parts of the country. Others include these details, even though they may not be appropriate for the area where the home will be built. As a result, the plans you receive might be overdesigned, resulting in extra costs, or underdesigned, leading to some serious problems.

If it's starting to sound like stock plans are a risky investment, that's not necessarily the case. These predesigned plans can be an outstanding value. The cost of having a home completely custom designed typically runs between 5 and 15 percent of the construction costs — that adds up to $10,000 to $30,000 for a $200,000 home. A stock plan, on the other hand, generally costs from $500 to $1,000 and may be your best choice, even though you'll likely incur some additional expenses for local engineering or drafting.

Materials Lists and Specifications

Some plans include a materials list specifying the exact quantity and quality of the building materials. In other words, they itemize all of the lumber, roofing, windows, doors, exterior trim, and other materials needed to build the house. Because of such variables as location and local construction techniques, your builder may want to provide a materials list instead.

The specifications provide information about such items as kitchen appliances, plumbing fixtures, countertops, door handles, and many more products necessary for the finish of the home. Typically you and your builder will spend a great deal of time completing these specifications. Since they can dramatically affect the cost of the home, creating accurate specifications is an extremely important part of the building process. If the plans you purchase happen to include a list of materials and specifications, you should still spend considerable time reviewing them with your builder to ensure that they include the exact items you want.

Professional Seal of Approval

More and more communities are now requiring that the plans you or your builder submit for a building permit must be *sealed* by a design professional registered in your state. Due to concerns about energy codes and structural issues, local building officials want a local professional to review the plans and certify their compliance with standard building codes and accepted structural techniques by literally stamping the drawings with his or her professional registration seal and signature.

At this time, very few (if any) plan services will be able to provide sealed plans for all geographic locations. Check with your local building authorities to see whether they require a seal. Then ask the plan service or firm from which you intend to purchase the plans whether a seal can be included. Be aware that most local design professionals will be extremely hesitant to place their seal on another firm's drawings. In most cases, the only way they will consider sealing the plans is if they can totally redraw the entire set of plans.

What are your options if local building codes require the plans to be sealed? Several possibilities exist:

- ***Contact the original designer*** of the plans you wish to use. Possibly that designer can seal the plans him- or herself for an additional fee, or he or she may be able to refer you to an engineer in your area who can help.
- ***If you've already selected a builder,*** talk with him or her about having the plans sealed. Builders often have long-established working relationships with local engineers and sometimes can take care of sealing the plans for you.
- ***If your plan provider and builder can't help,*** you may still be able to have the plans sealed as long as the provider will grant you written authorization to have the plans revised and possibly redrawn locally by someone who can get them sealed. Remember, a designer or plan service may be hesitant to offer such permission. If your provider agrees to grant you such authorization, you have to add the cost of having the plans modified locally to the original cost of the plans. Sometimes the total cost exceeds what you might pay a local design firm to custom-design your home.
- ***Consider working with a conceptual home design*** *(see facing page)*. A conceptual design is created with the assumption that changes will need to be made to the plans not only because of local codes but also simply because you desire them. Conceptual designs

TERMS TO KNOW

Beams. Sometimes referred to as a girder, a beam is a structural member that supports a specific load (weight) above it. It can be made of wood or steel, and the exact size usually must be determined by an engineer.

Building permit. After approving the plans, your municipal building authority will issue a building permit granting you authorization to begin the building process.

Framing. The structural material — such as joists, studs, and rafters — that are used to build the home. The term also refers to the process of framing: combining the various wood materials to create the frame or skeleton of the home.

Joists. Joists are lengths of wood that run parallel to one another and support a floor or ceiling above. They are supported by walls or beams.

Rafters. Similar to joists, rafters are attached to exterior walls at an angle and form the framing (skeleton) of the roof. Roof sheathing (typically sheets of plywood) and shingles are then attached.

Roof pitch. Pitch is the degree of slope (angle) of the roof.

Studs. The vertical lengths of wood that support the walls are called studs. These are pre-cut and available in three standard sizes for constructing walls with finished heights of 8 feet, 9 feet, and 10 feet.

should include written authorization for your builder and/or design professional to make any changes that are necessary for the plans to be sealed locally.

Conceptual Home Designs

For some, the experience of purchasing a stock plan and making the necessary changes is an economical and rewarding choice. However, others find the process stressful and confusing. If you've searched the Internet unsuccessfully for a stock plan and also decided the custom-design process is not for you, consider a relatively new option: the conceptual home design. Developed as an alternative to traditional stock plans, conceptual designs offer a practical, straightforward approach to selecting a plan for your new home.

Conceptual home designs are developed with the idea that the buyer will want to make some changes to the plans and that local codes and building conditions will also require certain modifications. They offer the essential design for a home, providing everything a local designer, architect, or builder will need to finish the plans to suit *your* style and preferences, along with any structural or other changes made necessary by local codes. In this way they combine the low cost of stock plans with the flexibility of custom-designed plans.

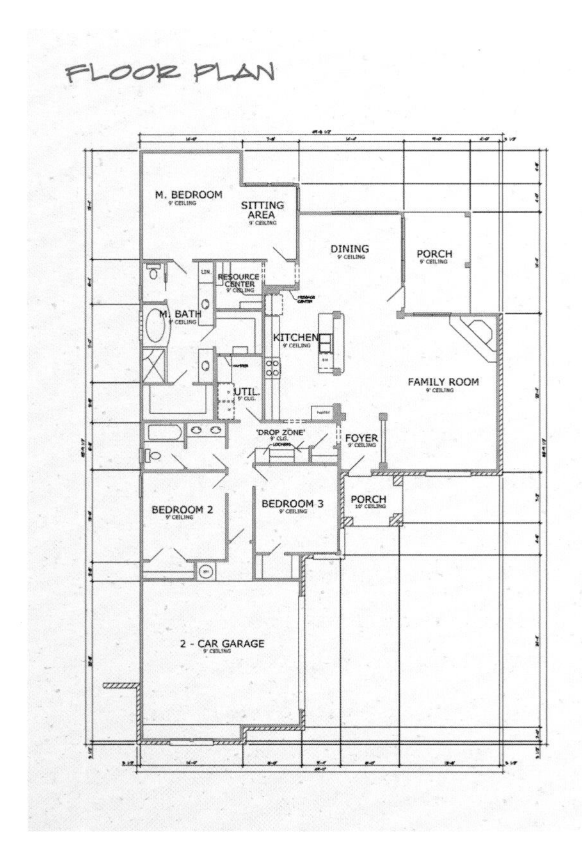

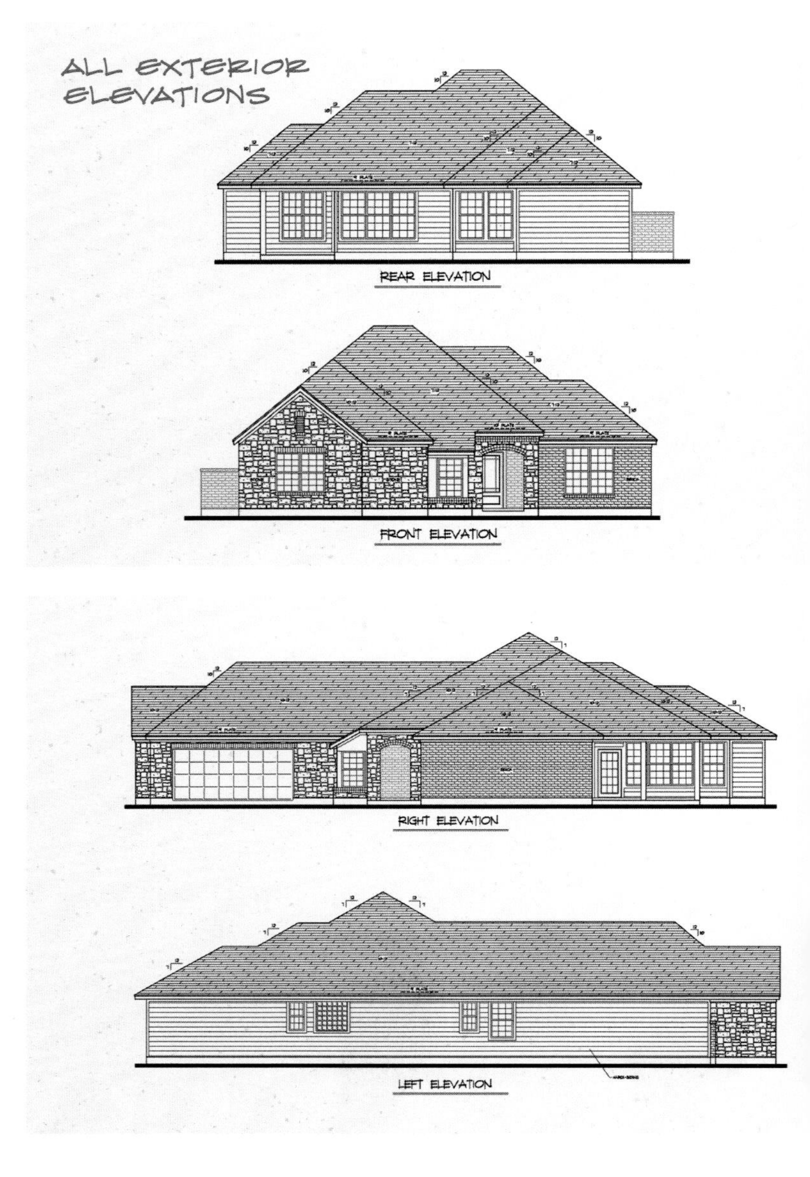

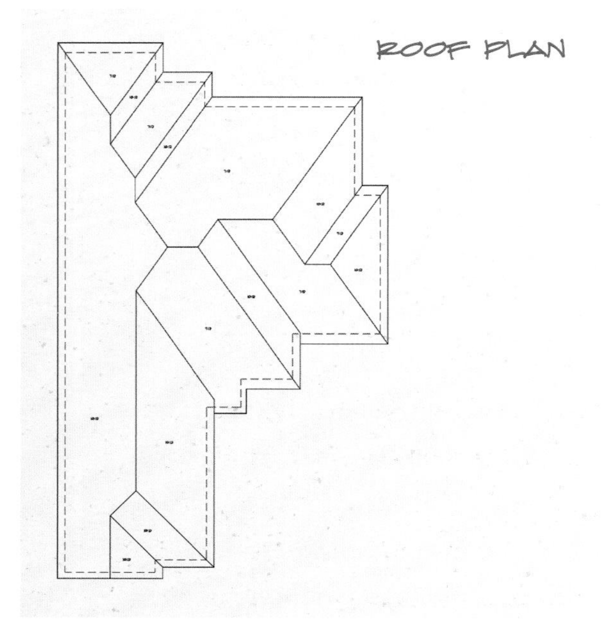

Conceptual design plans. Stock plans and conceptual designs look fairly similar at first glance, but there is a big difference in the level of detail. Stock plans (examples shown on pages 23 and 24) contain more detail in the floor plans and include information for the framing, interiors, and foundation.

Many builders either have someone in their office who can complete the drawings or work closely with a local designer. If you need to find a designer, however, you can obtain a list of local design professionals from the local telephone directory or online.

Conceptual home designs typically include the following:

- front, side, and rear elevations
- floor plan(s)
- roof plan
- plan customization form and step-by-step guide to help you make changes
- written authorization allowing the plans to be modified, completed, and copied as needed

With a conceptual design, you pay only for what you really need. Conceptual designs cost less than stock plans because you're not paying for all the detail work of the stock plans, much of which may need to be modified anyway. And when you bring your conceptual plan to a local home designer for finalization, he or she is able to work from that basic concept, rather than investing considerable time in the concept design phase. As a result, the designer's fees are less than for a completely custom design.

A conceptual home design may be your best option if:

- You want to be able to make changes to your home plan as it develops. (Almost everyone wants to make a few changes to a design — that's right, you're not alone!)
- Local codes require structural details specific to the local conditions.
- Local codes require that the plan be sealed by a certified design professional or engineer.

How to Proceed

If you decide you want to go this route, here's what to do:

- Select the conceptual design that comes closest to addressing your needs. (Sample plans are available at www.homeplandoctor.com.) Remember, virtually any changes can be accomplished, even in the exterior design.
- Conceptual plans are available in two formats: paper prints and CAD files. The CAD files will be extremely useful for a design professional to modify. If you're not sure which format you need, order the paper prints first. You can upgrade your order to the CAD files later.

- Complete a customization checklist. To make this easy, all conceptual designs include a step-by-step customization form with each plan order. The completed checklist will become an invaluable asset as you take the next step toward finalizing the plans.
- Once you've determined the modifications that need to be made, take the conceptual design and your customization checklist to a local design professional or to your builder. The designer or your builder will complete the drawings.

Making Modifications

Maybe you've already found the perfect stock plan — well, almost perfect. It just needs a few slight adjustments. While some changes may require little effort, others might mean a complete redraw of the plan. Remember, due to variations in local codes and especially local building conditions and construction techniques, *most* stock plans will need to be modified, if not redrawn completely.

Laying the Groundwork

So, how should you proceed? Although obtaining and modifying a stock plan may seem a bit overwhelming, some simple step-by-step solutions do exist. The guide that follows can help you prepare up front for the likelihood of modifications.

① Before you purchase your plan, review "What's in a Plan?" *(see page 21)* to make sure you understand the options and concerns.

② Contact your local building official to determine exactly what your plans will be required to contain in order for you to receive a building permit.

③ Contact the plan provider (designer, plan publisher, or Internet site) to determine the contents of the plans you intend to order. Compare this against the plan requirements specified by your local building official. If a specific drawing (such as a framing plan or foundation detail) is not included in the plans you will receive, you will require the services of a local design professional to add this information.

④ In the rare event that an existing stock plan is exactly what you want, order at least six sets of plans. Since it's illegal for you to make copies, make sure you'll be permitted to order additional sets at a later date.

⑤ If you determine the plans will need to be modified, contact the plan provider to verify that the purchase of the plans provides written authorization for you, your designer, or your builder to make changes and possibly redraw the plans. (If you cannot obtain this permission, you should seriously consider continuing your plan search.) From a practical standpoint, only one set of plans will be needed if you're sure you want to make modifications.

Typically, almost every plan will require some type of modification. Your builder can often make simple changes. However, be extremely cautious when it comes to larger changes such as enlarging rooms or changing the roof design. In most cases the services of a local design professional will be one of the best investments you make. The expense of consulting with a designer and having your plans revised by a professional will usually be far less than that of correcting a mistake once construction has started.

Taking Action

Before you talk with a design professional about your plans and the changes you desire, you might want to review chapter 3, "Defining Good Design." The more you understand the design process, the more easily you will be able to talk with the person making the changes. When you're ready to proceed, you have two options:

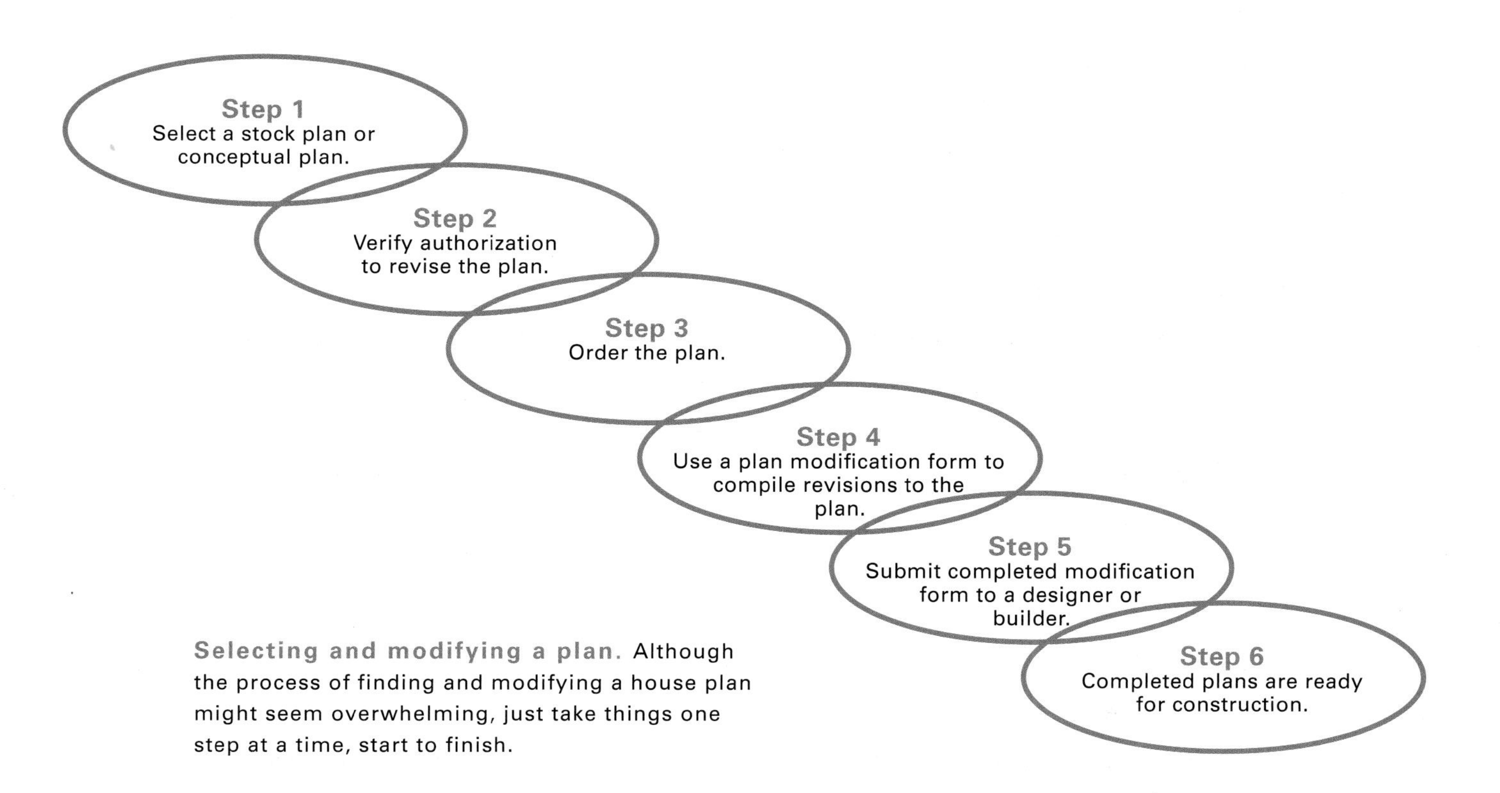

Selecting and modifying a plan. Although the process of finding and modifying a house plan might seem overwhelming, just take things one step at a time, start to finish.

• ***Option 1.*** Contact the designer or architect who originally created the plans. If you found the plans on the designer's own Web site, you'll probably also find information regarding his or her revision services. If you found the plans on a plan services Web site, the plan services company might be able to provide information on how to contact the original designer. Also, some of the plan services offer various revision services for the plans they market. This often becomes the most efficient way to have the plans changed.

• ***Option 2.*** Contact a local designer or architect to discuss your changes, or talk with your builder about having the changes made by his or her designer. Be sure to inform the person you choose to work with that you have written permission allowing him or her to work with the plans you purchased.

Make a detailed list of changes you would like to make, or photocopy and complete the Stock Plan Customization Form found in the appendix (or download it from www.homeplandoctor.com). Once completed, this form will help you communicate to your local design professional the exact modifications you wish to make. Conceptual designs will include a similar form with the plans.

Copyright Issues

The federal laws that protect intellectual property cover all home plans. Blueprints cannot be copied or used without the consent of the copyright owner, which is usually the designer or architect who created them. And designers and architects have become increasingly protective of their designs over the past few years; after all, they have invested considerable time and creative effort in developing them. Ignoring copyright issues can be an extremely costly mistake; the laws allow for statutory penalties of up to $100,000 per incident, plus legal fees and actual damages. As a result, many builders, designers, and drafting services have become quite reluctant to revise or redraw stock plans without written authorization from the copyright owner.

Conceptual home designs, like stock and custom-designed plans, are also protected from unauthorized use and copying. However, designers of conceptual plans *expect* that they'll be modified and *should* provide written authorization allowing the plans to be modified or redrawn and copied as often as needed. This permission should be printed directly on the plans, so your builder or designer will never have any hesitancy working with them.

Frequently Asked Questions

Q How much will my plan cost to build?

Ⓐ This is absolutely the most frequently asked question and also the most difficult to answer. First, material and labor costs differ considerably from one area of the country to another. We all know that the average cost of a home in Southern California far surpasses that of one in Missouri.

Furthermore, individual building sites play an important role in determining the cost of construction. For instance, a relatively level lot will require far less site preparation and foundation expense than a sloping site. Property in a development located in the city will likely already have utilities such as sewer and water, while a rural location generally will require that you drill a well and install a septic system. This could add thousands of dollars to your budget before you ever even begin building your home.

Finally, the ultimate cost depends on the amenities you select for your home. You'll find vast differences in the prices of countertops and flooring, along with windows, doors, and roofing. Consider this analogy: When you purchase an automobile, the final price depends on the accessories you select. The same proves true for building a home.

Q Should I be my own contractor and build my home myself?

Ⓐ Typically a builder charges between 10 and 20 percent of the total cost of construction. On a $250,000 home, that's $25,000 to $50,000 — a considerable amount of money. However, that's most likely *not* savings that pass directly into your pocket. Since full-time professional builders provide continuous work for the subcontractors, they receive better rates from these craftsmen than an individual who offers them only one job. For that same reason, the subcontractors will give priority scheduling to their longtime builders. In other words, you may wait for days — or weeks — for that plumber.

But the most important consideration is this: Do you have enough time each day to spend on the job site? You'll need to be there first thing in the morning at 7 A.M. to go over the day's schedule with the workers. Then you must be available at any time during the day when questions arise (which will happen almost every day!). If you're not immediately available, either the job will shut down or someone will make a decision for you (invariably the wrong decision!). Either way, you lose money.

So, should you build your own home? If you have a great deal of free time, perhaps so. You will undoubtedly save *some* money. But if you have another job, consider the real value of your time.

The Fully Doctored Plan

EXAMPLE 1

The original plan, shown below, was designed by my firm some years ago. While it may still appeal to some people, there are several areas that I've suggested updates on to meet today's lifestyle needs, including improved flow between the kitchen and living areas, and additional storage and informal living space.

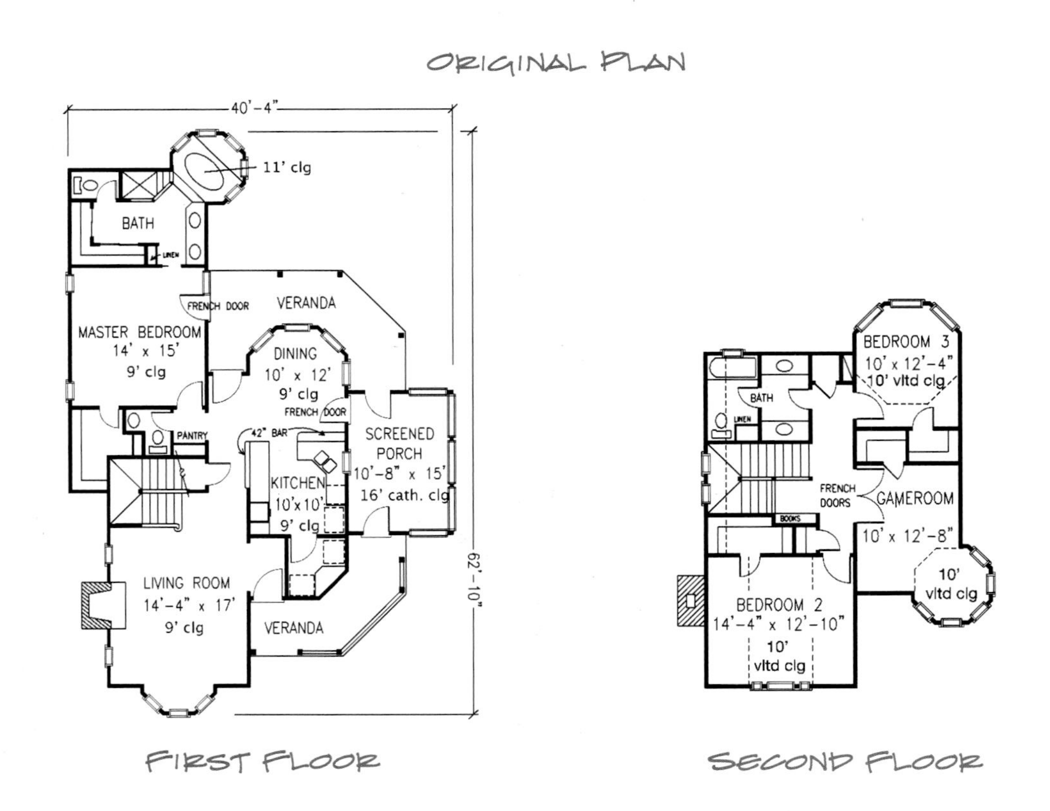

The Doctor's Solutions

- Open up the kitchen by adding an island sink and snack bar. This makes the kitchen, family room and dining areas all feel much larger.
- Add an extra-thick wall (10") between the foyer and kitchen to accommodate an additional 8" deep pantry cabinet.
- Add a sunroom. This is an economical way to add square footage to the living area, simply by replacing the screens with casement windows and installing heating and air conditioning.

The complete plans for both the original and revised versions are available at www.homeplandoctor.com.

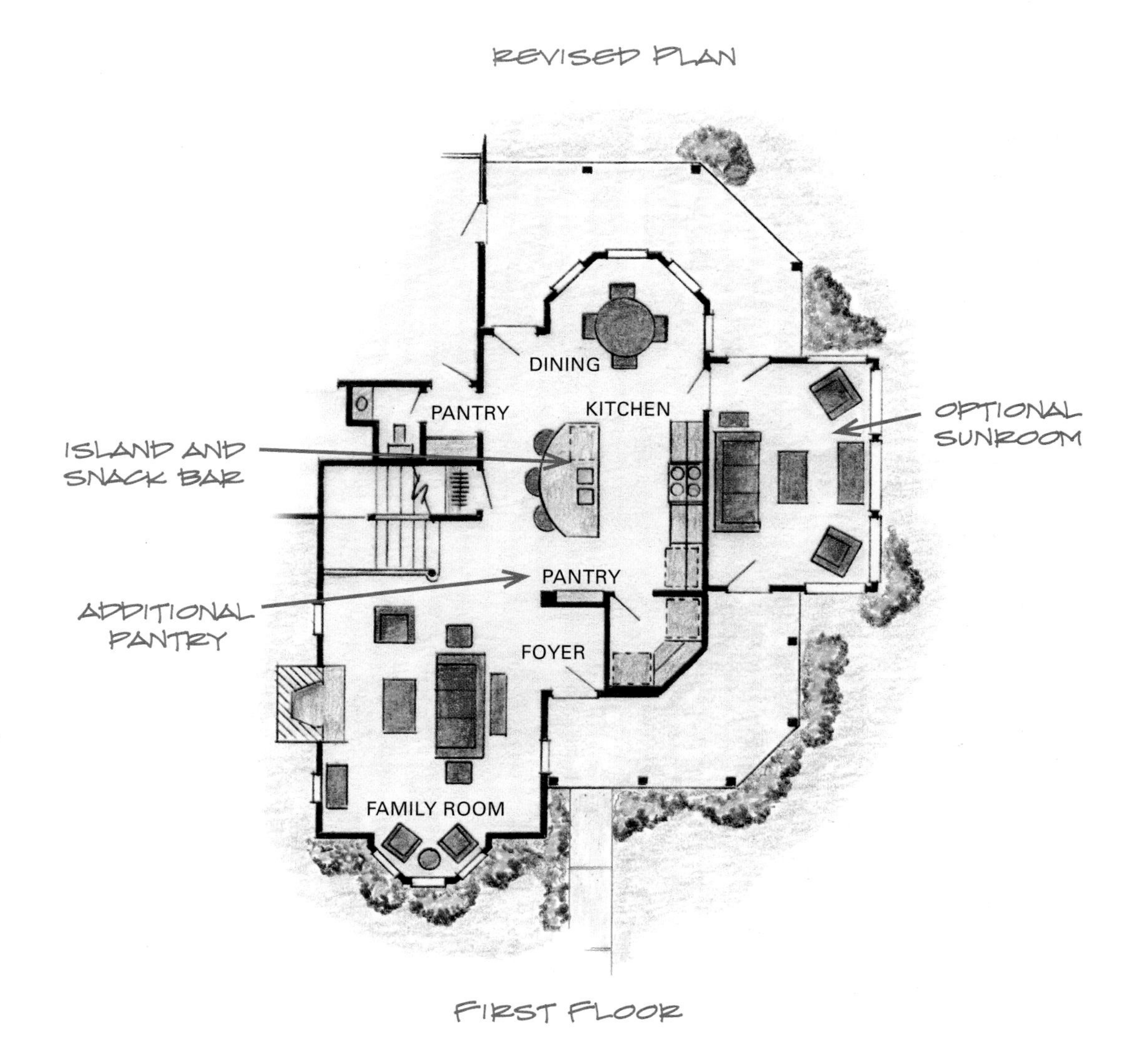

The Fully Doctored Plan

EXAMPLE 2

While the original plan may still appeal to some people, there are several areas that could benefit from an update to meet today's lifestyle needs. For instance, we've discovered the value of keeping a more open connection between the kitchen and family areas. In place of a gigantic tub in the bathroom and a fireplace in the master bedroom, some homeowners prefer having a larger shower and more storage for linens and clothes.

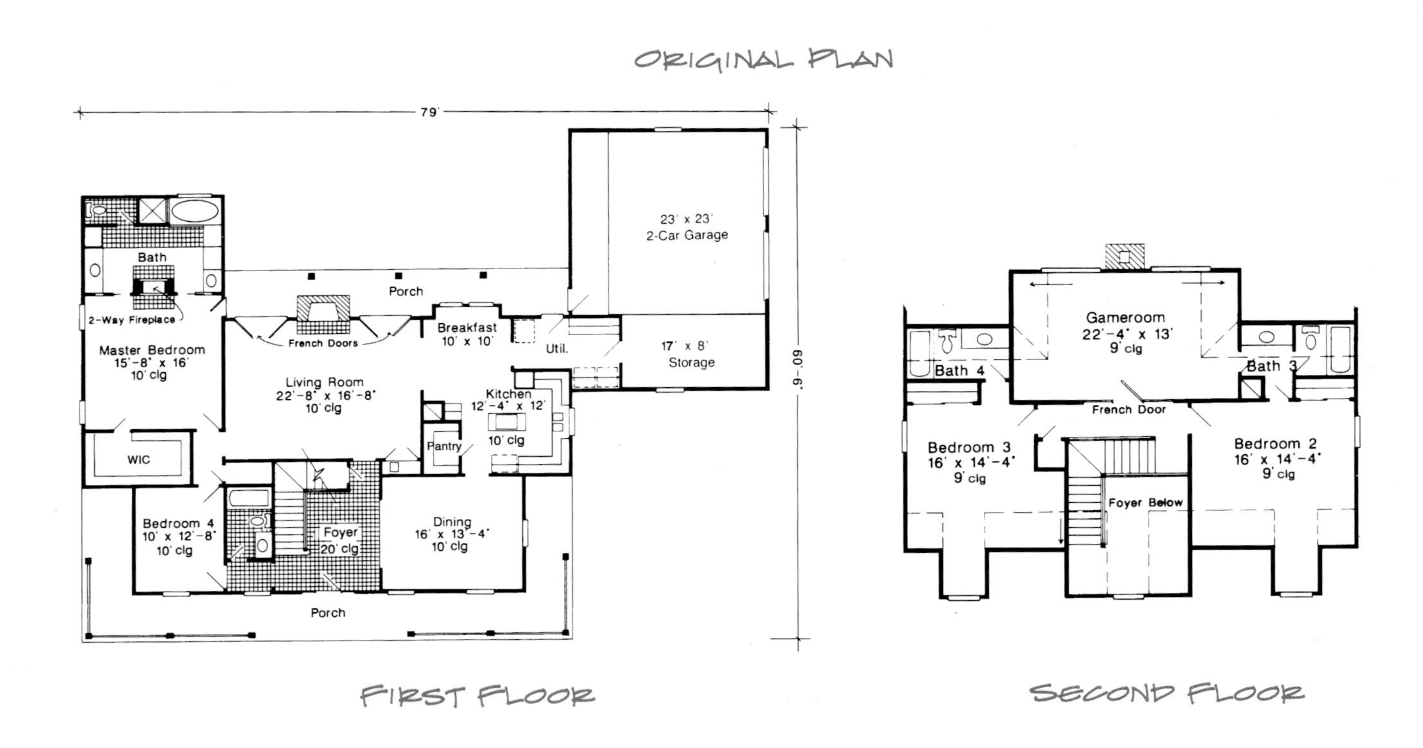

The Doctor's Solutions

- Open the kitchen to the family room (formerly the living room).
- Define a gallery area by adding 12" columns on opposite walls in kitchen and family room.
- Create a drop zone and family entry from the garage, eliminating traffic through the utility room.
- Replace wet bar with a coat closet in the foyer. This also opens up room to put in stairs for basement access.
- Redesign the master bath and bedroom, eliminating the fireplace and large tub to allow for a linen closet and larger shower.

The complete plans for both the original and revised versions are available at www.homeplandoctor.com.

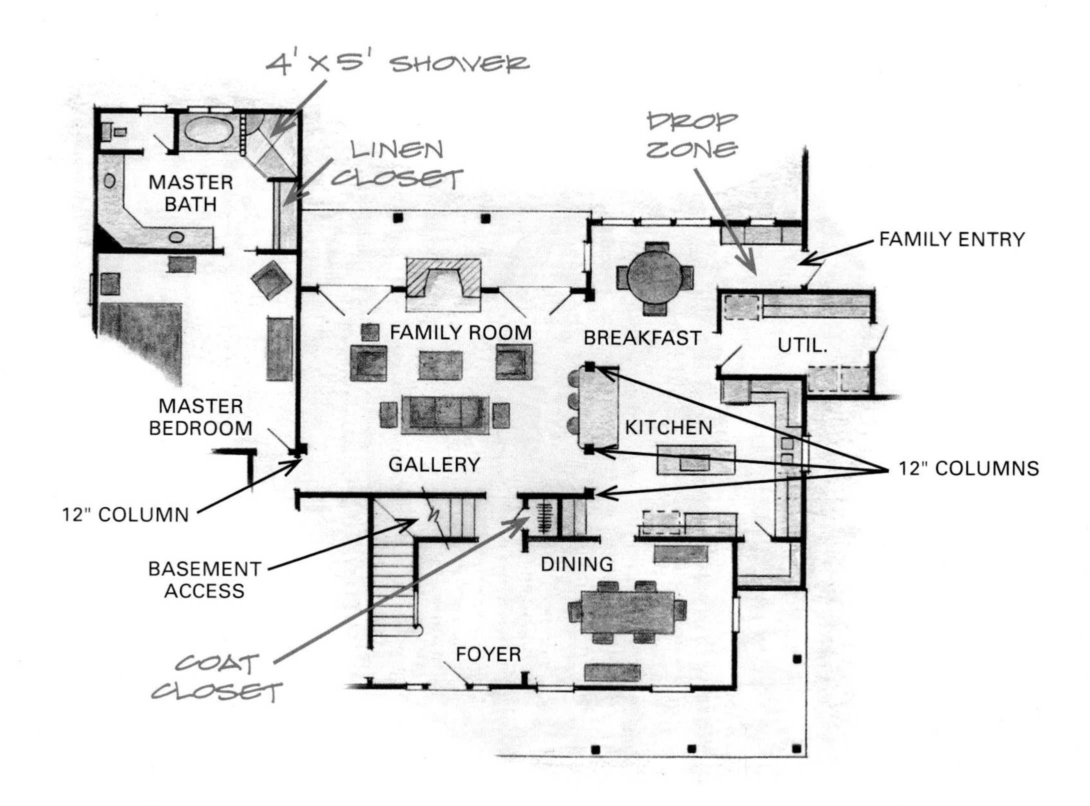

3

Defining Good Design

Ask any group of people what they think "good design" means, and you're likely to receive a range of responses. For most of us the easier question may be, "What is *bad* design?" We seem to immediately recognize what we consider unattractive. When the question of design relates to our homes, the wide variety of houses built all across the country proves that, as a society, we have some extremely diverse opinions about what we consider to be good design.

In the creation of both the exterior and the interior design of a home, four essential elements come into play: *scale*, *proportion*, *mass*, and *functionality*. *(See definitions on page 42.)* Adjusting one of these elements often changes the others. Thus, the impact of modifying virtually any aspect of a design must be carefully considered.

Design Sense

Although most people don't analyze why they are attracted to certain homes but not others, they often find themselves drawn to houses that have been designed and built with particular attention to details. Most of us have an innate sense of scale and proportion, and we respond to houses in which these elements combine to yield a feeling of permanence.

> **People often find homes built in the early part of the twentieth century attractive. Many of these residences were constructed during a period when architects and builders paid strict attention to craftsmanship and details.**

For example, the next time you look at a porch, consider the posts that support the roof above. For most porches 4 × 4 columns will suffice structurally, but somehow they seem too small. A porch with 8 × 8 columns just *feels* better. Thicker posts give us the sense that the porch is a safer and more secure place.

Another example of incorrect proportion is a roof that appears either too tall or too low for the rest of the home. The mass of the roof must be proportional to that of the house in order for the two to relate comfortably to each other.

Design Diagnosis

Incorrect proportions

⊕ **Roof pitch.** The roof's pitch (angle) determines its overall height. If the pitch is too steep, the roof will appear to be too tall, with its mass out of proportion with that of the rest of the house.

INCORRECT

CORRECT

⊕ **Windows and columns.** Proper proportions are the basis for good design. Compare the use of narrow columns and poorly sized shutters with wider columns and properly sized shutters.

By examining the exterior of any home, you'll find numerous areas where proportion and scale influence the design. One morning while I was driving with my family through a neighborhood of new, mass-produced homes, my youngest son commented, "Dad, those windows don't look right." When I asked him to explain, he answered, "Those pieces of wood [shutters] on each side of the window don't look very good." There's no need for a formal design education to notice that wide windows with narrow shutters simply don't seem appropriately sized. *(See page 39.)*

The same elements of scale and proportion relate to the interior of homes as well. To understand the importance of scale inside a home, consider the differences between

■ = 12"-THICK COLUMNS AND WALLS
::::::: = 12" × 12" HEADERS

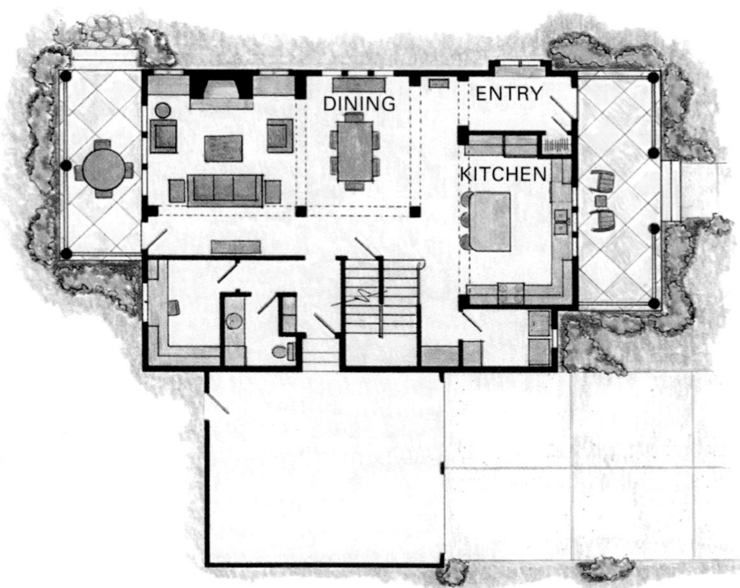

Design Diagnosis

Borrow visual space

Continuous flooring in the foyer, dining area, and kitchen allows these areas to "borrow" visual space so that each room seems larger than it is. In order to define the areas, 12-inch-square columns and 12-inch-thick walls, both with dropped headers, frame each room. A double column at the corner of the kitchen lends further weight to its definition.

public buildings and houses. Offices, malls, schools, and places of worship are intentionally built on a huge scale, often with soaring ceilings, walls of glass, and massive beams. This allows large numbers of people to inhabit them in comfort. However, homes that are designed and built on a massive scale can lose their sense of security and comfort. This doesn't mean that houses should never have vaulted ceilings or tall windows. Rather, it means that the scale and proportions of the room must be considered when determining ceiling heights.

Appropriate interior proportion involves ceiling height and room size. Although raised ceilings can create the illusion of space, they can just as easily make a room seem small. Basically, if a room is taller than it is wide or deep, you may feel as though you're in a cavern.

Wall thickness is another small detail where scale can make a substantial difference. The typical interior wall is framed with 3½-inch-wide wood studs. When this thickness is doubled to 7 inches (using two studs) at openings, there is a perception that all the walls are this thick and the entire home appears to be sturdier. In some cases, thickening the walls to 12 inches can offer an even more substantial look.

Rooms that are open to each other can be defined by columns with a *dropped header* (ceiling beam) that frames the area. For example, a dining area might be defined within a kitchen by the use of 12-inch-square columns and corresponding 12-inch-square dropped headers. Increasing the thickness at openings in this way involves little extra cost but, especially in an open floor plan, can have a big payoff in terms of giving each space an appropriate sense of scale and proportion.

Entry way drop zone. This spot provides a convenient place for keys, mail, and cell phones.

Design for Daily Life

Good design might be more appropriately described as *functional design*. Though we typically pay a great deal of attention to the surface appeal of our homes, the true measure of enduring design relates to function. Homes that offer practical solutions to the challenges of our daily routines become more valuable in the long term than those with

TERMS TO KNOW

Functionality. While this might seem an obvious point, a good design should be functional. From the flow of traffic throughout the home to well-conceived storage areas, a successful plan will offer thoughtful features that will be appreciated on a daily basis. From an exterior perspective, elements such as rooflines, porches, windows, and doors should be carefully placed on the home so that they appear to belong. Although window shutters might not actually operate, they should at least be the proper size to *appear* functional. Too much frivolous ornamentation will often result in a pretentious-looking home.

Mass. The mass of an object refers not only to its size but also to its volume and shape. Consider two homes with identical square footage and outside wall dimensions. If one has an extremely steep and tall roof, it will have more mass.

Proportion. Although similar to scale, proportion involves the relationship in size of adjacent design elements. Proper proportion occurs when adjacent elements coexist in a harmonious manner. For example, a typical 6-foot 8-inch door will seem proportionally correct in a room with 8- or 9-foot ceilings. However, if the ceilings increase to 10 feet in height, an 8-foot-tall door might be more appropriate.

Scale. Essentially, scale refers to the size of an object as it relates to our human scale or size. For instance, the scale of a typical 6-foot 8-inch door is appropriate for the average person between 5 and 6 feet in height. However, for a person who is 6 feet 9 inches or more, the scale of this door is obviously wrong. Adjusting the dimensions of doors, windows, ceilings, and roofs can transform the scale of a home or certain spaces within it, creating environments ranging from intimate and cozy to spacious or even overwhelming.

elaborate ornamental elements. Imagine if you could always easily locate your keys and cell phone when you're rushing out the door to work. How about having a convenient place to sort the daily mail? Entries with areas dedicated to these items and activities are invaluable *(see chapter 10)*.

Here's another example: Rather than building an expensive formal living room just so you'll have a place for your piano, consider creating an alcove for it adjacent to the family room. Not only will the piano become an attractive focal point, but the alcove saves at least 175 square feet of living room area.

Piano alcove. Lower the ceiling and add a recessed light with a dimmer switch to define a special place for a piano.

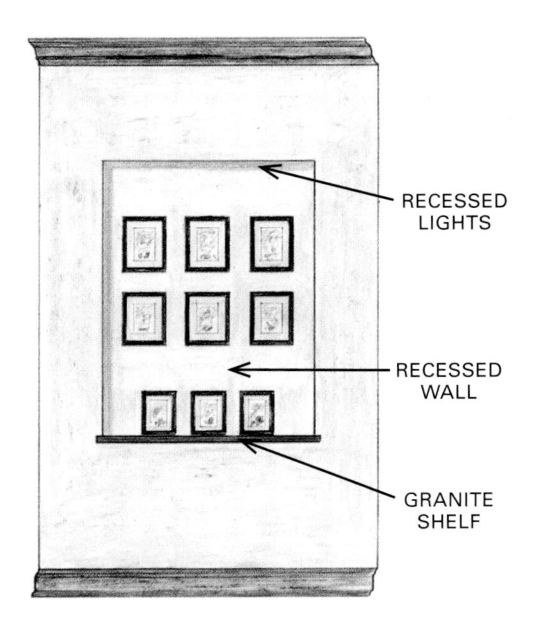

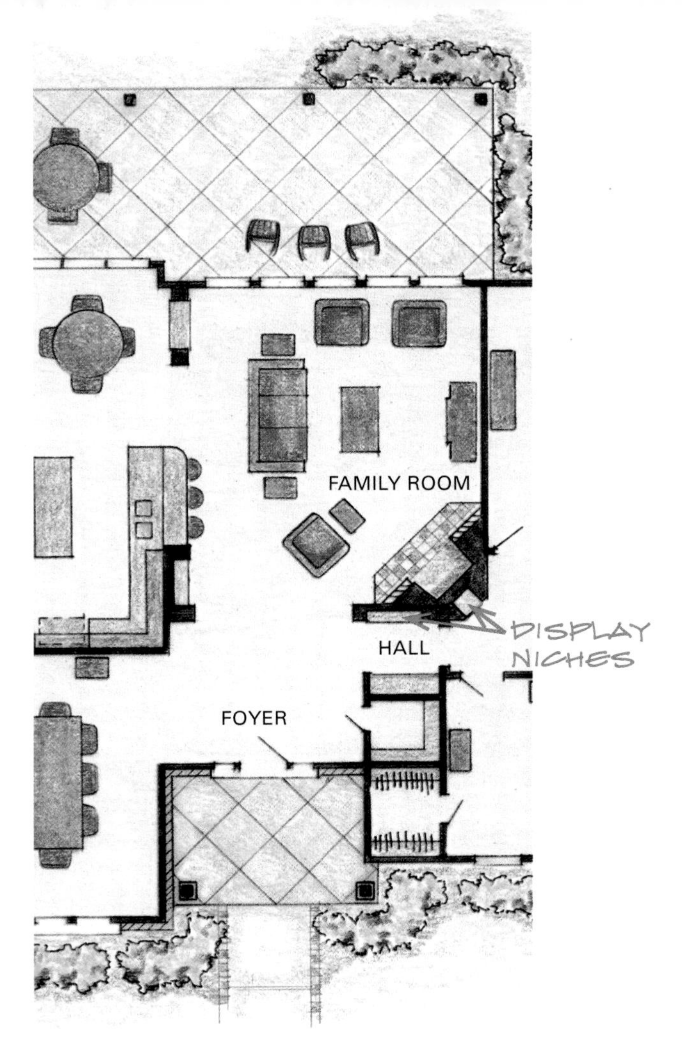

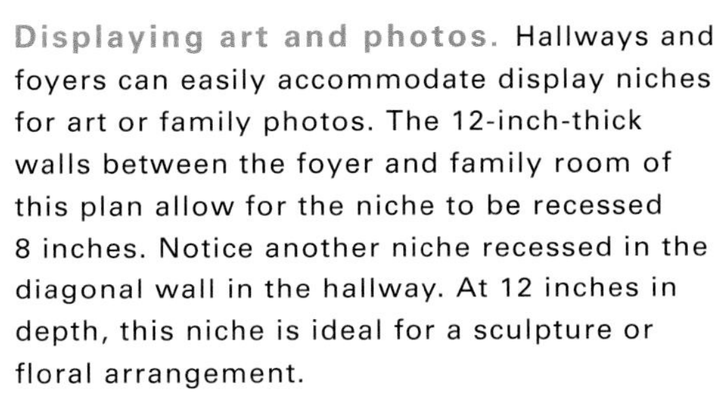

Displaying art and photos. Hallways and foyers can easily accommodate display niches for art or family photos. The 12-inch-thick walls between the foyer and family room of this plan allow for the niche to be recessed 8 inches. Notice another niche recessed in the diagonal wall in the hallway. At 12 inches in depth, this niche is ideal for a sculpture or floral arrangement.

If you enjoy collecting and displaying art, you'll certainly appreciate built-in niches (recessed areas in the wall). With the elimination of walls in many open-concept designs, finding a place for paintings and family photos can be a challenge. Hallways and foyers can easily become galleries for such items. A larger recessed area in a wall can transform a hall into a family photo gallery.

Most of us live at such a fast pace that simple daily tasks become stressful due to a lack of organization. An area I call the *resource center* provides an efficient place to manage the household administrative activities. For many homeowners this command center becomes the most important and functional area of the home. *(See the examples on the next page and in chapter 13.)*

Timeless or Trendy?

Although it may sound like a cliché, good design truly is timeless. However, often the line between timeless and trendy is extremely fine. Those of us old enough to be labeled baby boomers can recall a time when the latest kitchen designs all featured avocado green appliances!

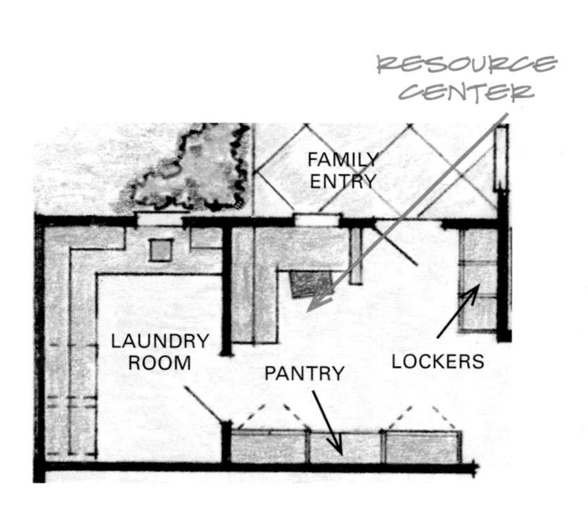

A resource center. Located next to the family entry and kitchen, this resource center is the most functional area of the home. A desk and computer, along with file drawers and bookcases, make it easy to pay bills, organize mail, and perhaps even run a small business.

Timeless design certainly involves much more than selecting the color of your refrigerator. Every home will eventually begin to show its age. But those avocado green appliances can easily be replaced; truly good design transcends such elements. If the kitchen has been designed to function properly, with logical appliance location, plenty of counter space, convenient pantry storage, and an abundance of natural light, the area will survive an array of trendy colors and finishes. Who knows, perhaps granite countertops will be considered a trend when we look back in twenty years!

Timeless exterior design can be more difficult to achieve. Drive through virtually any new housing development anywhere in the country and you'll see the effects of trendy design. Individually, many of these new homes have been created with an appreciation for proper detail and proportion. However, repetition is a problem. Rooflines with identical shapes and colors, along with front facades that mirror those of homes across the street, are doomed to be considered trendy at some point in time.

In general, the overall design of your home must first address the site. The appeal of any home depends on its relationship with the immediate surroundings. A farmhouse with wraparound porches might be a good design if you're building on a rather spacious site with views in every direction. However, placing such a design in a development where neighboring houses are 10 feet away may not be appropriate. In an area where houses are close together, a plan that turns inward and focuses on a courtyard might be a better approach. In other words, the home itself may be an exceptionally well-conceived design, but the context in which it exists will determine whether it's a good or bad design.

For those with the option of creating their own design, resist the urge to mimic the other homes in the neighborhood, but at the same time maintain a respect for the existing style and character. Most of the monotony of recent developments relates directly to economics. With the cost of housing rising at a frightening pace, cost obviously is the primary factor in determining the ultimate design. Nevertheless, options do exist.

Unfortunately, good design is not the result of a special formula or distinct set of rules. However, the more you understand the various elements of design, the better prepared you'll be to recognize both good and bad design when you see it.

The Challenge of a Narrow Lot

Perhaps you're building on a narrow lot in a planned subdivision. Since you'll have little or no choice in the orientation of the house, pay close attention to how your design relates to existing or proposed neighboring houses. Selecting a site with existing neighbors allows you the distinct advantage of being able to make adjustments to your plan that can help ensure privacy. At least you can avoid having bedroom or family room windows opening directly toward your neighbor!

While narrow lot designs can be amazingly successful, they can also end up becoming design disasters. Often a fine line separates the two extremes, with details making the difference.

If you're the pioneer in the neighborhood with no idea of what will be built next to you, a few options can still be considered. First, try to orient bedroom and family room windows toward the rear of the lot, where you'll have a better chance of maintaining privacy. Be particularly careful with second-story bedrooms that overlook a side yard. While your initial view may be toward that delightfully landscaped and private courtyard, you may eventually look directly into your future neighbor's bedroom. Often subdivision architectural restrictions will dictate window placement. While such rules may seem overly restrictive, they become essential to maintaining privacy in neighborhoods with narrow lots.

When the depth of your property is relatively shallow, you might consider a design with a side courtyard. Even though your neighbor may be only several feet away, you can still create a very private side yard with the use of a privacy wall. However, if your neighbor has a two-story home, this may not be a good alternative. I recall visiting some model homes in a neighborhood on the West Coast where land costs often dictate high-density developments. The two-story homes built on 35-foot-wide lots featured exteriors designed and built with meticulous attention to detail. Nevertheless, I didn't see many "sold" signs. As I entered the first house, I quickly began to understand why. Expansive windows filled the home with natural light *and* with unobstructed views of the neighboring home's expansive windows!

I'm sure most potential buyers reacted just as I did when climbing the stairs. Standing midway up the stairs on a landing, I immediately noticed a massive window located high on the wall. No problem with privacy here. But as I reached the top of the stairs, adjacent to the master bedroom entry, I looked back down the staircase. Although high on the wall at the landing, from the top of the stairs this massive window offered an uncomfortable view directly into a huge bay window in the neighbor's breakfast room. With only 10 feet between these windows, certainly more than pleated shades would be needed to achieve even a semblance of privacy for the residents of either home.

Garages are another important consideration. This rather massive area where we store our automobiles and an assortment of other items can easily overwhelm the rest of the home. Ideally the development in which you will be building will allow for an alley, so that the garage can be placed at the rear of the home. If the garage must be front-loaded, the lot width may be sufficient for the garage to be placed perpendicular to the front, so that the garage doors open to the side. If the garage must face the front, pay close attention to the design of the doors. Consider an extended roof overhang to create a shadow that will soften the appearance of the door. (*See chapter 5 for more information about garages.*)

HEALTHY EXAMPLES

Designs for privacy

Example 1

Inner courtyard. This plan, suitable for densely populated neighborhoods, includes an inner courtyard for privacy. Note the addition of an outdoor kitchen and cabana that further enhance the sense of seclusion. The exterior features a well-proportioned roof and a natural blend of stone and brick.

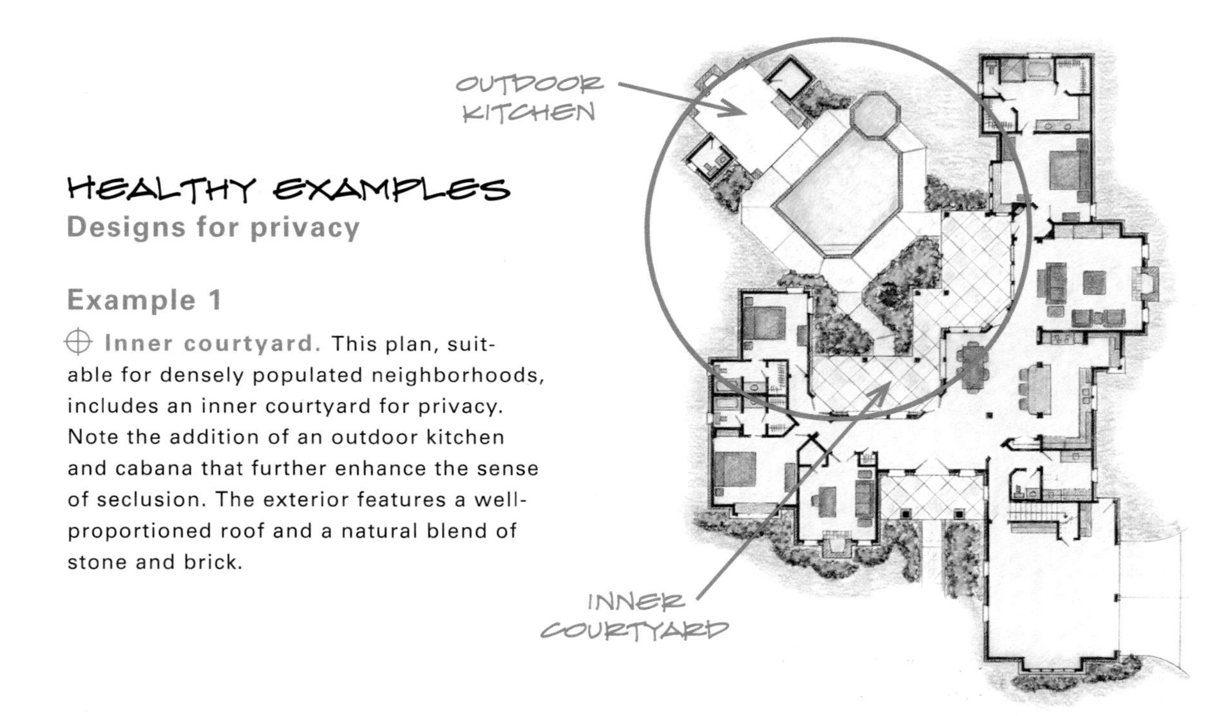

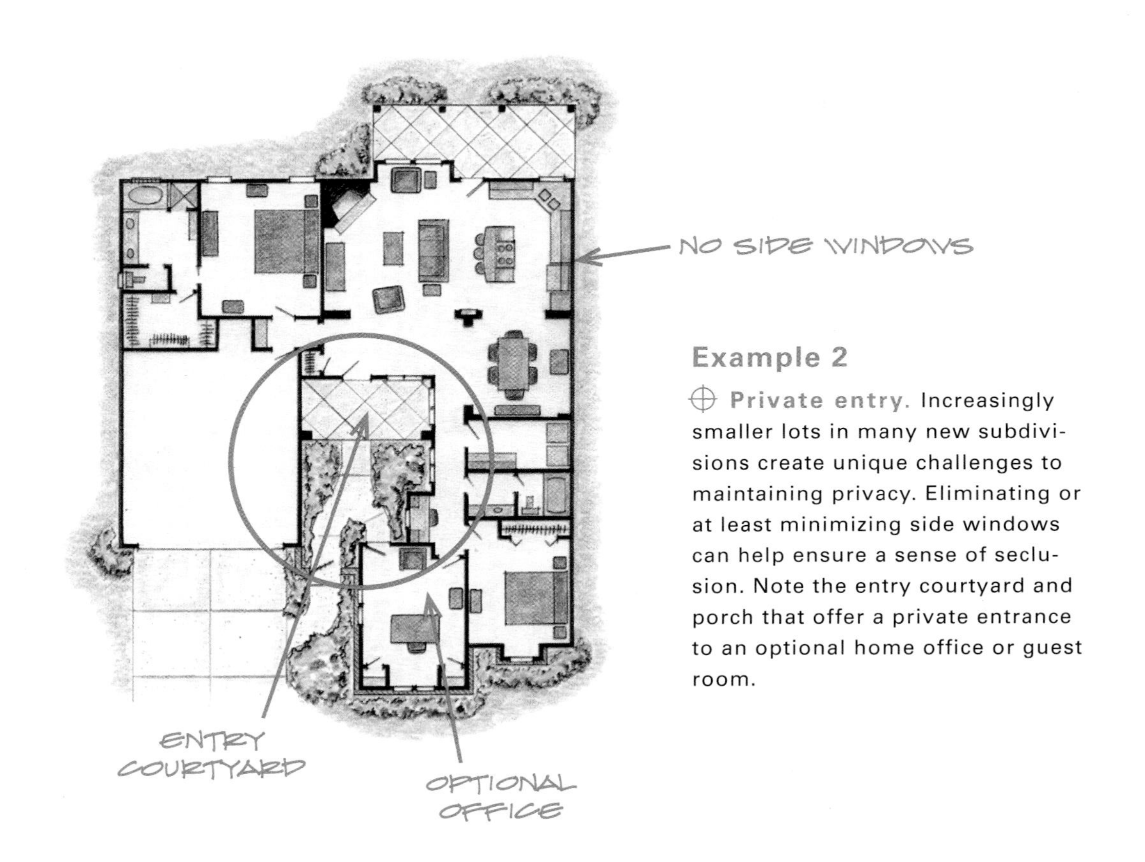

Example 2

⊕ **Private entry.** Increasingly smaller lots in many new subdivisions create unique challenges to maintaining privacy. Eliminating or at least minimizing side windows can help ensure a sense of seclusion. Note the entry courtyard and porch that offer a private entrance to an optional home office or guest room.

Example 3

⊕ **Window placement.** Careful placement of side windows along with an entry courtyard can help maintain privacy. Note that placing the garage well behind the front of the home greatly reduces its impact. *(See chapter 13 for more on casitas.)*

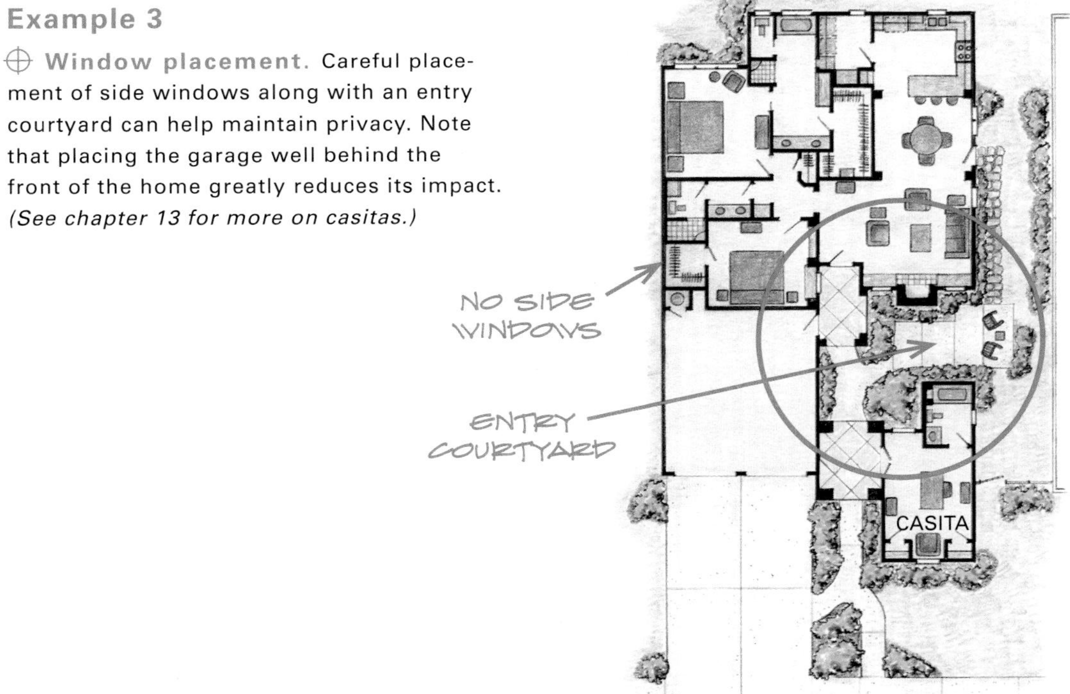

Frequently Asked Questions

What are some good indications that a plan is well thought out?

Ⓐ One of the most critical elements of a floor plan has to do with the traffic flow, or the path you take to travel from one room to another. Carefully designed plans address traffic flow with short hallways and galleries (open hallways) that connect the various areas of the home. For example, upon entering the home, you should be able to walk to the bedrooms or kitchen without being forced to cross through the family room.

Another indication of thoughtful design relates to storage areas. Bathrooms should have ample linen storage, and the kitchen obviously needs plenty of cabinets and pantry area. A walk-in pantry is not always the most efficient form of storage; cabinet-style pantries with multiple fold-out shelves often prove to be more functional.

Finally, while *open-concept* designs work wonderfully for most families, they must still allow for a certain level of privacy, especially for the master suite. Although hallways have been considered wasted space in recent years, they often provide the buffer for bedrooms. Be very cautious of selecting a plan that allows the master bedroom to open directly into the family room!

What are some pros and cons of having a main-floor master suite?

Ⓐ The location of the master bedroom has been debated for years. Strong arguments can be presented for locating it on either the first or the second floor.

A second-floor master bedroom is generally the preference in the West and East, while the Midwest and South seem to prefer a first-floor location. These preferences are probably based on what is customary in the area. Tradition aside, there are several practical considerations for where to place your master suite.

- A first-floor location may offer more privacy and eliminates the need to climb stairs. However, parents with small children might prefer to be close to the children's bedrooms on the second level for a greater sense of security.
- In the interest of energy conservation, locating all the sleeping areas on the same level allows for more efficient thermostat adjustment at night.
- A second-floor master bedroom may allow the homeowner to take advantage of a spectacular view the site might offer.

Part Two

Exterior Design Elements

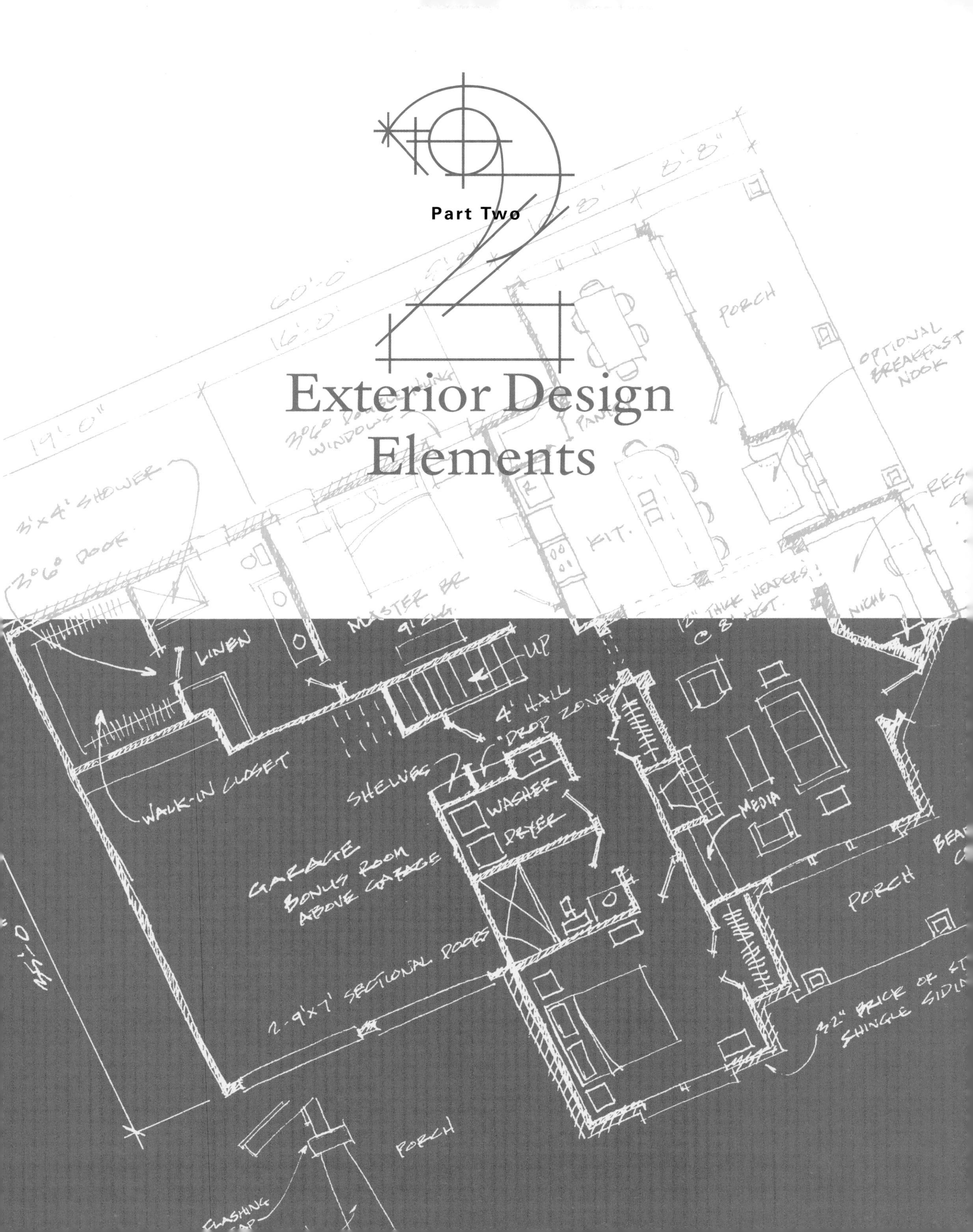

4

The Right Style for You

Why do some homes instantly appeal to us? They have what realtors, builders, and others in the home construction business refer to as *curb appeal* — something that immediately grabs our attention and invokes a sense of attraction to a house. I'm not sure a definitive explanation for it exists. After all, while we may consider our neighbor's home to be less than attractive, our neighbor probably thinks it's magnificent! We all possess different tastes and sometimes have drastically diverse opinions regarding aesthetic qualities of architecture. If not, every home would be almost identical.

Well, you might say that the houses in many new developments *do* look almost identical. Perhaps this indicates that we all have more in common than we thought. Or perhaps our sense of individuality has simply been ignored by the large-volume builders who insist on creating sprawling subdivisions of monotonous homes with little or no character. Drive through virtually any new housing development in any part of the country and you'll notice two things immediately: First, if you didn't know what city you were in, you'd never be able to tell by the style of houses — they look almost identical from one area to the next. Second, the roof designs and colors tend to be so similar that groups of homes almost appear to be large apartment complexes.

Money and Materials

As I've noted earlier, economics has a great deal to do with the overall appearance of the majority of our current new housing. However, by paying more attention to various exterior details, much of the sameness could be eliminated, or at least greatly reduced, even in the most basic of homes. Explore neighborhoods developed prior to World War II and you'll find an amazing number of quaint homes that were built on tight budgets. The same could be done today.

Let's explore why older homes appeal to so many of us. Specifically, I'm referring to those built virtually all across the nation from the early 1900s until the Great Depression. Ranging from small cottages to estate-size homes, many were built from pattern books that were local builders' primary source of designs. The wide availability

Design Diagnosis

Include variety

Details are critical when creating homes with a sense of character. The combination of materials, along with window and shutter proportions, must be correct. Notice the variety of window designs and siding in this exterior plan.

of these pattern books explains why many of the same homes dot the landscape from coast to coast. Most of these plan books featured intricately drawn details created by architects who seemed passionate about their work.

These homes' lasting appeal has to do in part with the era in which they were built. Although industrialization had enabled certain materials to be mass-produced and transported by railroad, builders still relied on local carpenters and craftsmen to fabricate many of the fine details and trim. For example, if the plans called for window shutters, the carpenters carefully measured and built each shutter for a precise fit. (Compare this to today, where readily available plastic shutters of random sizes can be nailed beside the window with no regard to proper proportions.) Many of these homes portray a certain sense of substance and permanence. They are usually composed of simple forms, and their visual impact comes from their humble and unpretentious design. Attention to detail and scale, along with expert craftsmanship, has provided many of these older homes with their inherent charm and lasting appeal.

Today, partly because materials are readily available, many new homes are an architectural hodgepodge. Such chaos sometimes begins with the designer. Computer-aided design (CAD) has enabled architects to select predrawn windows, gables, dormers, and other ornamental elements and easily place them on home plans. I call this "cut-and-paste architecture." The thought process that used to be involved in creating such details has in some cases been short-circuited by our technology.

This is not to imply that all computer-generated drawings should be considered inferior. On the contrary, the ease of revising plans electronically can (and often does) increase the architect's ability and freedom to refine the designs. However, even if the plans have been produced with meticulous attention to the details and proportions, the builder might still reach for those plastic shutters to save some time and money.

I often hear the comment, "They just don't build houses like they used to!" Well, that's true. Furthermore, we should be thankful that they don't! Today we have technology that provides us with better insulation, superior mechanical systems, and stronger structural components. Why, then, can't we create new homes with superior design and personality? There's no doubt that we can! We have all the essential ingredients at our disposal, from authentic siding made with durable concrete to meticulously replicated columns and window trim.

A growing number of builders are starting to pay strict attention to the proper application of these materials. Additionally, a significant portion of the design community has acknowledged that lessons of scale and proportion proven over time don't have to be ignored when creating new designs. Although some design professionals insist that good design must be totally unique to be considered original, many more realize that using rules of proportion along with practical and functional forms can still result in innovative and original designs.

The ultimate solution to good design involves you, the homeowner. The more educated you become in learning about scale, proportion, and quality, the better able you'll be to insist that your home be built with these essential elements of style.

Use time-tested design principles. The proven lessons of scale and proportion, along with attention to detail, don't have to be ignored in order to create innovative new designs.

Design Diagnosis

Placement of gables

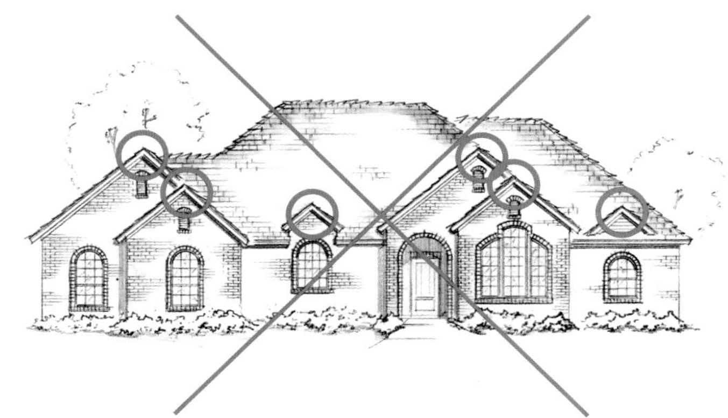

Every home should have a central focal point, or a design element that attracts and holds our attention, usually located at the front door or entry area. Certainly arch-top windows and gables can be a focal point, but when these elements are overly repetitious the focus is lost. The top plan has two well placed gables and an arched doorway. The original plan (at right) has six gables and too many arched windows.

A Matter of Personal Taste

In a meeting years ago I asked my clients what style they had in mind for their new home. They both emphatically replied, "Victorian!" I then asked whether they preferred Queen Anne Victorian or Folk Victorian. When I saw the blank expression on the husband's face as he looked at his wife, I quickly described the distinguishing details of each style. They politely listened as I spoke about the elaborate gingerbread fretwork of the Queen Anne style and the orderly, symmetrical details of the Folk style. My enthusiastic description of Victorian architecture was abruptly interrupted when the husband blurted out, "We just want a front porch!"

I could relate similar stories regarding clients' requests for "French" or "Spanish"-style exteriors. However, I have learned that trying to define a particular style often is confusing or misleading. Of course, if you consult an architectural history book, you'll find very specific descriptions and wonderful examples of various styles. While studying the evolution of architectural styles can be quite fascinating, most people just want a simple label to describe their home. In reality, however, most homes borrow elements from various styles to create a blend of details and features. We sometimes call this an *eclectic* style.

TERMS TO KNOW

Elevation. The flat (two-dimensional) drawings of the front, sides, or rear of a house are typically referred to as the elevations.

Facade. Often used in place of "elevation," facade refers to the exterior "faces" of the house after it is built.

Four-sided architecture. Quite often, houses are designed and built with attention paid only to the front and possibly rear elevations. Four-sided architecture refers to designs that consider all four elevations important.

Rather than dwell on a label, concentrate on the elements of various exteriors you find pleasing, along with materials you prefer. Perhaps you're attracted to steeply pitched roofs. Maybe a combination of stone and cedar shingle siding has always caught your attention. Instead of adhering to a certain style, focus on finding a plan that seems appropriate to your building site. The most appealing homes typically are those that blend with their surroundings, including not just natural conditions such as topography but also existing structures close by. Think about an exterior design that looks as though it belongs on the land and in the neighborhood.

Give careful attention to selecting exterior materials that are appropriate for the building site. Native materials, in particular, can help a home feel as though it *belongs* to a building site. For example, using local fieldstone in the exterior can make a home seem to harmonize with the land it sits on; using imported white limestone on that same site may result in a structure that seems out of place.

If you have a lot in a neighborhood with homes nearby, respect the existing architecture. Consider, for example, visiting a neighborhood filled with quaint cottages built in the early part of the past century. The sudden sight of a new stucco and glass home with a flat roof would be quite jarring. This design and use of materials would show no regard for the existing homes in the neighborhood. A growing concern for such lack of architectural respect has prompted more and more towns to enact laws and restrictions that prevent this very situation.

Craftsmanship. Attention to specific details can provide an elegant and inviting entry. Properly scaled beams (4×12) protrude from the stone, offering a sense of substantial structural integrity. The slight curve of the stone wall and the arched stone opening are subtle indications that this home has been carefully crafted.

Match the landscape. Consider an exterior style that reflects the land around it. For instance, if there are cedar trees and stone outcroppings, utilize some of these same materials in your home.

Now, this caution certainly isn't meant to imply that you should duplicate the look of your neighbor's house. On the contrary, select a design that offers at least subtle differences. Vary the slope of the roof, or the roof design itself. However, carefully select materials and colors that will complement those of the existing homes. For example, if you're building in a New England neighborhood composed of traditional homes built with brick and siding, you might consider using stone with stucco or shingle siding, and avoid trying to import the Southern California plan with low-pitched tile roofing that you fell in love with on your vacation. While it's lovely in California, it will look totally out of place in a New England neighborhood.

I've often been asked how I begin designing a home. Do I create the floor plan first, or do I start with the front elevation? The answer is both! Typically I have an idea of the essential exterior elements. For example, perhaps I want the elevation to reflect details of the Craftsman style. In this case I might use a combination of stone and shingle siding. To create the proper roof mass, a lower pitch would be required. Continuing with elements of the Craftsman style, window designs and locations begin to emerge.

With these images in mind, I begin to develop very basic floor plan diagrams, paying strict attention to both the building site and the specific requirements, such as square footage, number of bedrooms, and so forth. Although I have an exterior look in mind, the design and layout of the floor plan will ultimately become the determining force. The final design will include specific details and elements of the Craftsman style — and will probably be labeled as such by those who insist that every home has a style. However, the overall style of the home will actually have been dictated by the creation of the floor plan and its relationship to the site.

Certainly it's possible to design a home by first selecting a style and then manipulating the floor plan to conform to the style's unique forms and proportions. However, as you might imagine, this usually leads to compromises in the floor plan layout. For example, an authentic Georgian-style design will require a very symmetrical plan with precise window locations, while a design with only selected elements of the Georgian style might allow more flexibility in the floor plan. Once again, there's no right or wrong here. However, careful attention must always be paid to the particular details. An authentic Georgian-style home will fall short if the precise proportions and trim details are ignored. Similarly, the use of Georgian elements must also follow the rules of scale and proportion.

The fact that you're reading this book may indicate that you haven't yet found the plan that pleases you. Perhaps you have a particular style in mind, or maybe you are open to a variety of exterior designs. Either way, remember this: As you browse through the plans in this book or any collection of house plans, *resist the urge to pass over plans with an exterior you don't like.* If you quickly pass by that Mediterranean design because you have your heart set on a Country French style, you might overlook a floor plan that addresses many of your requirements. Exterior design can usually be easily changed. In fact, exteriors can often be revised with much less effort than it takes to dramatically alter a floor plan.

Harmonize with the neighbors. Even a well-proportioned stucco design with a tile roof may appear out of place in a New England neighborhood.

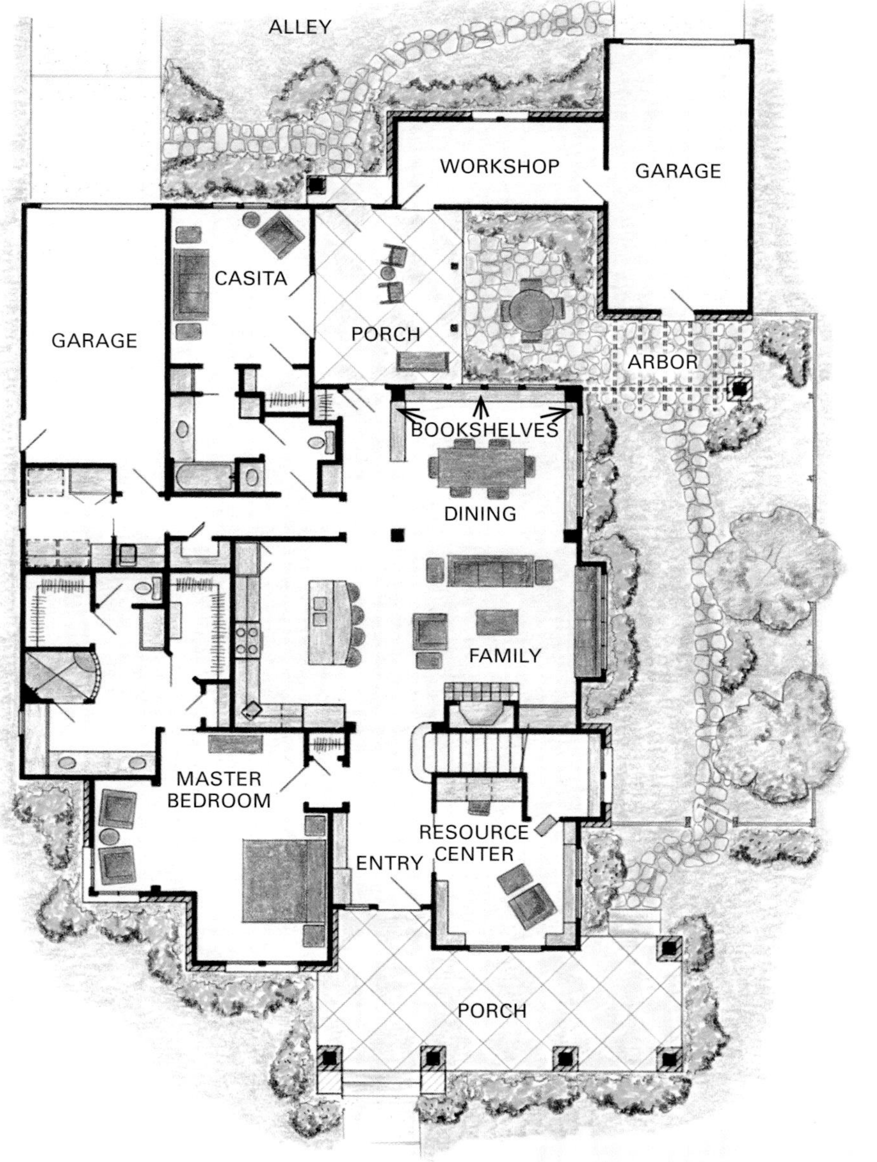

HEALTHY EXAMPLES

Customize the exterior to fit the plan and the site

This exterior design (below), though based on Craftsman details, is actually dictated by the floor plan and site. Garages are placed at the rear of the property and are accessed from an alley, while the front of the home opens to a public greenbelt. Although the front porch offers a welcoming invitation to passing neighbors, the side courtyard provides privacy for the homeowner. This rather unique custom design addressed the client's extensive book collection by creating a dining room that also functions as a library.

HEALTHY EXAMPLES

Customize the front exterior to fit your style

These alternate front exteriors show how dramatically different designs can be created for the same floor plan.

Example 1

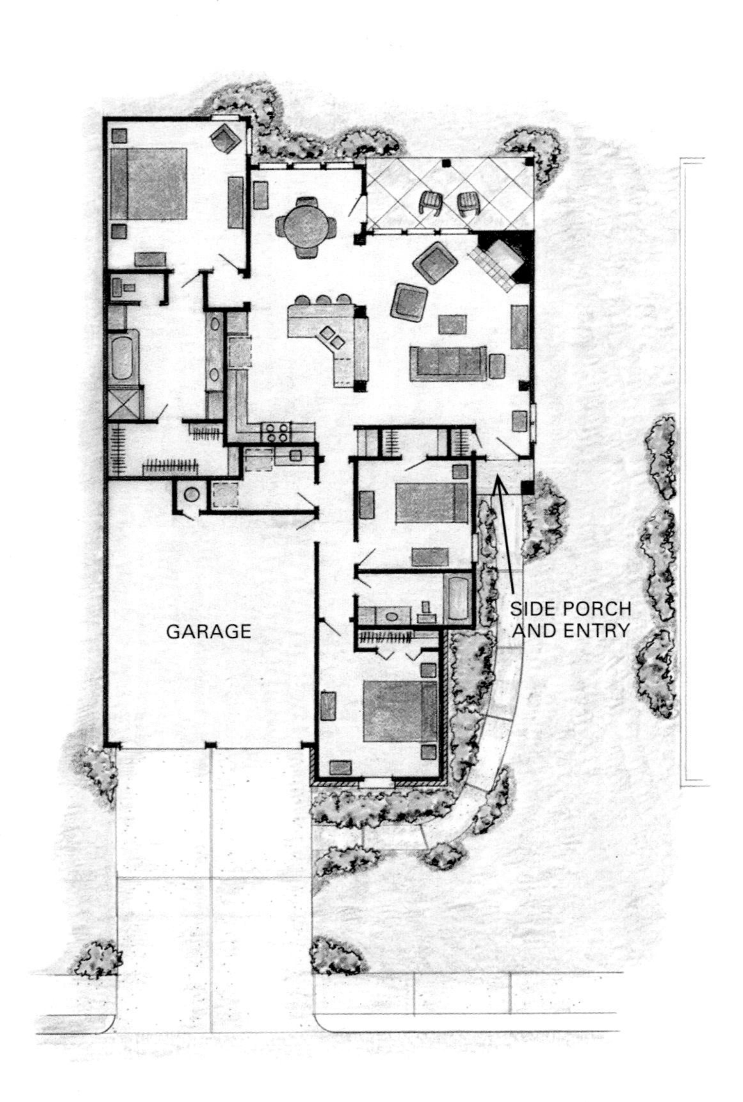

Exterior option Ⓐ

Exterior option Ⓑ

Example 2

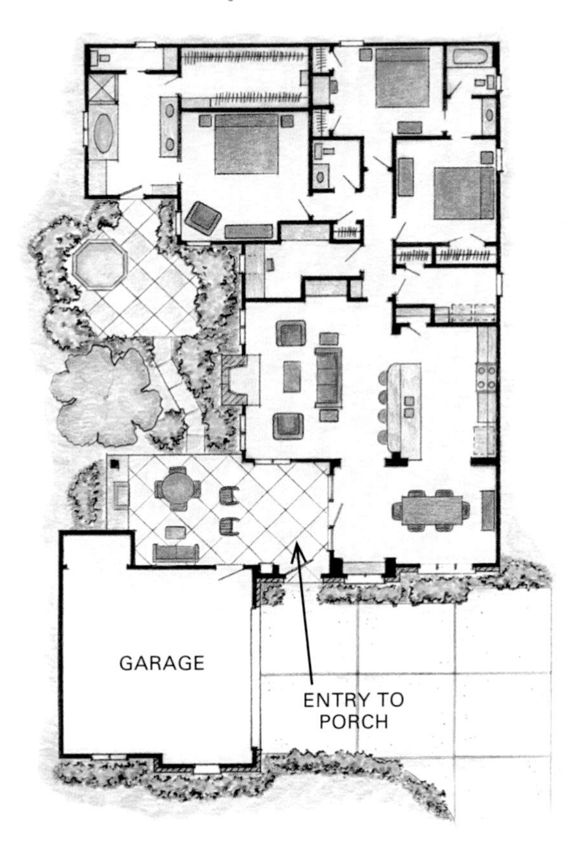

Exterior option Ⓐ

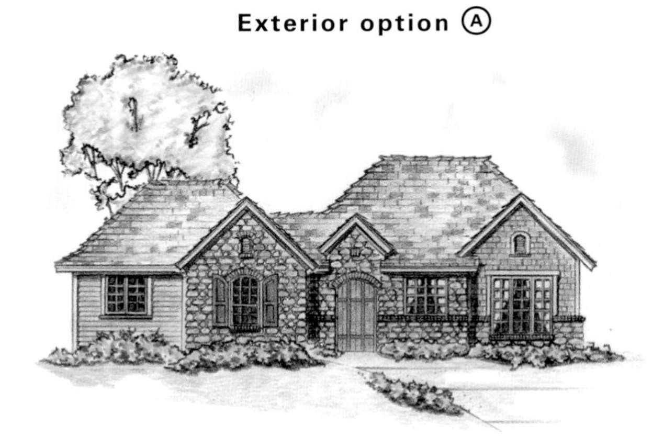

Exterior option Ⓑ

Example 3

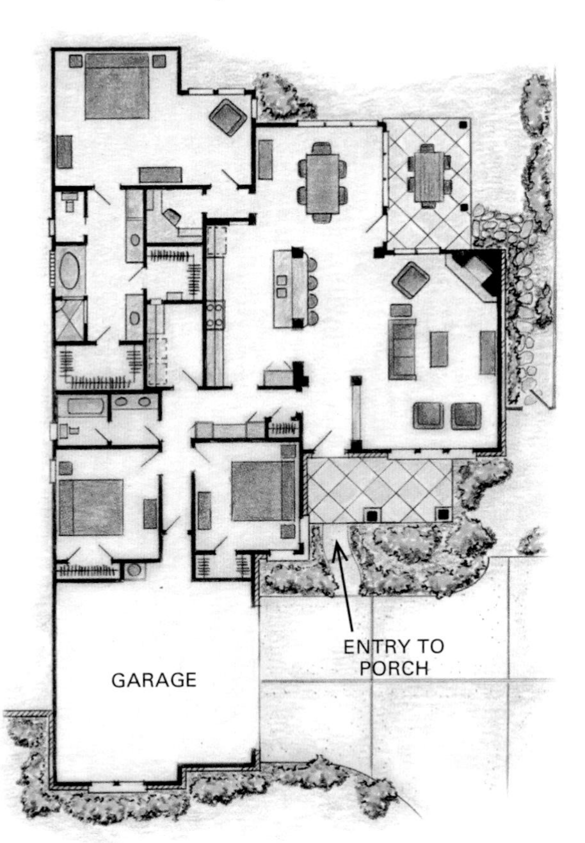

Exterior option Ⓐ

Exterior option Ⓑ

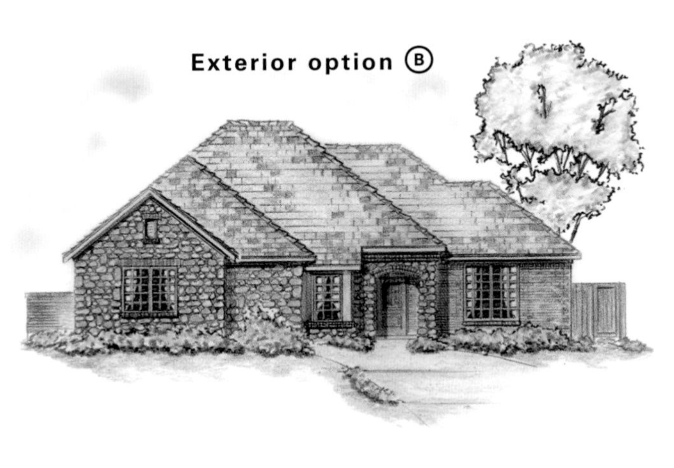

A range of styles. The right style for your home should be based on the materials that you prefer or that the site seems to suggest. While avoiding a design that mimics that of your neighbor's house, respect the overall theme of the neighborhood.

Styles allow us to exert personal tastes regarding our homes. While no one style is inherently better than another, there are some basic attributes that can make any home more appealing. The proper use of exterior materials, roof design, window placement, and garage location become vitally important when designing your home.

All Four Sides

All too often, designers and homeowners consider only the front facade when selecting or creating a home design. However, exterior design involves more than just the front of your home. In many cases the sides and back elevations are seen more often than the front. For instance, consider a floor plan designed to take advantage of views towards the rear of the property. If you spend a great deal of time in the backyard, you'll see the back of your home more frequently than the front. Furthermore, with a lake or golf course behind you, others will be looking at the design of the rear, possibly never even seeing the front.

Side elevations also become critical on very narrow lots, which generally call for plans with side yards. Since this area serves as your outdoor living and entertaining space, attractive architectural design will be important. Also, for homes on a large building site with plenty of surrounding open area, all four sides should be carefully planned. Builders in many new developments with homes ten feet apart often pay little or no attention to the side elevations. Of course, if no one ever sees the sides of your home, it can easily be argued that this becomes a logical place to save some money.

Budgets, of course, must always be considered. However, creating what we call *four-sided architecture* doesn't necessarily require an increase in the overall building cost. Rather, materials and details must be selected with even greater care. For instance, instead of using all of the budgeted brick on the front of the home, use some of it along the side and especially the rear. The budget remains the same regardless of where the brick might be located. Simply paying attention to details can also enhance side elevations. For example, adding a band of 12-inch horizontal trim can transform a two-story wall from an overwhelming sea of siding into an elevation with much more pleasing proportions.

Homes built in the late nineteenth and early twentieth centuries rarely ignored the design of side and rear elevations, even when budgets were tight. If a person could afford a brick home, the brick was applied with proper care and details throughout the entire house. For those whose budget didn't allow for brick, siding would be utilized, again paying strict attention to such details as window and door trim. In other words, straightforward principles of design and craftsmanship were followed whatever the size of the budget. Today, if the budget can't justify brick, a builder may decide to offer the illusion of a brick house by placing it only across the front. Assuming no one will really notice, the sides and back reflect little attention to material selection and details. This is something to watch out for when reviewing plans for the exterior of your home. *(For more on siding strategies, see chapter 6.)*

Design Diagnosis

Add trim for impact

Simple details can make a tremendous difference. By adding a band of 12-inch horizontal trim, the large area of siding is defined by floor levels. Overall paint combinations are also key. Although the contrast between trim and siding must be definite, complimentary colors usually work best.

HEALTHY EXAMPLES

Consider all four sides of the house

Example 1

⊕ **Side courtyard.** With designs calling for side courtyards, the side elevation becomes extremely important. After all, this becomes your outdoor recreational and entertaining area.

RIGHT SIDE ELEVATION

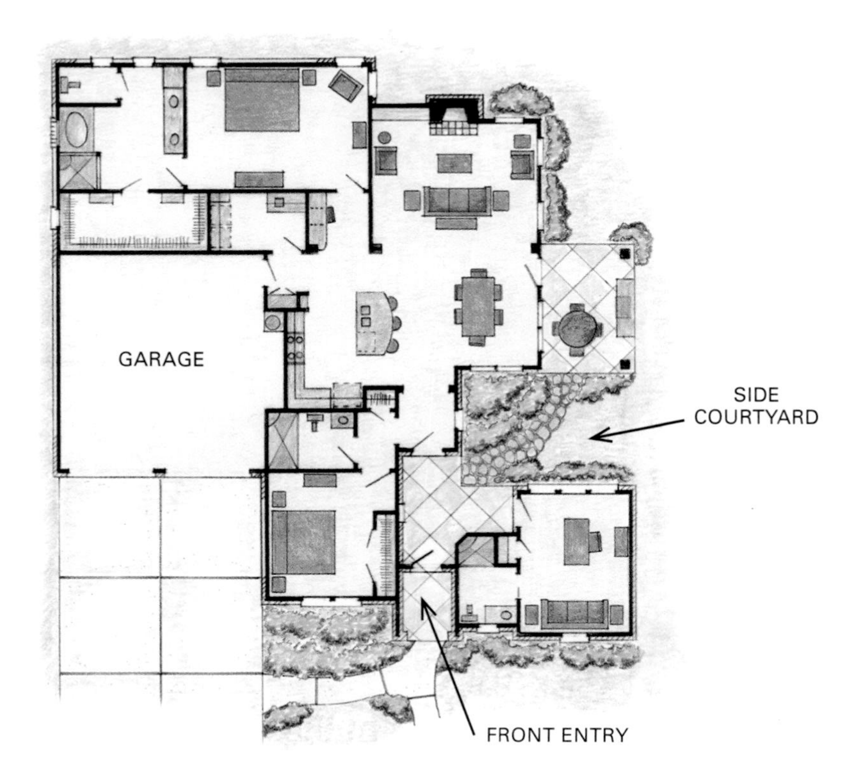

Example 2

⊕ **Matching details.** Ideally, all four sides of the home should be properly detailed. By carefully selecting appropriate materials, four-sided architecture can be created while maintaining the required budget.

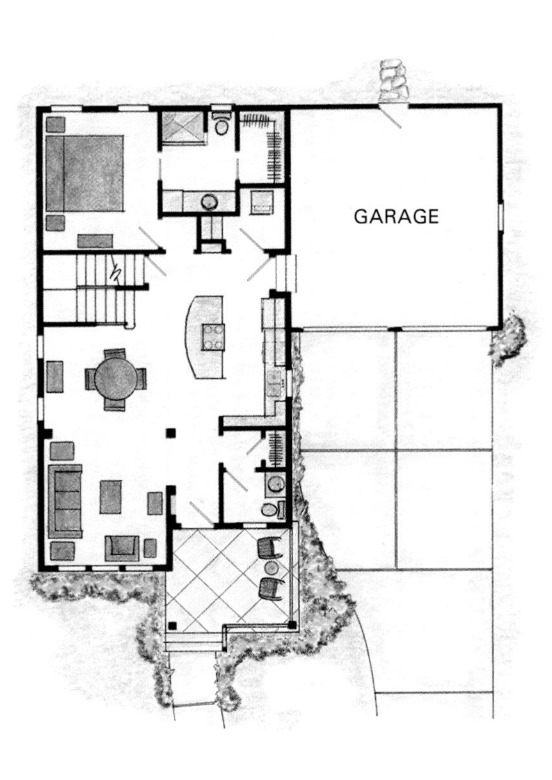

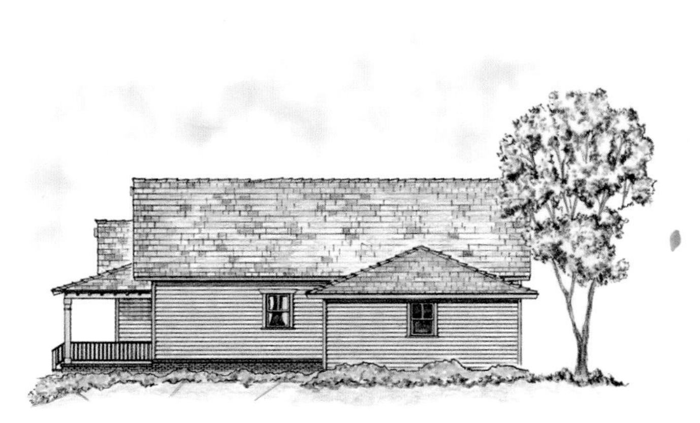

Evaluating Model Homes

Another time to pay attention is when reviewing model homes. I recently watched a television program that featured new planned developments and homes across a major metropolitan area. Instead of including the concrete driveways, elaborate landscaping concealed front-facing garage doors. **Some of the builders even replaced the garage doors with windows to give their model a homier appearance. However, these models do not accurately represent what the houses will look like when built. Don't be fooled by gimmicks.**

A growing number of builders are paying strict attention to the proper application of these materials. Additionally, a significant portion of the design community has acknowledged that the lessons of scale and proportion proven over time don't have to be ignored when creating new designs.

5

Approaching the Home

Generally we hope our guests will approach the front door and allow us to greet them in the foyer. However, this just doesn't happen in many homes, because we all tend to use the entrance that's most convenient. And that is most often the entrance closest to where cars are parked. If visitors park their cars in your driveway near a back door, that's the entrance they're most likely to use. Since many plans locate the utility room at this back door, everyone entering the home is welcomed by the dirty laundry and other undesirable items we place there. If your garage offers entry to the house and you usually leave the garage door open, people will tend to come in by that route. For many of us, garages offer an even less attractive entrance than the utility room.

Any discussion or analysis of entries must include automobiles and parking. Garage location and driveways often dictate where family and guests enter your home. Later we'll talk about formal entryways and foyers where you *hope* your guests will enter. We'll also discuss family entries. However, where automobiles are parked will ultimately determine where everyone enters the home.

Driveways and Walkways

The driveway and walkways should encourage guests to naturally gravitate toward the door you prefer they use. In other words, we can use careful design and landscaping of the avenues of entrance to our property to draw our guests toward the front entry.

If possible, place the driveway so that visitors see the front door as they approach your home. For example, if your plan has been designed with a garage at the right side of the house, try to bring the driveway in from the road on the left side. This will force you and your guests to drive in front of your home (and the front door) in order to reach the garage. If you allow adequate space along this drive for parking and create an inviting entry walk, most people will sense that the front door is the entry they should use. You might even use the front door yourself, since it will be so convenient!

HEALTHY EXAMPLES

Entry way options

Example 1

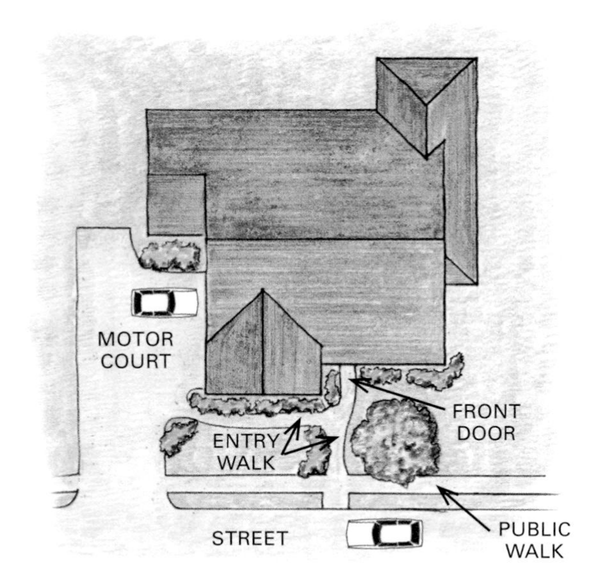

⊕ **Landscape a direct path.** People usually take the most convenient path and enter a house by the nearest door. Thoughtful placement and landscaping of the garage, driveway, and walkways will encourage guests to enter your home through the front door.

Example 2

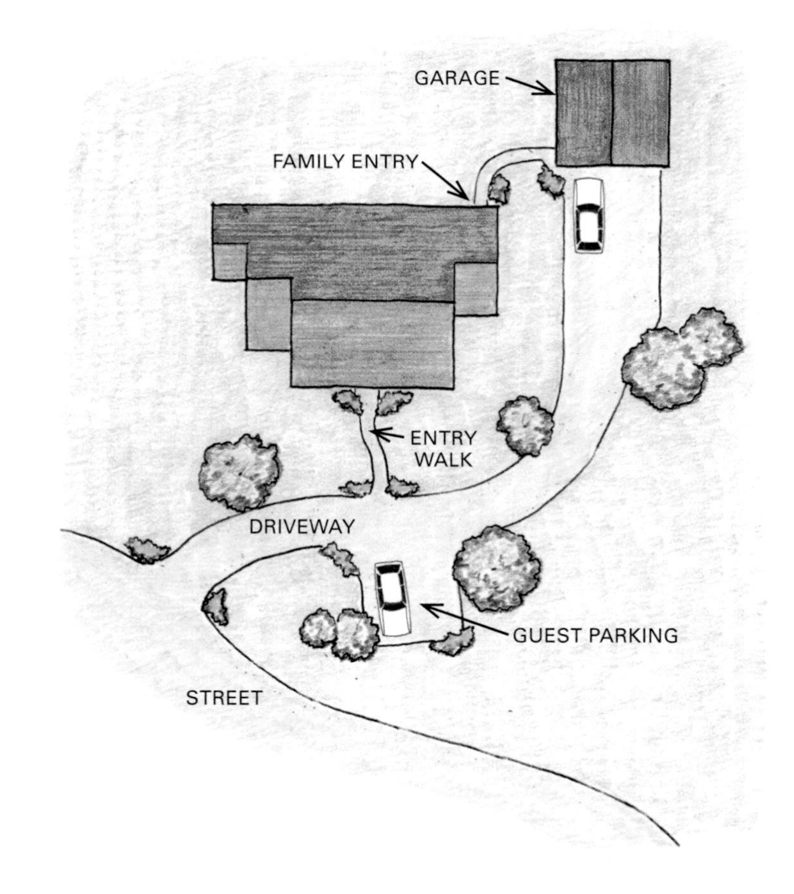

⊕ **Feature the front entrance.** If your building site will allow it, design the drive to enter the property from one side and travel across the front of the home to a garage on the far side. This will encourage your visitors to stop and enter through the front door. As an added benefit, you and your family will experience the pleasure of viewing the entire front facade of your home each day as you come and go from the garage.

Example 3

⊕ **Handling a rear alley entry.** Homes built along a rear alley present a unique challenge. Ideally, your guests will park along the front street and enter through your foyer. However, some will invariably decide to park in the driveway. Make sure there's a landscaped walkway that invites everyone to travel around the garage towards a side yard and entrance.

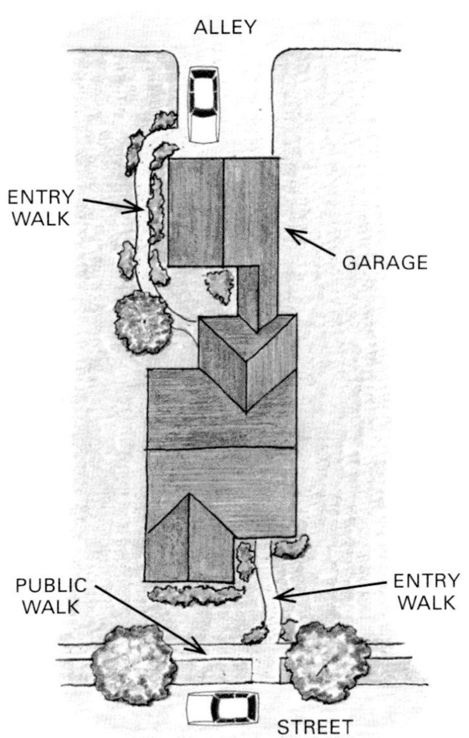

Example 4

⊕ **Planning on entry walk.** A garage facing the street should be located behind the front of the home. An inviting entry walk will lead people towards the front door. Make sure there's also an entry walk that will allow guests to park on the street and easily travel to the front door.

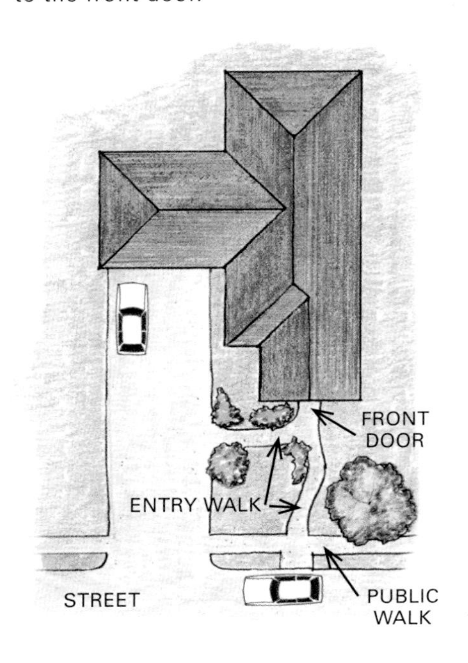

Example 5

⊕ **Separate family entry.** From a practical standpoint, a family entry adjacent to the garage is both convenient and functional. It can feature lockers, drop zones (for cell phones, keys, handbags, and mail), and benches for organizing the comings and goings of your family.

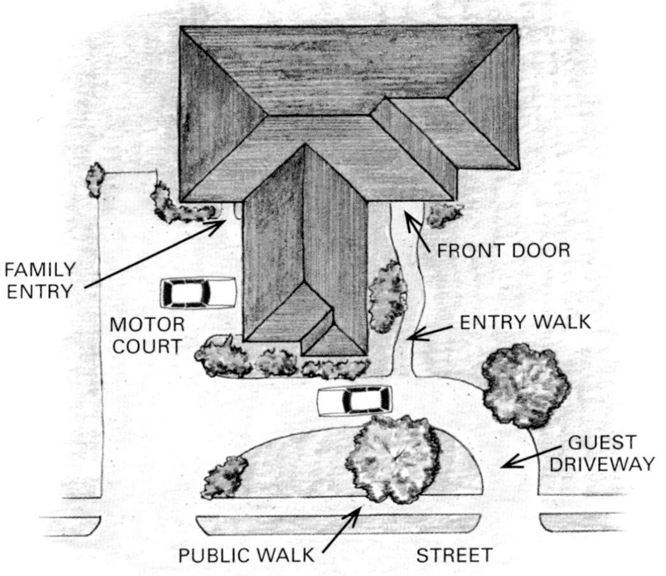

Remember, it's our nature to take the path of least resistance. If the front entry is just that, it will quickly become the entry of choice. There's another benefit of winding the driveway across the front of the house. I'm a firm believer that we, as homeowners, should enjoy the design and beauty of our homes each day. Often houses are designed and located on sites that don't allow this; instead, we back away from the garage each morning and return to the exact same location in the evening without ever seeing our own front door. By driving along the entire front of your home each time you come and go, you'll experience this pleasure on a daily basis.

With narrow building sites that force the garage doors to face directly toward the street, a welcoming walk leading to the front door will help direct everyone as they decide how to enter your home. Placing the garage as far back as possible also helps. If your guests drive past an inviting walk leading to the front door, they'll be inclined to use that path. If your garage is attached to the house, the key becomes keeping the garage doors closed at all times. Remember, we'll take the first available entrance; don't allow that to be through your garage!

Always make sure there's an attractive entry walk from the public sidewalk. I'm amazed that this path is so often forgotten, forcing your guests to walk up your driveway (and probably toward the garage). Of course, in far too many new developments there's no public walk in the first place! Obviously, if you're intent on building in a pedestrian-friendly neighborhood, make sure that it includes public walks.

Homes located in developments with rear alleyways present another set of challenges. A garage behind the home certainly has advantages, but the question is how to best direct guests to the front entry. If you and your guests park in the driveway at the rear of your home, make sure there's a landscaped walkway that invites everyone to travel around the garage toward an attractive side yard. Depending on the layout of your home, you might direct visitors to enter into the dining room or some other appropriate area.

In theory your guests will park along the front street and be easily directed to your front door. Some new developments encourage this by placing designated guest parking in convenient locations. Of course, in this case pedestrian walkways along the street that allow easy access to your front walk become absolutely essential.

As much as we might strive to direct traffic to our front door, in certain situations this simply doesn't work. In some cases we may actually *want* our family to enter elsewhere. For example, if your family has a lot of outdoor activities, an entrance that serves as a mudroom may be essential. Perhaps you live in a cold climate where an entrance with storage for boots, gloves, and heavy coats would be greatly appreciated. Realizing these special circumstances, a family entry *(see pages 135)* might become an integral part of your new home.

Garages

On the most basic level, housing is meant for shelter and automobiles are meant for transportation. However, we all know that each is much more. For some, cars are a necessary evil — loud machines that pollute our environment but are necessary for getting around. Others cherish them as works of art that are almost like members of the family. While most of us fall somewhere between these extremes, automobiles have an enormous impact on all of our daily lives.

Ideally garages will be of secondary importance in the design of a home. However, our dependence on automobiles dictates that we pay considerable attention to the design and placement of the garage. Consider this: A two-car garage will consume as much square footage as a large family room. A three-car garage will typically be the largest "room" in the home.

The term *cookie-cutter houses*, once used only by builders and architects, is common among homebuyers these days, expressing their disillusion with current housing developments. The placement and design of garages probably has more to do with this negative response than any other single detail. Of course many builders understand this. They build model homes with French doors in place of garage doors and place elaborate landscaping where the concrete driveway will be located. While creative landscaping has often been used to hide architectural mistakes, it does not fool today's buyers.

Avoid a dominant garage. Homes built on narrow lots with front-facing garages often seem more like garages built with small houses attached.

So, is there a solution to the garage design issue? If you're building on a larger lot or outside of a planned development, your options are many. But within planned developments with narrow lots, unless the development allows for garages to be placed along a dedicated back alley, the options are more limited.

As developers continue to carve out smaller and smaller lots, homeowners and builders face the difficult challenge of finding plans that accommodate two or more automobiles without allowing the garage to become the focal point of the home. When a 20-foot-wide garage with front-facing doors is set to the front of a 35-foot-wide home, it often seems as though the garage is being built with a small home attached.

If you select a plan with the garage doors facing the front, try to find one that places these doors behind the front line of the house itself. In other words, if the front porch or another portion of the home protrudes further forward than the garage, the front door will likely remain the focal point of the home, with the garage fading into the background. This concept has the added bonus of providing additional driveway area for parking.

Since so many homeowners dislike front-facing garages, some developments now prohibit garages from having doors that face the front of the lot. While I admire their attempt to help control the often overwhelming presence of garages, such restrictions readily allow garages that protrude entirely in front of the home as long as the doors face

Design Diagnosis

Add garage door details

Details such as single doors, detailed carriage house doors, and attention to rooflines can help soften the impact of front-facing garage doors. Although a gable roof above the garage may work, it's usually best to simplify this area in order to draw less attention.

HEALTHY EXAMPLES

Garage location

Example 1

Recessed setting. By moving the garage location behind the front of the house, the front door remains the focal point. Also, the additional driveway length provides extra space for cars to park.

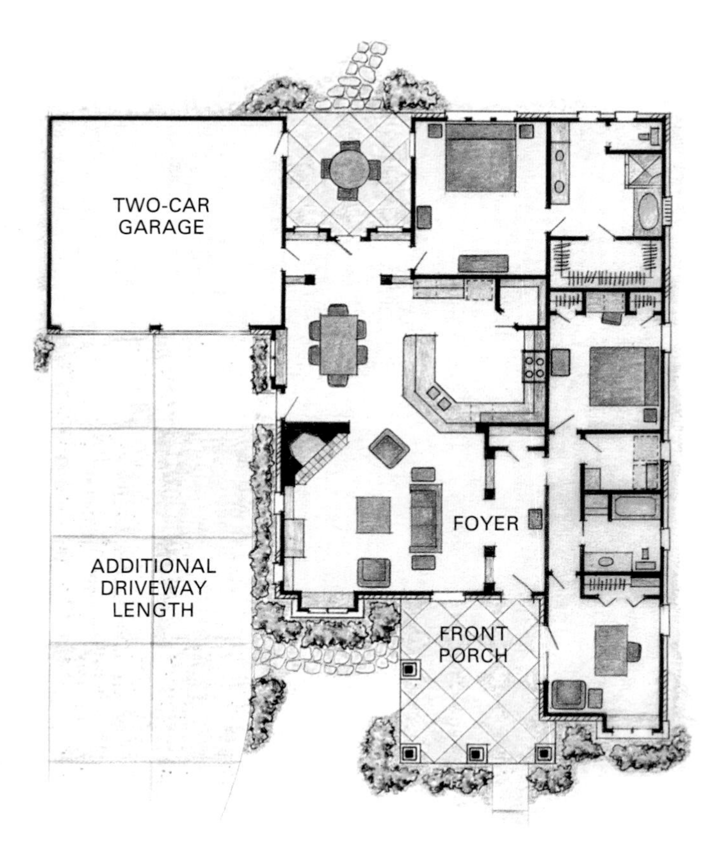

Example 2

Facing to one side. Wider lots offer the opportunity for an attached garage with doors facing towards the side. This not only eliminates the front-facing doors but also makes the home appear larger and avoids having parked cars block the view of the front door.

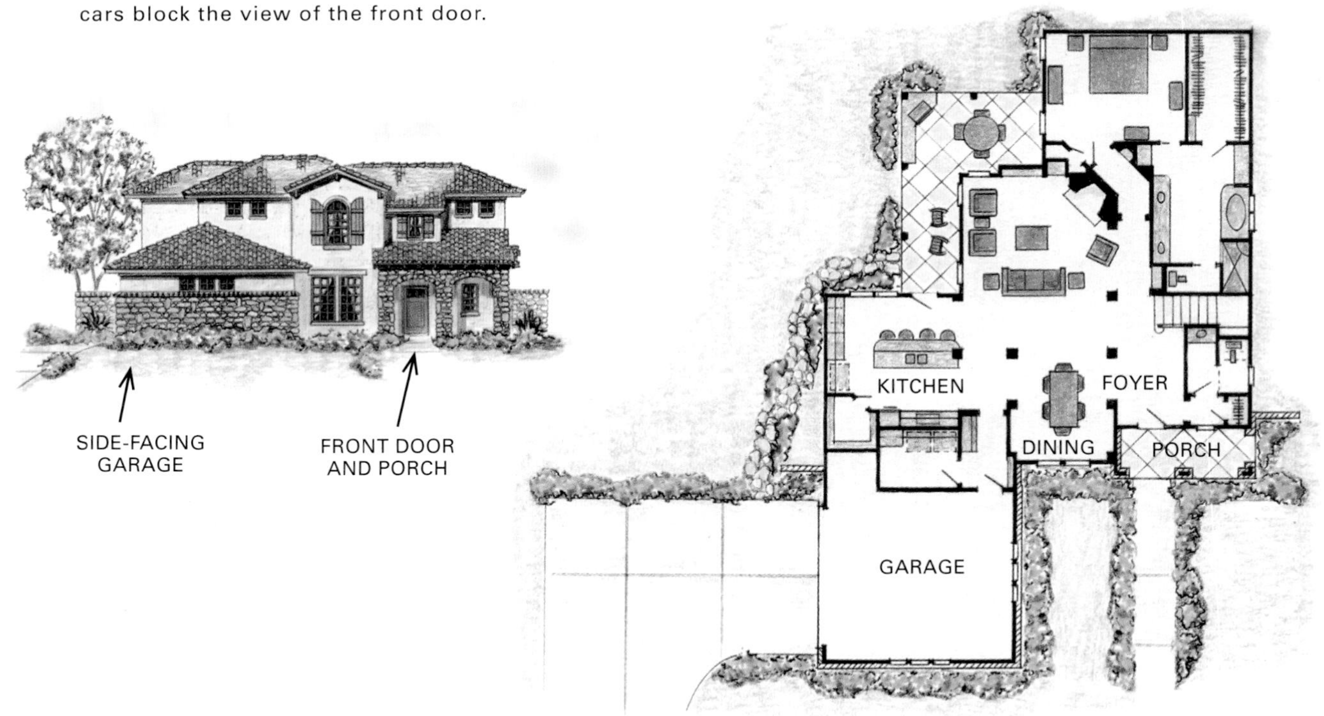

to one side. They are a classic example of two-dimensional thinking. In other words, on paper it appears that the garage doors will be obscured as they open to the side, but in reality, when viewed in three-dimensional real life, the doors are just as obvious as if they faced directly to the front. In fact, the garage itself can become even more massive in appearance.

Regardless of which direction its doors face, its exact location, or the number of cars it will hold, close attention to the overall placement and details of your garage can definitely reduce its impact on and improve the overall appearance of your home:

- Careful attention to rooflines can help, for example. Essentially, try to draw attention to another portion of the house, such as the entry, while downplaying the garage itself. Although a gable roof at the garage with detailed vents or windows above may work, often it's best to simplify this area as much as possible.
- A garage placed at the front of the home can be arranged so that an offset in the roof covers it, and wider roof overhangs can create deeper shadows that minimize the view of the doors.
- As for the doors themselves, two single doors usually look better than one large door. If your budget allows, new doors that are reminiscent of intricately detailed carriage-house doors are now available from several manufacturers. Using these doors can result in a garage that actually contributes to the architectural appeal of your home.

Wider lots offer the opportunity for an attached garage at the edge of the house with doors facing toward the side. Not only does this eliminate garage doors facing the street, it also gives the home a much larger and more impressive appearance. With the driveway at the side of the house, parked cars do not block the view of the front entry.

As if dealing with the two-car garage isn't enough of a challenge, many buyers now request space for three automobiles. Typically the three-car garage is pushed forward with garage doors opening toward an interior motor court that can hide the front entry. As an alternative, the garages can be separated into two-car and one-car areas, creating an attractive and functional side motor court.

Due in part to the traditional neighborhood design (TND) movement *(see page 9)*, detached garages are finding renewed acceptance in many markets. Whether placed at the rear of the lot and opening to an alley or simply set back from the front of the house with front-facing doors, the detached garage becomes secondary to the home itself. A covered walkway connecting the garage and house can extend the porch and outdoor

HEALTHY EXAMPLES

Three-car garage

Example 1

⊕ **An L-shaped arrangement.** As an alternative to the typical three-car garage located at the front of the house, this L-shaped arrangement also creates a functional motor court.

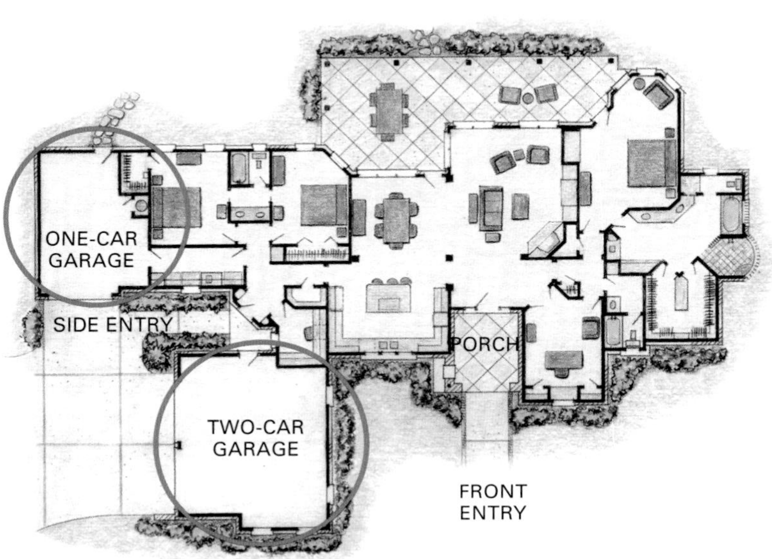

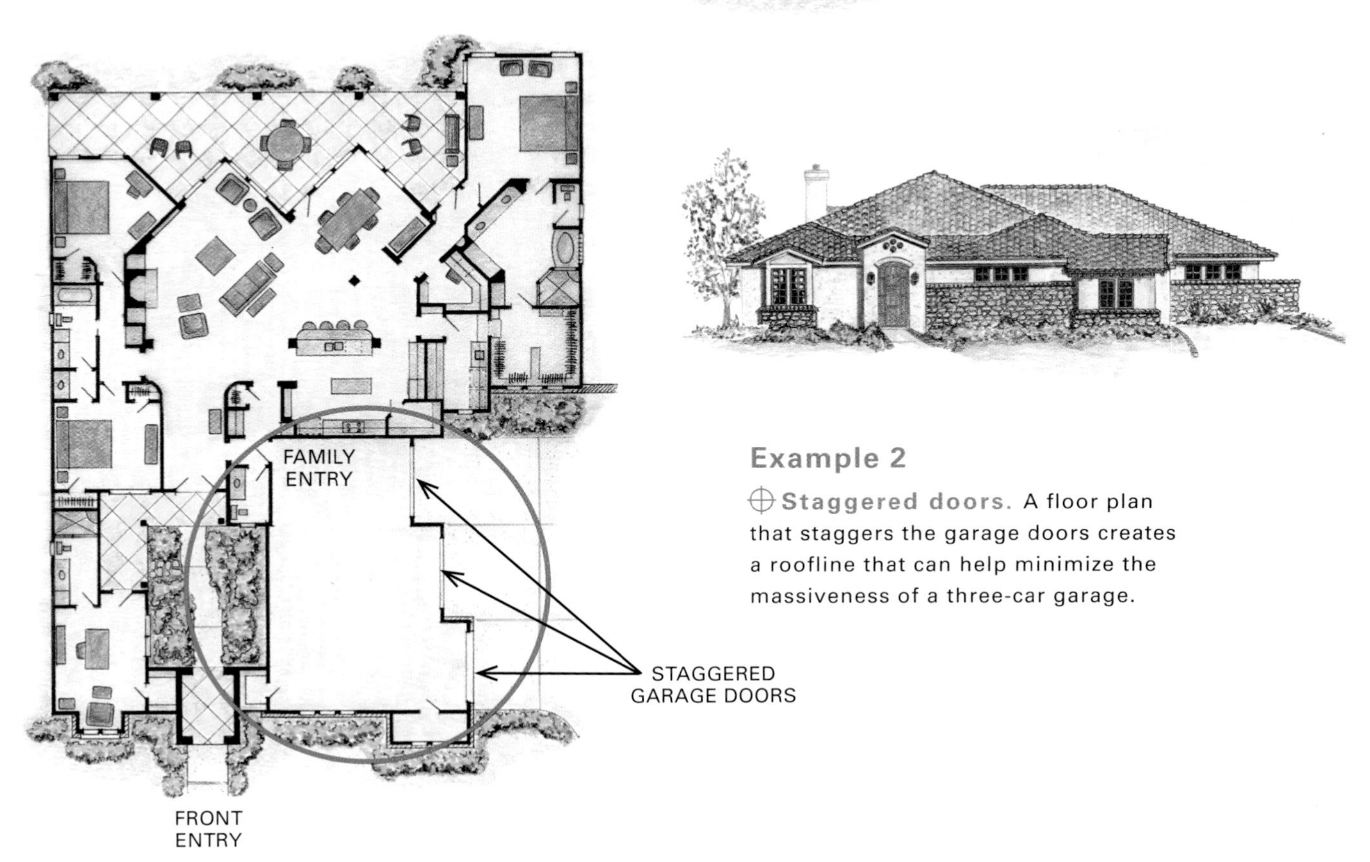

Example 2

⊕ **Staggered doors.** A floor plan that staggers the garage doors creates a roofline that can help minimize the massiveness of a three-car garage.

entertainment area. In severe climates, the walkway might be enclosed, creating a sunroom.

Ideally driveways will be wide enough to accommodate two vehicles. Narrow drives force the homeowner to constantly move one car in order for another to enter or leave the garage.

Once we become comfortable with the actual appearance of the garage itself, it becomes obvious that the real culprit behind the disenchantment with garages and driveways is the automobile itself. After all, the cars parked in front of the garage are the real distractions. Carefully designed garages with finely detailed doors are of little value if parked cars obscure them. The simple solution here is a remote-control door opener that will encourage you to keep the cars inside the garage. Perhaps more important, the garage should provide enough storage space that you can find room in it to park the cars. We all appreciate generous storage areas. A small alcove with a window easily transforms into a hobby area with a workbench. Simple shelving can help keep small tools and supplies organized. Dedicated space for lawnmowers and other outdoor gear is essential. And for homeowners with younger children, bicycle and toy storage is key.

Another reason we often find automobiles in the driveway, rather than the garage, is that garage sizes have not always kept pace with typical automobile dimensions. Many plans still feature garages that were appropriate for the compact cars popular in the 1980s. SUVs and large trucks are now more popular than ever, but many garages just cannot accommodate them. Certainly you'll find it worthwhile to measure your cars and make sure your new garage will be large enough for them before you finalize your plans.

Sometimes, of course, we must leave a car in the driveway. But if a front-facing garage is located only 20 feet from the sidewalk or street, there may not be enough room to leave a car in the driveway without having it protrude into the sidewalk or street. Ideally, any plan with a front-facing garage will place the garage doors so that a driveway of at least 35 feet in length can be built.

HEALTHY EXAMPLES

Detached garage

Example 1

Rear location. This detached garage becomes secondary to the home. A covered walkway connecting the garage and house can extend the porch and outdoor entertainment area.

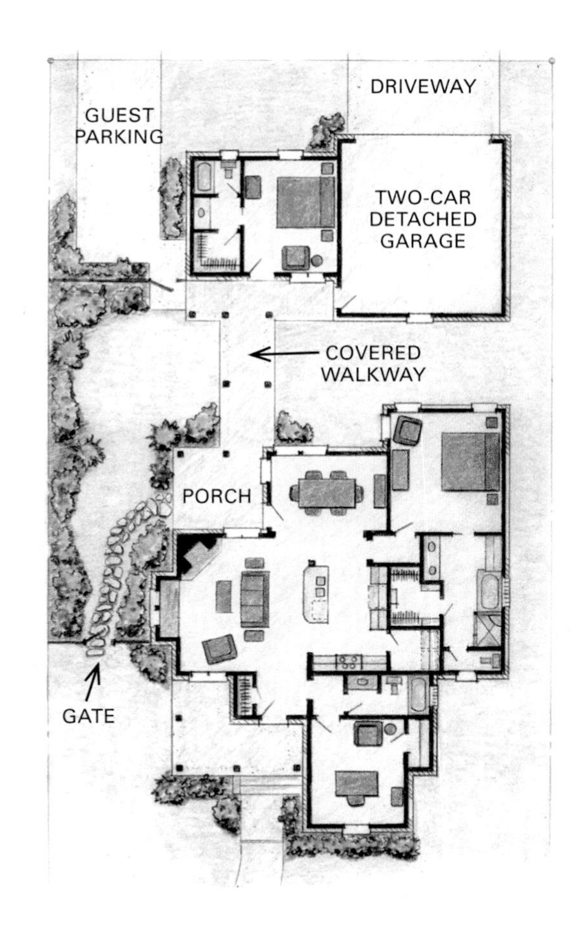

Example 2

A wide lot. This plan offers the opportunity to detach the garage and face the doors towards the side. Once again, the covered walkway becomes part of the porch. For sites with less width, the garage doors can easily be located at the front of the garage.

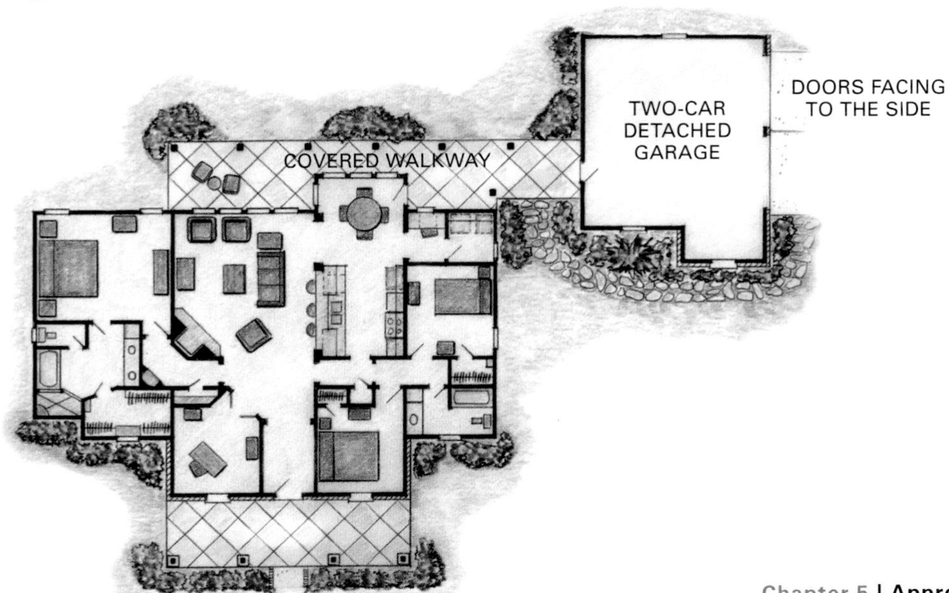

Frequently Asked Questions

Q *What size garage doors should I consider?*

Ⓐ For years standard garage doors have measured 8 feet in width and 7 feet in height. This was adequate until we tried to fit massive SUVs through these openings. Even the traditional double door with 16 feet of width is an issue due to the 7-foot height. Today an assortment of door sizes can be found, ranging from 6 to 20 feet in width and 6 to 12 feet in height. Since the typical ceiling height on most homes has increased from 8 to 9 feet, we now have the opportunity to easily increase the height of garage doors. As a result, while the typical door now is 9 feet by 7 feet, it's not unusual to see 9-foot × 8-foot doors.

Materials are another consideration. While the current trend favors finely detailed wood, steel and fiberglass continue to be good options. You should also investigate insulated doors, especially if your design calls for an attached garage.

Remember to make sure the overall width and depth of the garage will provide enough space for your cars. Unfortunately, I've seen beautiful oversize doors on garages that don't allow enough depth to accommodate some vehicles.

Q *What are the advantages and disadvantages of a detached garage?*

Ⓐ Historically all garages were detached. Automobiles displaced the wagons and carriages from carriage houses, and for many years the fear of gasoline combustion prevented any consideration of actually attaching automobile storage space to our houses.

As discussed in this chapter, the garage is a design issue due to its massive size. Detaching the garage allows more options from a strictly aesthetic point of view. However, the detached garage typically requires more building area. Also, a detached structure normally adds to the cost of construction, since it doesn't share one of its walls with the house.

Of course, climate and security must also be considered. The attached garage offers you and your car much more protection from the elements. With an electric door opener you can literally drive your car into the "house" and never endure severe heat or cold. Additionally, the security of closing the garage door behind you and being in the confines of your home may be a comfort.

6

Cladding and Windows

The materials you select for the exterior of your home, known as *cladding*, not only play an important role in its overall appearance but also can dramatically affect its cost. Cladding options essentially break down into two choices: masonry and siding. Although masonry costs more than siding, it has traditionally offered less maintenance and a longer life span. However, some of the new building materials make this comparison less distinct. Let's start with a closer look at some of these cladding options.

Brick or stone cladding creates additional wall thickness. As a result, a home with a brick or stone exterior will have a greater square footage than an otherwise identical home with siding or stucco.

Brick. Composed of kiln-fired clay, brick is available in a variety of colors and textures and will last for many years with little or no maintenance.

Stone. Stone has been used for centuries as a building material, and its natural appearance and strength make it a favorite for home exteriors. However, increased costs in recent years have limited its use to larger-budget projects or exterior accents.

Veneer stone. A relatively new alternative to natural stone is synthetic stone veneer, which is made of aggregate materials. When installed properly this product appears almost identical to natural stone. Due to its light weight and an average thickness of only 1½ inches, it's often an excellent choice for chimneys and other areas where natural stone might become an expensive structural issue.

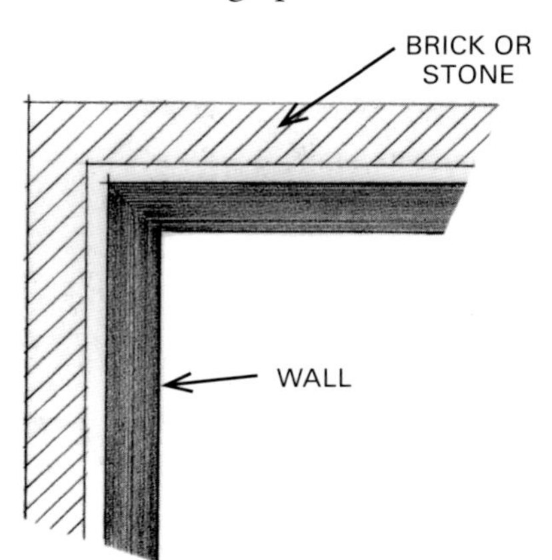

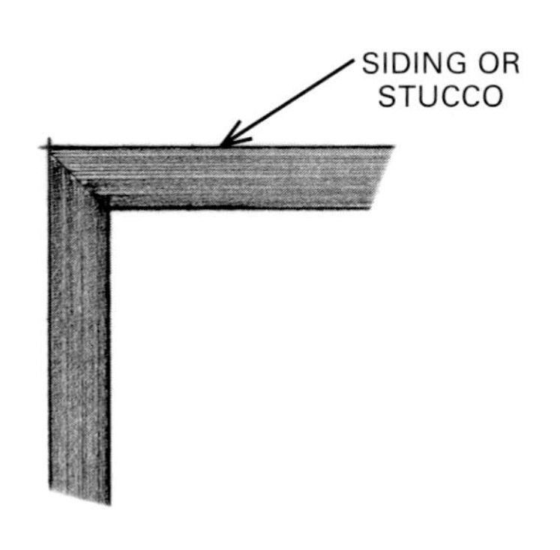

Siding symbols. When reviewing floor plans, you'll know whether a design calls for siding or masonry cladding by the drawing symbols. An extra crosshatched wall layer indicates brick or stone walls.

Stucco. Although brick and stone normally come to mind as the only masonry materials, stucco should also be included in this group, since its basic ingredient is concrete. Used for centuries as exterior cladding, stucco provides a pleasing, textured appearance with excellent moisture resistance when properly applied. In recent years several synthetic materials that resemble stucco have gained acceptance. In some cases, however, these synthetic materials do not offer the same durability as authentic stucco. Both authentic and synthetic stuccos do not usually add the extra wall thickness that brick and stone do.

Wood siding. Another exterior material with a rich historical tradition, wood siding might be milled from pine, cedar, redwood, cypress, or Douglas fir. A variety of sizes and textures can be found from a number of manufacturers. Although wood siding is far from maintenance-free, regular painting or staining can extend its life span for many years.

Vinyl, aluminum, and steel siding. Essentially maintenance-free except for periodic cleaning, these products strive to resemble wood. Each product should be evaluated for appearance and cost.

Cedar shingles. Often referred to as *shakes*, cedar shingles can be applied one shingle at a time or as lengths of plywood with factory-applied shingles. Although normally stained or painted, shingles can be left to weather to a soft, gray color. Depending on the thickness and quality, cedar shingles can literally last a lifetime with minimal maintenance.

Fiber-cement siding. This durable and natural-looking siding has revolutionized the homebuilding industry in recent years. In addition to being fireproof and termite-proof, fiber-cement siding has outstanding manufacturers' warranties and is considered to be masonry by many insurance companies, thereby lowering rates for homeowner's insurance. It is available in various sizes, profiles (shapes), and textures; some manufacturers also offer factory-applied colors.

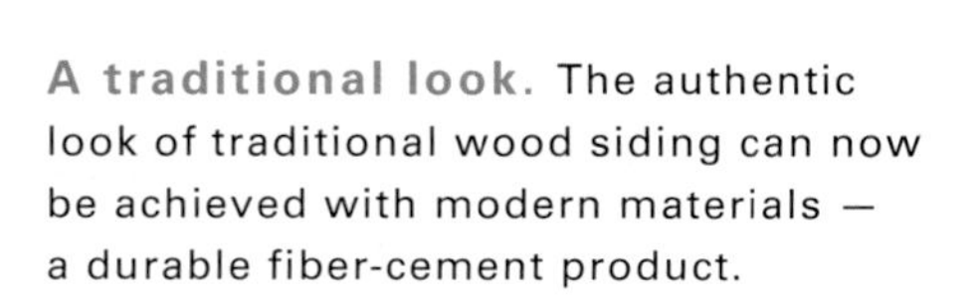

A traditional look. The authentic look of traditional wood siding can now be achieved with modern materials — a durable fiber-cement product.

Stone vs. Brick

Transporting stone or brick over long distances can dramatically increase the cost of these materials. In the past, the native stone readily available in many parts of the country was far less costly than man-made brick. The exact opposite is now the more common situation. Even for stone that is quarried locally, the labor involved in the installation will typically result in a higher price than you would pay for a brick exterior.

Combining Cladding Materials

Combining various exterior materials is a longstanding practice, undertaken sometimes in the interest of aesthetics or, more often, because of budget constraints. While using expensive materials in combination with less expensive materials can be a good way to get the high-quality look you desire without breaking your budget, care must be taken to ensure that the combination appears to be a design choice rather than a cost-saving measure.

We often find homes from previous centuries appealing because of the way they combine exterior materials. For example, a New England home in which a central red brick structure contrasts with an adjoining section clad in white clapboard seems to have character. But don't imagine that these charming homes were designed simply with charm in mind. Some of their most appealing details resulted from practical solutions to design and budget challenges. In that New England farmhouse, for example, the brick core was probably built first, and the flanking white clapboard section was added later, as the family expanded or finances allowed, and clad in wood because it was less expensive than brick. As another example, we frequently see homes from the nineteenth and early twentieth centuries built predominately of stone, with brick used only to surround windows

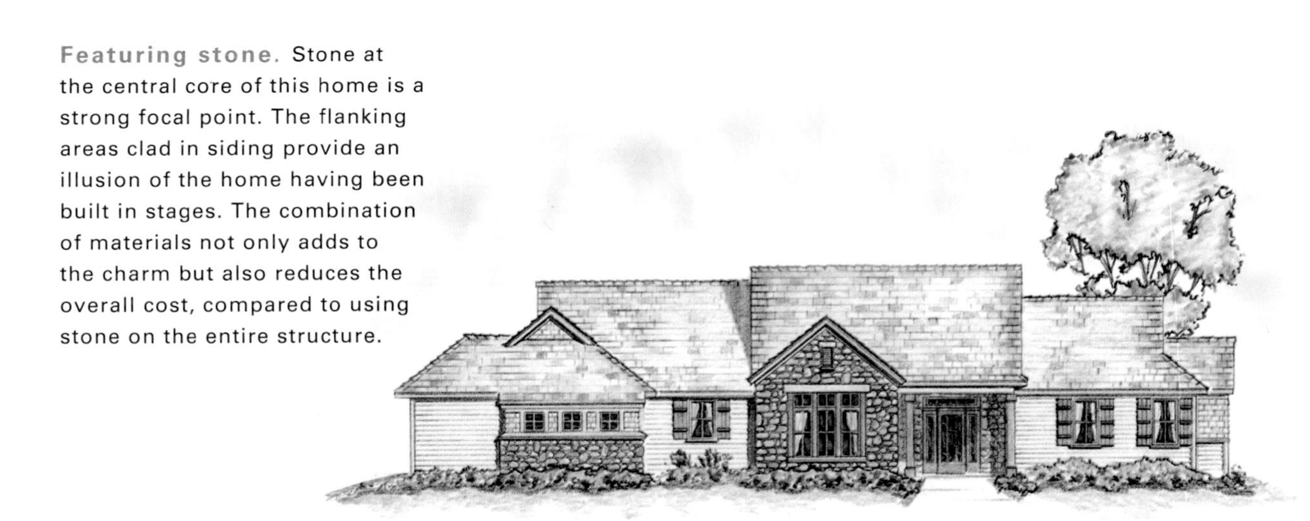

Featuring stone. Stone at the central core of this home is a strong focal point. The flanking areas clad in siding provide an illusion of the home having been built in stages. The combination of materials not only adds to the charm but also reduces the overall cost, compared to using stone on the entire structure.

and at corners. In these cases stone was the exterior material of choice simply because it was readily available. Man-made brick was at the time a costly luxury but provided the uniform straight edges that would be labor-intensive to shape from stone, and so it was used only in those places where uniform straight edges were necessary.

When it comes down to it, a large expanse of any single material can be boring. We've probably all seen homes clad entirely in brick or stone that seem very monotonous. The careful combination of materials can highlight each material and enhance the overall appearance of the home, while at the same time saving money. For example, you might consider having brick on the front of your home and less expensive siding on the other three sides. Instead of having the brick run across the entire front of the house but abruptly stop at the corner, make the transition on an inside corner of the front of the house, so that the house seems built of two sections, each with a different type of cladding. In this way the change of materials is an element of design, rather than a budget constraint.

Although combining materials can lend charm and interest to a home's exterior, a great deal of commercial architecture currently utilizes an overwhelming number of materials to create visual impact. It's not uncommon to see stone (perhaps even two types) combined with brick, stucco, and tile. These seemingly drastic contrasts have been designed to capture our attention. Although such combinations might be visually appealing on a retail structure, the use of so many vastly different materials on a home will likely result in a jarring and trendy facade. **In general, no more than two or perhaps three different materials should be used on the exterior of a home.**

Always consider the exterior in three dimensions. A few years ago Georgian-style homes were the rage. Considered by many to be the most elegant and tastefully designed homes in our country's rather brief architectural history, these perfectly proportioned red brick homes with dark green shutters became the inspiration for many large production builders all across the South. At first glance these boxlike structures must have seemed economical to build. However, as with all styles, the details proved critical.

The crucial mistake made by these builders involved the use of brick. Their construction budgets allowed for only enough brick to be placed across the front of the homes, and they used siding on the sides. While this likely looked fine on paper with two-dimensional drawings, the actual homes appeared more like those of a Hollywood movie set, where only front facades are built. From almost any viewing angle, the drastic transition from the brick front to the siding destroyed the character of these Georgian-inspired

HEALTHY EXAMPLES

Combining exterior finishes

Example 1

⊕ **Transitioning from brick to siding.** The home on the left probably looked fine when viewed in drawings that showed just the front, with handsome brick cladding. However, when seen in perspective, the brick abruptly terminates at the outside corner, in awkward contrast with the siding on the side of the house. In the home on the right, the transition from brick to siding takes place at an inside corner. Though it may have been a cost-saving decision (siding being less expensive than brick), the combination of materials has a charming result and seems more like a design decision.

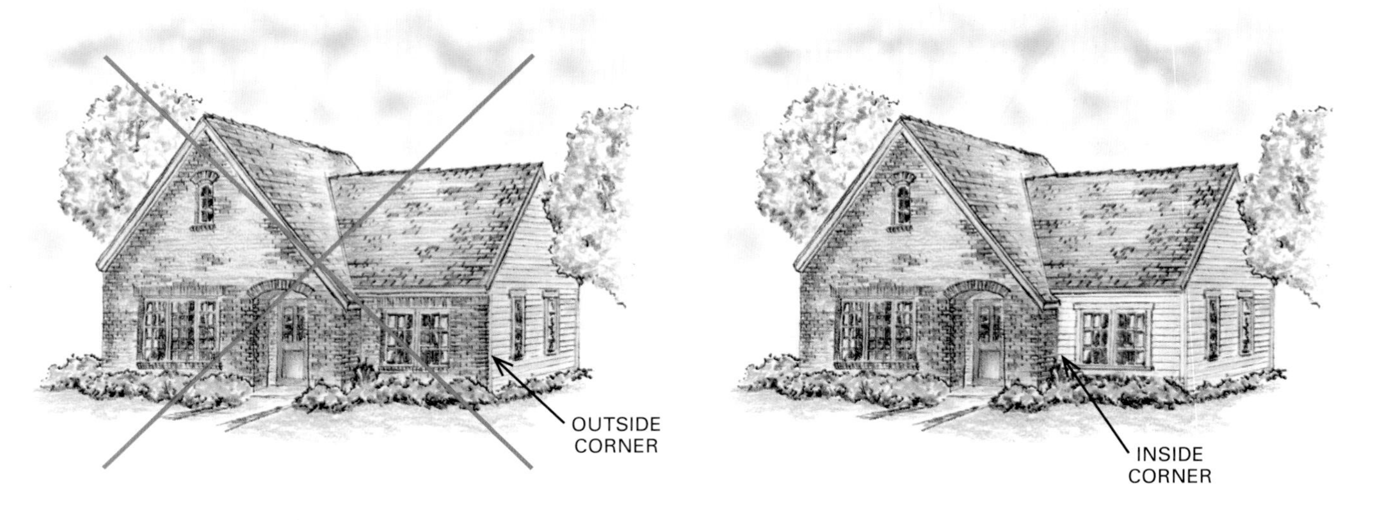

Example 2

⊕ **Blending brick and stone.** The brick surrounding the windows of this predominately stone exterior provides a comfortable transition to the brick wall that wraps around the right side of the home. The stone on the left side will need to continue to a point at the rear of the home where an inside-corner transition can be made.

Design Diagnosis

Combine materials

This home effectively uses three different exterior materials: brick, shingle siding, and horizontal siding. Note the slight contrast in colors used on the horizontal siding and the shingle siding in the gable. Using more materials than three, however, would lend the home a chaotic, unsettling appearance.

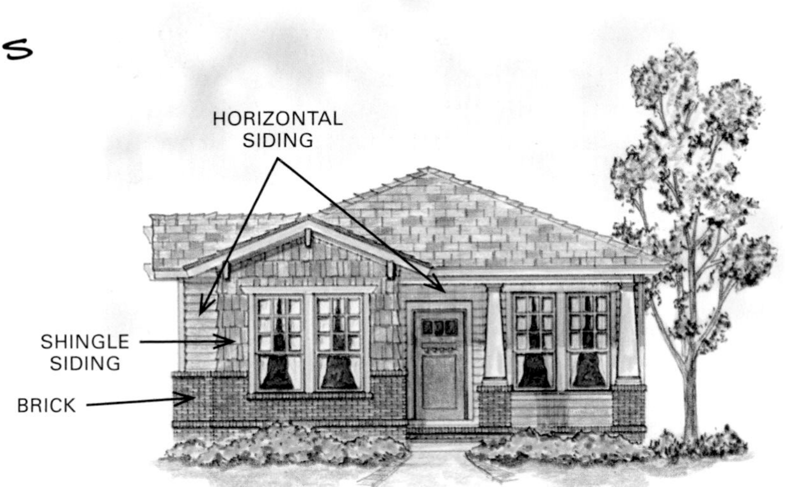

homes. (Of course, improperly sized window shutters and other ignored details exacerbated the problem.)

In some ways I consider this approach to designing and building homes an insult to the homeowner. Essentially it's implying that since you can't afford to build a home with proper materials and details, you'll settle for a cheap imitation. Of course we all must deal with budget constraints. However, an honest approach to selecting or designing a plan with the appropriate materials can result in a home in which you'll be proud to live, and which you'll also be able to afford.

Windows

Windows should be considered one of the most important elements of any home. They not only create a connection to the outdoors but also provide a barrier against the heat and cold. And of course if you just paid a premium for an exceptional view, you want windows sized and placed to emphasize that view. Unfortunately, window selection is often the most neglected aspect of home planning. For many builders there is only one factor: use the cheapest windows that can be found!

The location and orientation of your building site will play a large role in the selection of windows. Window quality is always a critical factor in this selection, particularly if many of your windows face towards the intense western sunlight or cold winds of the north. Many manufacturers offer special designs that minimize heat and cold transfer and block damaging ultraviolet rays.

WHAT IS A CLAD WINDOW?

Clad windows are constructed with wood frames that have cladding on the exterior. This cladding protects the wood from the rain and sun and provides a permanent color that will never need to be repainted. Some manufacturers clad their wood windows with aluminum, while others utilize vinyl or other composite materials. Although more expensive than solid vinyl or solid aluminum windows, clad wood units often perform better from an energy standpoint, since wood is a much better insulator than either vinyl or aluminum. Also, since the wood remains exposed on the *interior* of these windows, they can be either painted or stained to match the other interior trim. When you browse through design magazines you will rarely find interior photos of windows other than those with wood interior surfaces. There's simply a drastic difference in the appearance of a wood window and one made of some synthetic substitute.

Consider this: Even though you may spend time, effort, and money insulating your new home and installing high-efficiency heating and air conditioning, if you don't complete the job with high-quality windows, you'll be making a serious mistake — one that is extremely costly to correct!

High-quality windows, especially clad wood units, are expensive. One way to keep the cost under control is to use standard-size windows. Still, it might be worth investing some extra money in a special window that enhances the front of your home. A bay window or a series of windows with arched transoms can provide a breathtaking effect. Note, however, that an arch top adds significantly to the cost of a window — so much so you'll believe that arches really are golden! Also, be aware that window coverings for unusual window shapes cost significantly more than those for standard sizes. Since specially shaped windows have always been expensive, architects and designers constantly face the challenge of designing appealing exteriors without resorting to costly windows. As a result, some of the most attractive homes feature very straightforward window selections.

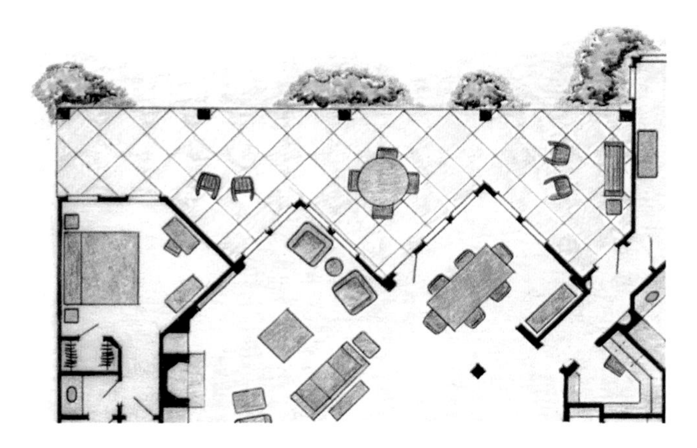

Appreciate the view. Expansive windows are a critical design element for a home that faces an exceptional view. This plan features an angled row of windows (top) overlooking the back porch.

Window Shutters

In times past construction details were based largely on practical and functional concerns. Perhaps the best example is the use of window shutters. Originally louvered shutters were installed with hinges so they could be closed; they provided protection for the windows while allowing light and air to filter through the louvers. Obviously, in order for the shutters to fit properly, they had to measure exactly one-half the width and the exact height of the window.

While we rarely see functional shutters in today's market, proper scale and proportion remain important details. Though selecting the appropriate-size shutter seems relatively simple, more often than not houses feature shutters too narrow for their windows. Sometimes a wide window tempts us to use shutters of less than half the window width. Resist! *All* shutters should be half the width of their window. Adherence to this detail of proportion can become the single most important element that sets your home apart from neighboring houses.

The design codes in some new planned communities require the use of functional shutters that open and close. While this requirement might seem extreme, the hinged shutters actually make a remarkable difference in a home's appearance. They form deeper shadows on the walls, since they are suspended by hinges rather than being attached directly to the walls. If you happen to live in a coastal area subject to high winds, you'll find these operating shutters quite useful. After all, consider the original reason shutters were invented!

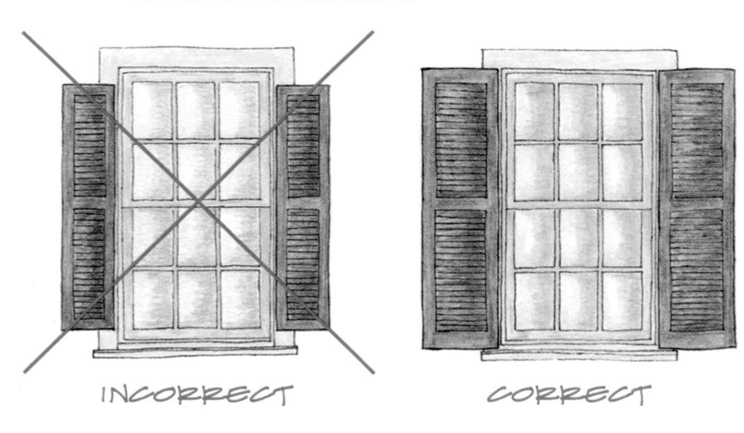

Shutter proportions. Proper proportions require shutters to be exactly half the width and exactly the same height of the window. Too often we see shutters that are both too narrow and the wrong height.

Shutters that actually work. Authentic shutters with operating hinges might be appreciated in an area with high winds. Also, the deeper shadows cast by shutters that are suspended by hinges can add to the appearance of a house.

Terms to Know

Flashing. Usually a small piece of galvanized or other non-corrosive material, flashing is installed above a window to keep water from seeping behind a wooden window frame.

Header. Similar to a lintel *(see below)*, a header refers to the wood support in the framing directly above a door or window. Usually, this consists of two 2×6s or two 2×12s nailed together.

Jack arch. While most arches are curved along the top, a jack arch is flat. Although horizontal with no curve, the arrangement of wedge-shaped bricks or stones support one another by mutual pressure.

Lintel. A lintel is a horizontal structural member such as steel, stone, or wood that supports the load (weight) above an exterior opening such as a window or door.

Shaped stone. While some stones are placed on walls in their natural shape, most are hand-chiseled and chipped to form shaped stones.

Soldier. Bricks or rectangular-shaped stones placed in vertical alignment — like men in a uniform line — are called soldiers. One technique involves placing the bricks so that every other brick protrudes at an angle, called a marching soldier course.

Transom. A transom is a window located over another window.

Brick and Stone Lintel Details

In the past the use of stone and brick lintels or jack arches above windows was a practical necessity for framing window openings. These spans of segmental brick or cut stone supported the weight of the wall above the window. Today, with the use of steel supports for windows, stone and brick lintels are ornamental details. Nevertheless, the proper application of these details adds tremendously to the traditional appearance of a window.

A simple soldier course of brick across the top of a window provides a relatively inexpensive yet attractive lintel detail. Adding a course of shaped stone as a header will be slightly more expensive, since the stone mason will have to create the rectangular shapes from natural stone. However, such a detail can easily transform the windows into the focal point of the home.

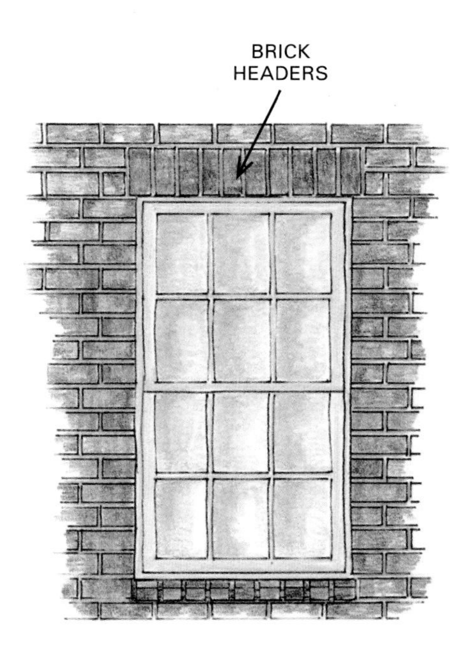

Brick headers. Vertical brick or stone headers should extend approximately 2 inches beyond the edge of the window opening.

A properly proportioned lintel, whether a solid piece or a soldier course of stone or brick, extends 2 inches beyond the edge of the window opening below. A lintel that stops short at the edge of the window advertises the fact that it is an ornamental piece. A lintel that extends beyond the window, on the other hand, looks like the lintels of times past that were actual load-bearing structural pieces.

Trimming with Wood

Windows surrounded by any type of siding will naturally utilize wood (or composite wood product) as trim. While a simple 3½-inch or 5½-inch trim is the typical choice, historical homes offer numerous examples of alternative trim details. The addition of cap molding at the top piece of trim can easily enhance

Stone soldiers. The simple addition of vertical-shaped stones above a window can enhance it, much like a frame that surrounds a picture.

HEALTHY EXAMPLES

Window framing options

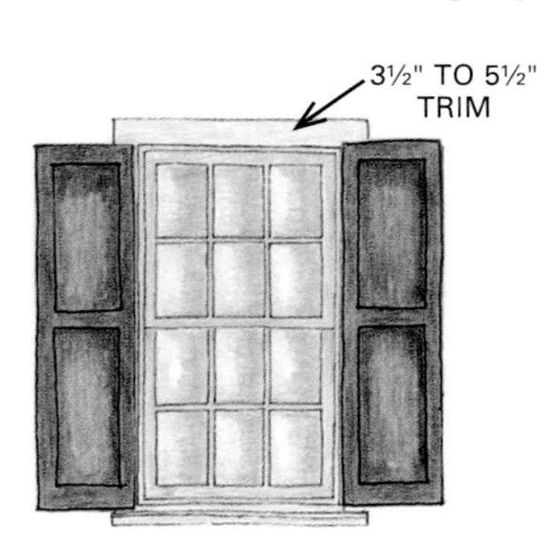

Example 1

Standard treatment. Windows surrounded by siding are usually framed with 3½" to 5½" trim. Note that the shutter proportions remain important. Flashing should always be installed at the top trim boards.

Example 2

Adding cap molding. A small piece of cap molding at the top piece of trim provides a subtle, yet important detail.

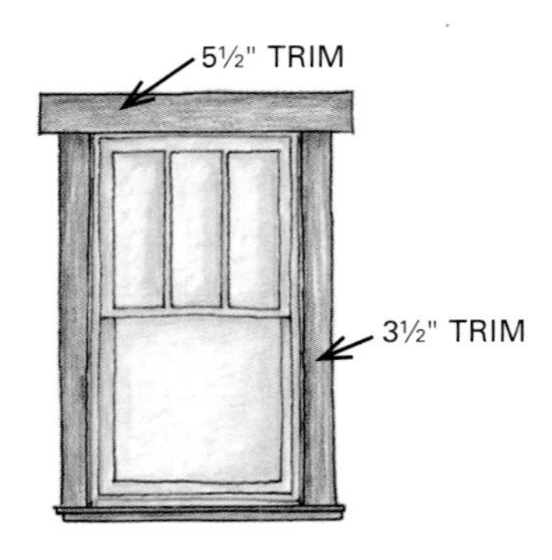

Example 3

Extending the length of the trim. For Craftsman Style designs, the top piece of window trim can be extended past the vertical side trim 3" to 5".

the overall appearance of the window. Make sure appropriate flashing is installed.

Arch-Top Windows

Good-quality clad wood windows with arch tops are expensive, and matching shutters add to the cost. Of course, the appeal of properly proportioned arch windows might justify the added expense. This is particularly true when the windows become a focal point of the interior design.

One way to achieve the look of an arch window without the cost is to create an arched opening for a rectangular window and a curved filler piece of wood or cast stone above. This innovation has been in use for years, since arch-top windows have always been an expensive item.

Shuttering an arched window. Shutters placed on windows with an attached arched transom should maintain proper proportions, with a curved top to match the transom. Note how the horizontal framing on the shutters matches that of the window sash and transom.

If your design calls for arched windows (or an arched opening) with shutters, proportions once again become critical. Not only should the shutters be half the width of the window, but the shutter tops should be curved to match the arched opening. This rather simple detail, while requiring some effort and expense to carry out, adds a sense of quality to any exterior design.

Design Diagnosis

Optional arch treatment

⊕ A simple, economical way to create the look of arch-top windows is to use standard rectangular windows topped by an arched filler piece made of wood or cast stone. Make sure the shutters are properly sized to cover both the window and the arch at the top.

Pay careful attention to windows that are topped by an arched *transom* (a window over a window). As with an arched window or a rectangular window topped by an arched filler piece, the shutters should be constructed to be half the window width and with a curved top to match the transom.

Keep It Simple

If you haven't already guessed, I have a strong bias towards clad wood windows. From the energy benefits to the unmatched natural beauty of the wood frame when viewed from inside the home, I sincerely believe clad wood windows to be one of the best investments you can make. Since these windows will greatly impact the cost of your home, my suggestion is this: Seriously consider limiting or even eliminating the specially sized and shaped windows, including those arches. By utilizing standard sizes and shapes, you can significantly reduce the costs. In the long run I think you'll find that the warmth and overall appeal of these simple yet elegant wood windows will surpass the novelty of those "synthetic" arches!

Design Diagnosis

Feature an arch window

Although quite expensive, a properly proportioned arch window may be worth the investment, especially if it becomes a focal point of the exterior and interior design.

main roof to allow for windows in the attic space.

Some of the plans you'll find for roofs will feature a large assortment of gables with various window details. While intricately designed roofs can add to the appeal of some homes, many of the most renowned homes have very simple roof forms. Nevertheless, a certain degree of complexity adds interest to the overall appearance of most homes. The challenge is to combine these different shapes and masses in a way that seems proportionally correct.

How can the average individual looking at a series of exterior drawings and sketches feel confident that the roof will be attractive? Here are a few ways to help with this analysis.

First, the home should have a clear central core with a corresponding central roof mass. The projecting roofs, whether hip or gable, must appear secondary to this main roof.

Consider the complexity of the roof. If the home has a number of gables, take a look at each one to determine its necessity. Quite often a designer will add an artificial gable, or in other words a gable that exists simply to interrupt the roof line. In some newer neighborhoods, it often seems as though builders have a competition among themselves to see who can put the most gables on the front of a home!

Consider the mass of the roof. Carefully look at the drawings and artist's renderings and consider whether the roof makes the home appear to be top-heavy. Remember, the roof pitch (degree of slope) determines the overall height of the roof. A home with a steep pitch on all sides may create an extremely tall and massive roof that's also quite expensive to build. I've been in many homes where the attic has enough space for

Not all roofs are alike. A variety of roof shapes, colors, and textures results in homes and neighborhoods with distinctive character.

Design Diagnosis
Determining roof pitch

When the pitch from front to rear is too steep, the roof seems out of proportion to the body of the house.

INCORRECT ROOF PITCH

CORRECT ROOF PITCH

another one-and-a-half-story home! Some styles, such as English Tudor, require steep rooflines and massive roofs. However, keep in mind that these types of homes almost always have at least two floors. Here we go again with proportion: a two-story home can support a much taller and more massive roof than a one-story home because of the increased height and mass of the body of the house.

Finally, if you're building in an area with existing homes, take a look at your neighbors' roofs. Although development restrictions may dictate minimum roof pitches, consider selecting a home with a different pitch, and perhaps a different style (hip or gable), than that of your neighbors. While you want to blend with the existing architecture, you don't want your home to look like a clone of your neighbors' houses. Drive through many of the newer developments where a handful of builders constructed all the homes, and more often than not you'll find almost all of the homes have an identical roof pitch, style, and color. Compare this with what you'll find as you drive around many older neighborhoods, in which you'll see an assortment of roof styles, textures, and colors. This variety is key to distinctive and visually pleasing homes and neighborhoods.

HEALTHY EXAMPLES

Roofing options

Example 1

⊕ **Variation in pitch.** The roof over the front porch has a 4:12 pitch that extends out from the 8:12 pitch of the main roof.

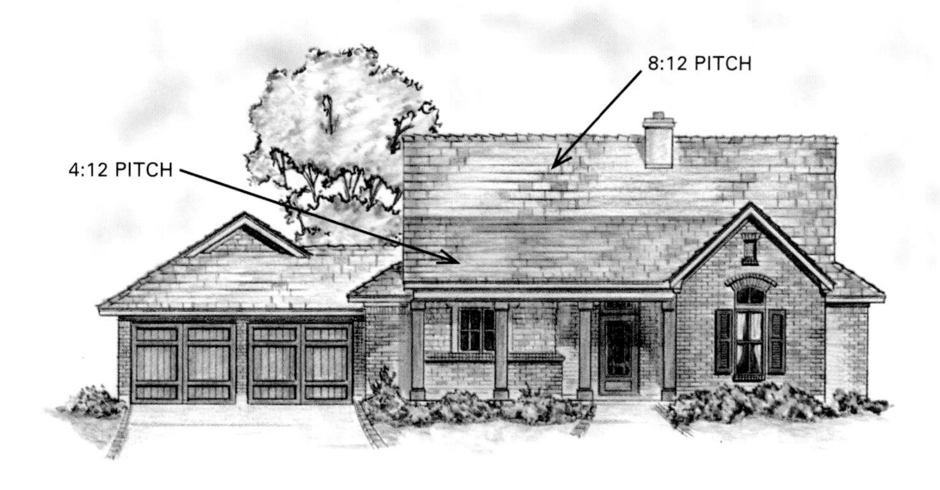

Example 2

⊕ **Combining roofing materials.** Using more than one kind of roofing material — for instance, using metal roofing on a porch roof — is a practice with a long historical tradition.

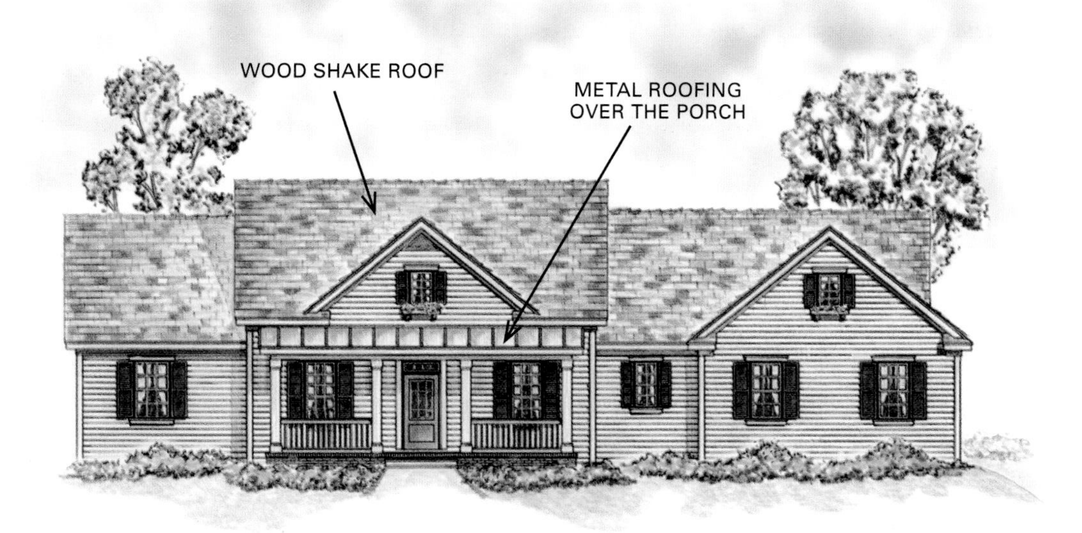

Porches

There's something about a front porch that many of us find extremely appealing. Perhaps it's the memories of relaxing in a rocker on your grandmother's front porch. Or maybe it's just that the front porch symbolizes a slower, simpler, less stressful lifestyle. Many older homes in neighborhoods throughout the country feature spacious front porches that were gathering places for families and neighbors, where adults discussed the day's activities while watching children play in the front yard. We may not be able to return to the slow-paced life, but we can recreate the serenity of the front porch.

As discussed in chapter 1, an increasing number of traditional neighborhood developments (TNDs) are experiencing unprecedented success throughout the country. An important feature of these people-friendly communities is a large front porch that invites residents to spend time on the street side of their home. Any neighborhood where people spend time in their front yards will obviously be more secure and friendly.

However, not all of us are lucky enough to be building in TNDs. Would a front porch be functional in a typical subdivision of porchless houses? Frankly, the answer is "Maybe, maybe not." Unless the neighborhood has been designed with a focus on public sidewalks and landscaping along the streets, your front porch likely will not seem too inviting. Of course, exceptions always exist.

Years ago, when my parents asked me to design their retirement home, my mother insisted on a large front porch. I pointed out that no other homes in the entire development had such a porch, but her mind was set. I had to concede that the client is always right, especially if she's your mother! Not long after my parents moved into their new home, we were all relaxing on the porch, enjoying the rocking chairs I assume my mother had dreamed about for years. To my amazement, neighbors walking by began to wave and say hello. Within a few weeks some of these people would venture up to the porch and accept an invitation to "sit for a spell and visit." (Note: I *am* from the South!) This was for me an early lesson on the immense value of a front porch.

Sometimes people get so caught up with the idea of porches that they decide to build them on both the front and back, and sometimes even down each side. In most cases they eventually discover that only one area enjoys regular use. It's a rare situation (found usually in TNDs) when residents actually spend time on both front and back porches.

If the building site offers a nice view, whether toward a golf course, a lake, mountains, or your personally landscaped backyard paradise, that's where your porch needs to be located.

HEALTHY EXAMPLES

Porch options

Example 1

⊕ **Porch frieze.** A detail often ignored on newer homes is the porch frieze. This perimeter beam should extend about 10 inches below the porch ceiling and rest on the columns.

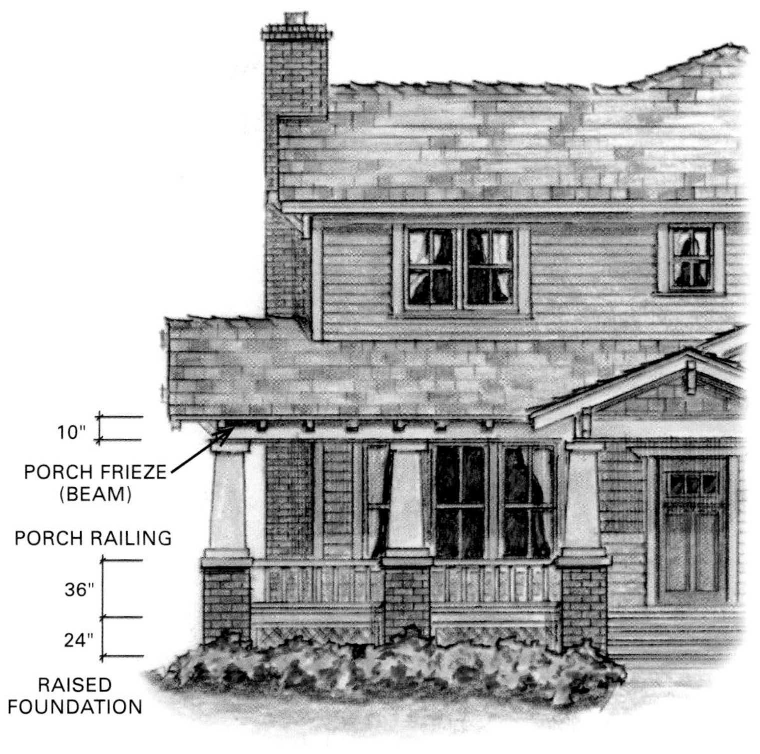

Example 2

⊕ **Elevated porch.** A front porch seems to symbolize a simpler and less stressful era. If possible, elevate the porch at least 24 inches above the ground to provide a sense of privacy and security.

In order for any porch to be a practical place that invites people to gather, it must be spacious. While the minimum depth should be 6 feet, dimensions of 8 to 10 feet are required for a swing and several chairs.

Proper proportion and scale along with strict attention to detail also prove essential. Columns must be large enough for not only structural but also aesthetic purposes. A column that is just big enough to be structurally adequate may still appear to be too small; an oversize column, on the other hand, gives the sense that the porch is securely supported and is a comfortable place to rest. *(See page 95.)*

A porch *frieze* (an exposed perimeter beam) is another important element that enhances the overall appearance of the porch. The frieze extends 10 inches or so down from the porch ceiling, resting on the columns and supporting the roof above. When exposed, it gives the porch a sense of sturdiness and frames the interior, making the porch seem like a haven. In newer homes this detail is frequently overlooked, with the frieze hidden above the porch ceiling. Although this might seem like an insignificant detail, it's like hanging a picture without a frame.

HEALTHY EXAMPLES

Creating an outdoor kitchen from a porch

Example 1

Screened porch. In many climates an outdoor kitchen located on a screened porch becomes the primary cooking and dining area. Be sure you add a ceiling fan or two for those days without a breeze.

Example 2

⊕ **Expanding a porch.** Most porches can easily be expanded to accommodate an outdoor kitchen. This 9-foot by 11-foot area has been increased to allow room for a cooking center and additional seating.

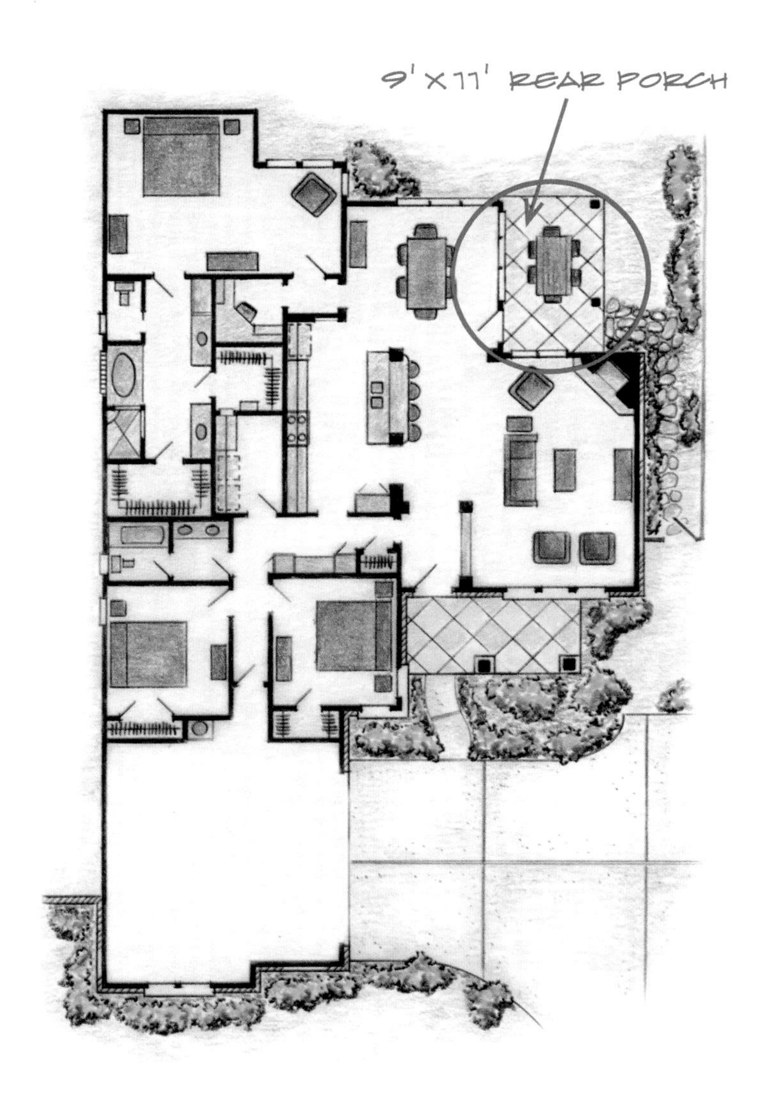

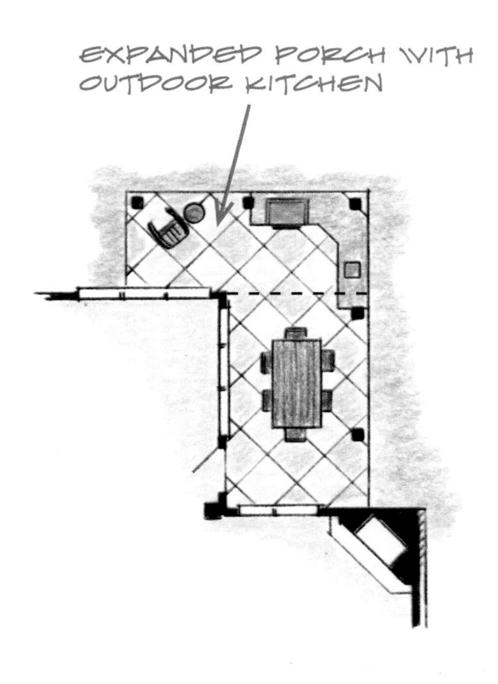

If possible, raise the porch at least 24 inches from the ground. This elevation provides an amazing sense of privacy and security. Also give consideration to the potential need for ramps for those unable to negotiate steps to an elevated porch.

The addition of an outdoor cooking area might be a consideration for a rear porch. It's not at all unusual to plan an elaborate outdoor mini kitchen that includes a sink, refrigerator, icemaker, and stainless-steel grill. For some the outdoor kitchen is a wonderful investment. Others may be completely satisfied with a charcoal grill alone. Either way, make sure the porch has adequate space for the equipment you plan to use. For a cooking porch, anything less than 10 feet in depth will not allow for proper furniture.

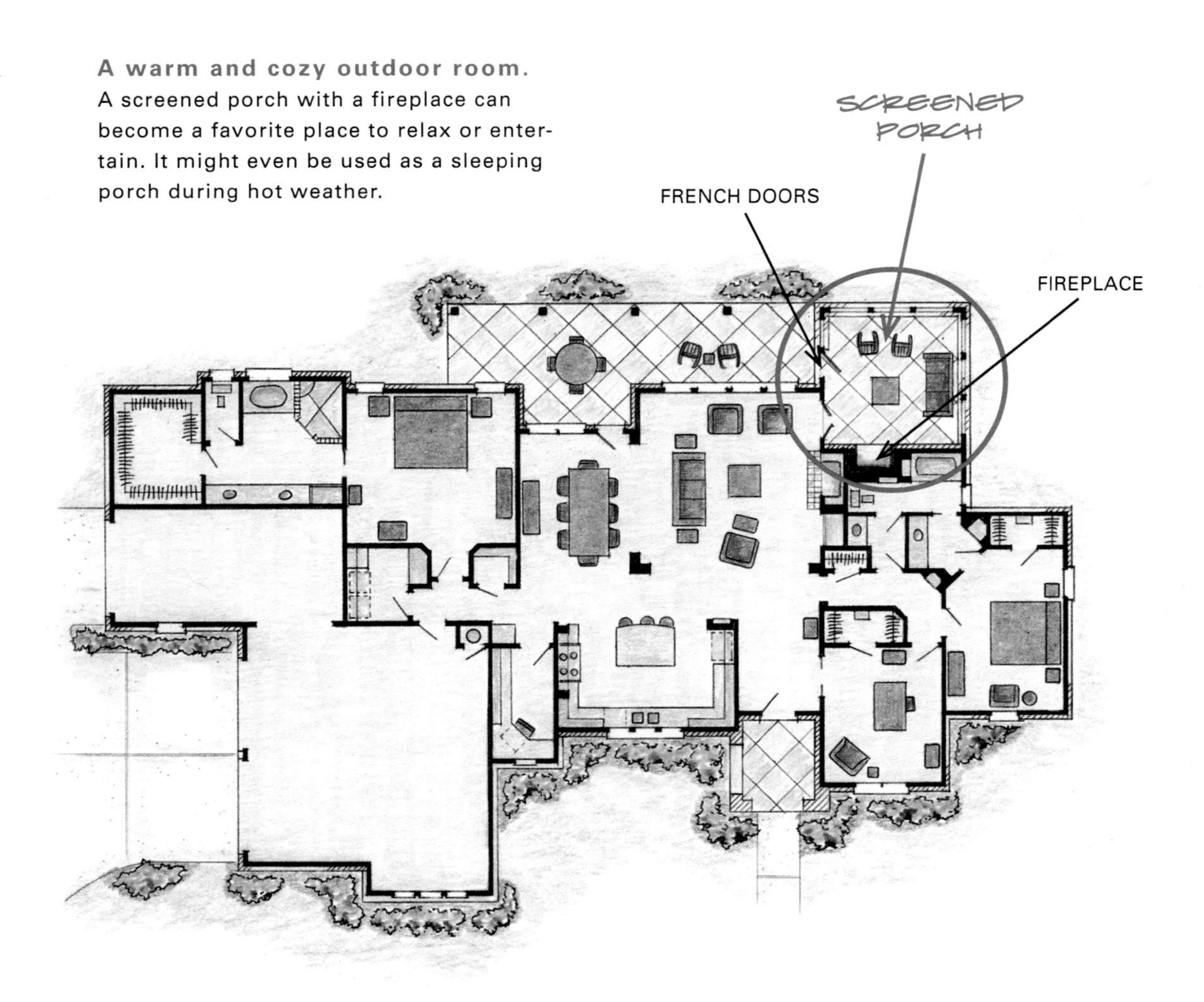

A warm and cozy outdoor room. A screened porch with a fireplace can become a favorite place to relax or entertain. It might even be used as a sleeping porch during hot weather.

You might also like to consider installing an outdoor fireplace on a back porch as an extremely cozy amenity. In fact, clients often tell me they use the fireplace on their porch more than the one in their family room.

A screened porch is the best way to create an insect-free outdoor environment. Before air conditioning became common, screened sleeping porches provided a cool and comfortable place to spend hot summer nights. Some of my fondest memories relate to the summer nights my favorite cousin and I spent on our grandmother's screened porch. I still recall the sounds of the crickets and the fresh cool breeze that made us crawl further under the covers as the night progressed.

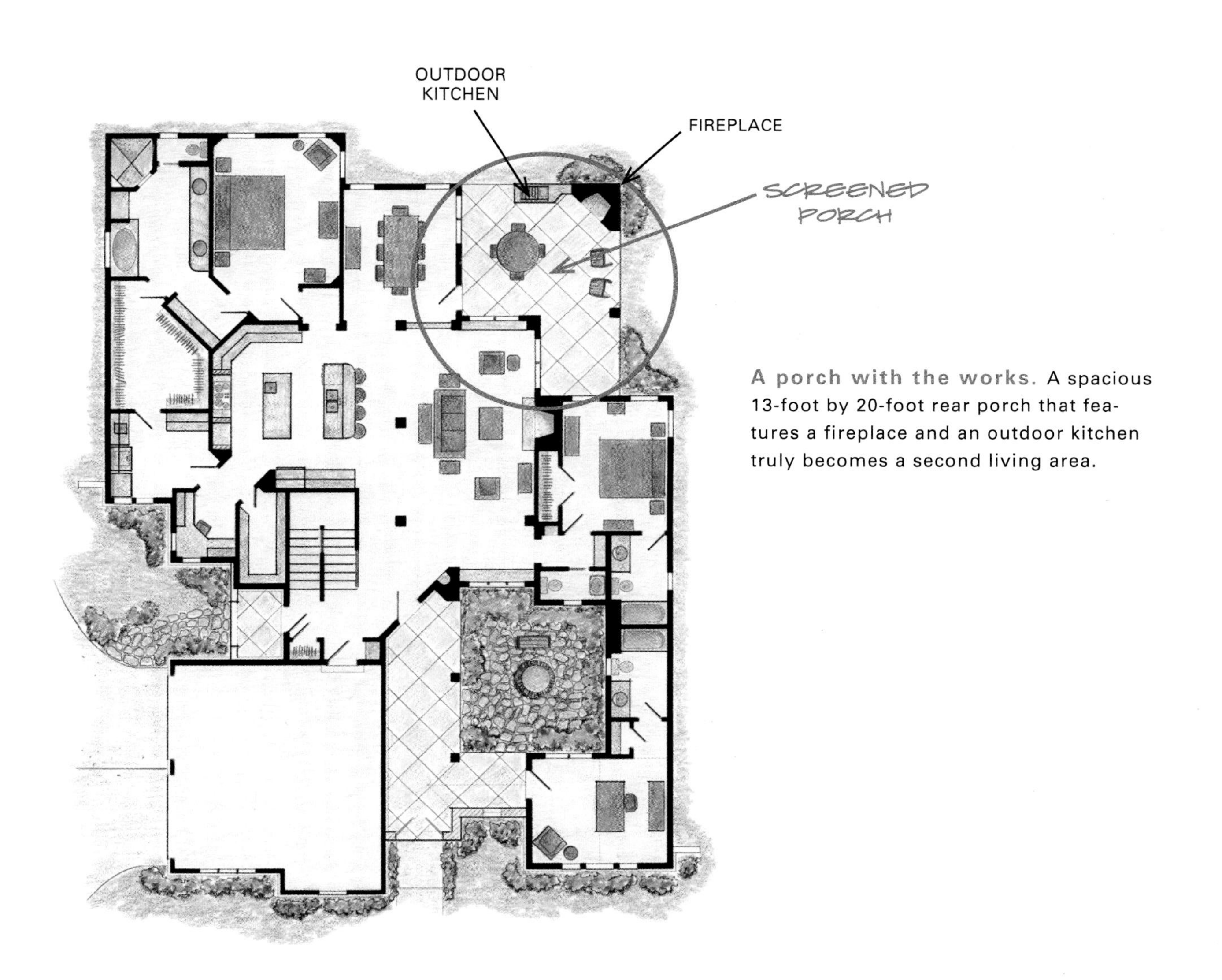

A porch with the works. A spacious 13-foot by 20-foot rear porch that features a fireplace and an outdoor kitchen truly becomes a second living area.

Frequently Asked Questions

Q *What exactly is roof pitch?*

Ⓐ *Pitch* refers to the angle of the roof's slope. This angle is determined by the ratio of vertical rise to horizontal run for the rafters (the wood beams that support the roof). Essentially the ratio specifies the number of inches a rafter rises for each 12 inches it runs. For example, a 4:12 pitch specifies rafters that rise 4 inches in height for every 12 inches in horizontal length. Thus, an 8:12 roof would be much steeper than a 4:12 roof.

Some designs may use more than one pitch. For example, the roof over a front porch might extend out at a lower pitch than that of the main roof.

Q *What are the cost differences between tile and composition roofs?*

Ⓐ Because of the vast number of tile and composition roof products now available, an accurate comparison proves difficult. However, in most cases you will find tile substantially more expensive. A large part of this increased cost involves the additional framing material and the size of rafters required to support the heavy weight of the tile.

Q *The plan we like has a composition roof. Can we use tile instead?*

Ⓐ The simple answer is yes. However, tile typically requires additional framing and support due to the extra weight and works best on lower-pitched roofs. If the design you've selected has a steep pitch, you may not be pleased with the look of tile, since the texture and massive scale usually seem overpowering. Also, due to the extreme weight of tile and the application techniques, it's usually not a good idea to place it on steeply pitched roofs.

Q *What are the advantages or disadvantages of low-pitched roofs?*

Ⓐ The lower the pitch, the smaller the roof mass. This translates into less roofing material and less framing lumber, so the overall cost is reduced. However, low-pitched roofs may create problems with snow accumulation in areas with heavy snowfall. Also, keep in mind that the lower the pitch, the less usable attic space you will have.

Q *Is it okay to combine different roofing materials, specifically on a home with a front porch?*

Ⓐ Absolutely. You may have seen homes from the late 1800s with metal roofing on the front porch that contrasts with the wood shake roof of the main house. This mixture of roof textures is often emulated in current designs. It's interesting to note that the historic home was probably first built *without* the porch. At a later date, quite possibly when a barn or other outbuilding was under construction, some of the extra material such as the metal roofing was used to add the porch.

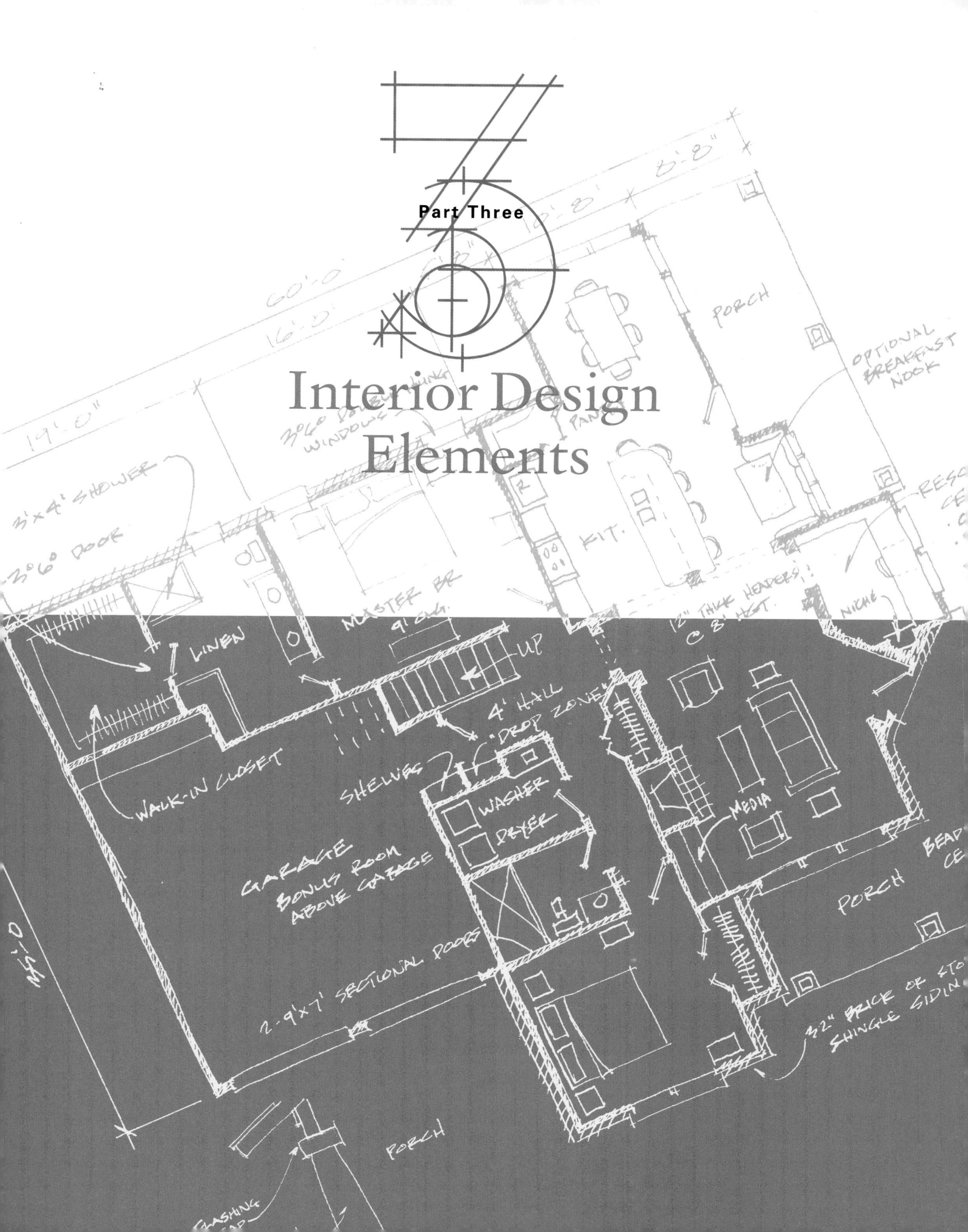

Part Three

Interior Design Elements

8

A Space of Your Own

What makes a home inviting? As with any discussion of design elements, the answer is usually quite subjective. Diverse personal preferences make it difficult to nail down specifics, but a few general guidelines can help increase the attraction and comfort of several areas in your home.

The front door and entry, for instance, require special attention, since this area normally provides the first and last impression of any home. The size allocated to a foyer continues to be the subject of debate within the design community. While grand entries with elaborate staircases and 20-foot ceilings continue to be built, some designers and architects consider a more subdued space with lower ceilings and a functional stair design to be what many people prefer. Entering a home with an enormous expanse of white walls can be rather overwhelming, as opposed to the warm welcome one might feel in a cozier space.

Consider borrowing an idea from Frank Lloyd Wright. Instead of designing massive entries, Wright often used lower ceilings as transitions to rooms with larger proportions and higher ceilings. Rather than being overwhelmed by the foyer, you have a sense of being drawn toward the next room. However, Wright stood about five feet five inches and stubbornly thought everyone should relate to spaces just as he did! Nevertheless, Wright's theory seems valid in most cases. The overall success of individual rooms and their relationship to one another are the essence of any home. The experience of traveling through a home can be either uneventful or emotionally gratifying.

While this may sound a bit too philosophical, consider why you're building your new home in the first place. Though housing must first be considered as shelter, we all know that our homes are much more than mere protection from the elements. Regardless of the size or cost of our homes, they become a reflection of our personalities. Part of this statement bears repeating: *regardless of the size.* You may have had the experience of walking into an enormous house that obviously was built with an unlimited budget but somehow, beyond its uniqueness and grandeur, simply doesn't feel inviting. It is not

Design Diagnosis
Define entry ways

⌖ The front door and entry require special attention. In this example, thick walls with an arched opening define the foyer and adjacent gallery. A 12-foot vaulted ceiling in the family room seems even more impressive when you enter from the foyer with its lower 9-foot ceiling.

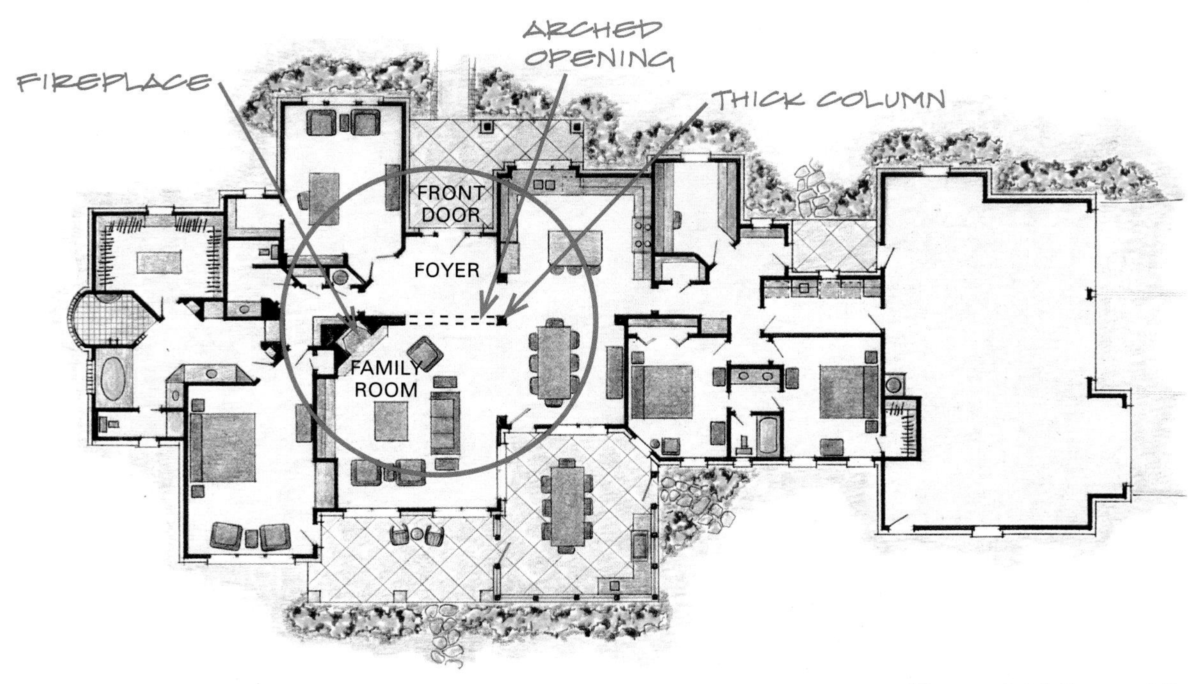

Design Diagnosis

Directing traffic

⊕ The family area in this efficiently designed cottage is a comfortable place to watch television or enjoy conversation. Traffic flows *past* the seating arrangement instead of *through* the room, eliminating the need for large square footage. The compact size and built-in bookcases are key to the room's wonderful sense of warmth and coziness.

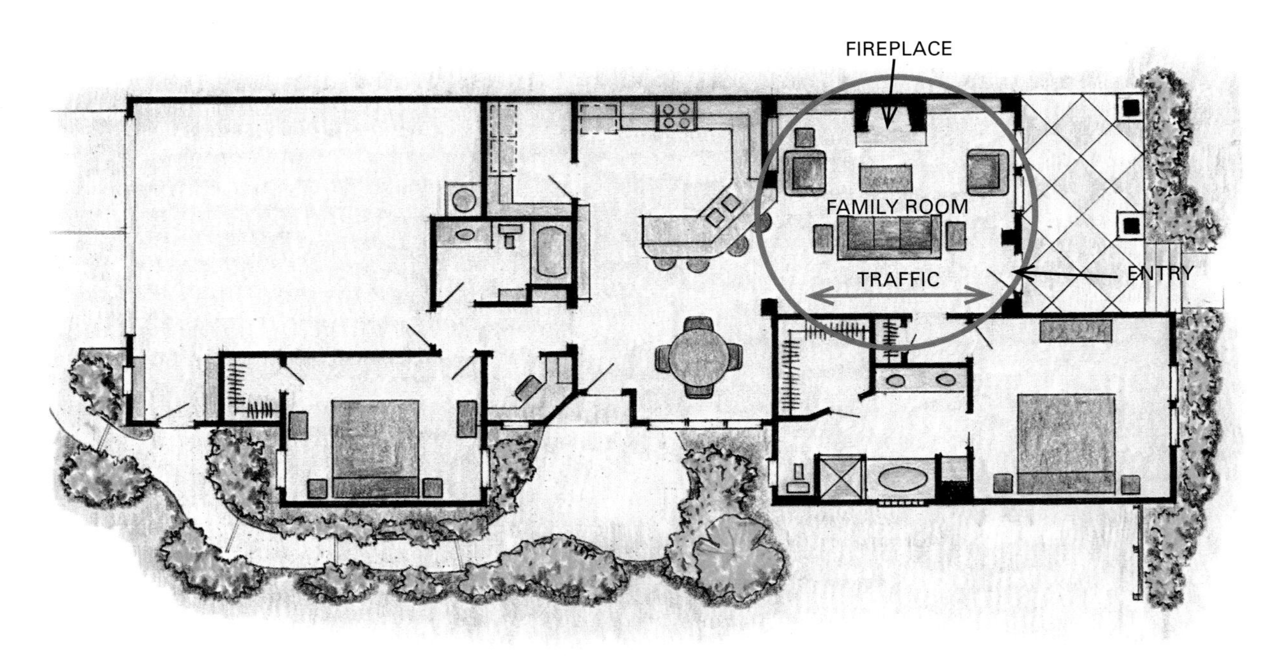

Terms to Know

Volume ceiling. A volume ceiling is raised in height with some form of slope or simply elevated higher than the ceilings in adjacent rooms.

¼-inch scale. Architectural drawings are typically prepared in ¼-inch scale, in which 1 inch equals 4 feet.

Offset. A wall is said to be offset when it protrudes beyond the basic rectangular shape of the house.

a place where you would feel comfortable relaxing with a good book, watching television, or simply interacting with your family. On the other hand, recall some of the small and often inexpensive homes you've visited that exude a wonderful sense of warmth and invitation — homes that say, "Come on in, kick off your shoes, and relax!"

Designing for Comfort

Making your home an arrangement of comfortable, inviting spaces involves thinking carefully about how you and your family will use each of those spaces and designing them accordingly. Ceiling height, window type and placement, and unique focal points such as built-in bookcases or small alcoves all contribute to the feeling of a room.

Ceiling height has an enormous impact on any room. High ceilings create a sense of grandeur, while lower ceilings promote a sense of coziness. Many current house plans call for a raised ceiling in the family room. If you entertain often, with large numbers of guests congregating in the family room, a volume ceiling will certainly offer a feeling of spaciousness. However, the tradeoff might be a loss of warmth and coziness. If you want a feeling of spaciousness in a certain room, consider adding some exposed beams or trusses to help maintain a personal scale.

In general, the comfortable height of any room relates to the size of the room itself. A 16-foot ceiling may work fine in a room measuring 25 feet in width. However, a hall or bathroom with a 10-foot ceiling can feel like a canyon. A good guideline is that either the width or the depth of a room should be greater than its ceiling height.

Windows also play a large role in creating comfortable and inviting spaces. Careful placement of windows within a room can make the area seem much larger. For example, locating two windows at the corner of a bedroom extends the view diagonally across the room.

Focal points can add character to a room. High ceilings allow the use of transom windows (windows above windows), which offer additional natural light and can become a major design element in a room. Window seats also make charming focal points, as they create cozy alcoves for sitting and enjoying the natural light.

When quizzed about the details they find appealing in older homes, many people invariably mention the nooks and crannies that are abundant in homes built in the late nineteenth and early twentieth centuries. Such unique home features, such as window seats, small alcoves, and built-in bookcases, seem to add a great deal of charm to any room. These areas provide private spaces to read, study, or just get away. A small offset in a bedroom with a built-in desk and bookcase, for example, gives the homeowner a secluded place to work or pursue a hobby.

In recent years our attempts to create open floor plans have often eliminated such delightful areas. However, most designs can easily be reworked to include these spaces.

Make a room seem larger. Corner window placement can allow for expansive views and an increased sense of spaciousness.

As the design community strives to create more innovative floor plans, remember that it's often the subtle details that make homes inviting and comfortable. Instead of trying so hard to create something new, perhaps we need to pay more attention to design elements that have worked for many years.

Size versus Function

Possibly the greatest misconception about home design is the assumption that simply enlarging a room will make the space more inviting and functional. Room size is far less important than such elements as window placement, finish materials, colors, ceiling height, and the overall shape of the room. On a practical level, room *size* should be dictated by the *function* of an area. For instance, a family room must be large enough to comfortably accommodate the required furniture. If the room dimensions are not adequate, the space will seem cramped. However, a family room that's too large can swallow the furniture and leave you with an uninviting and, perhaps, overwhelming sensation.

Bring in more natural light. A family room with high ceilings (at least 10 feet) is a good place to use transom windows (windows located above other windows).

Design Diagnosis
Plan a window seat

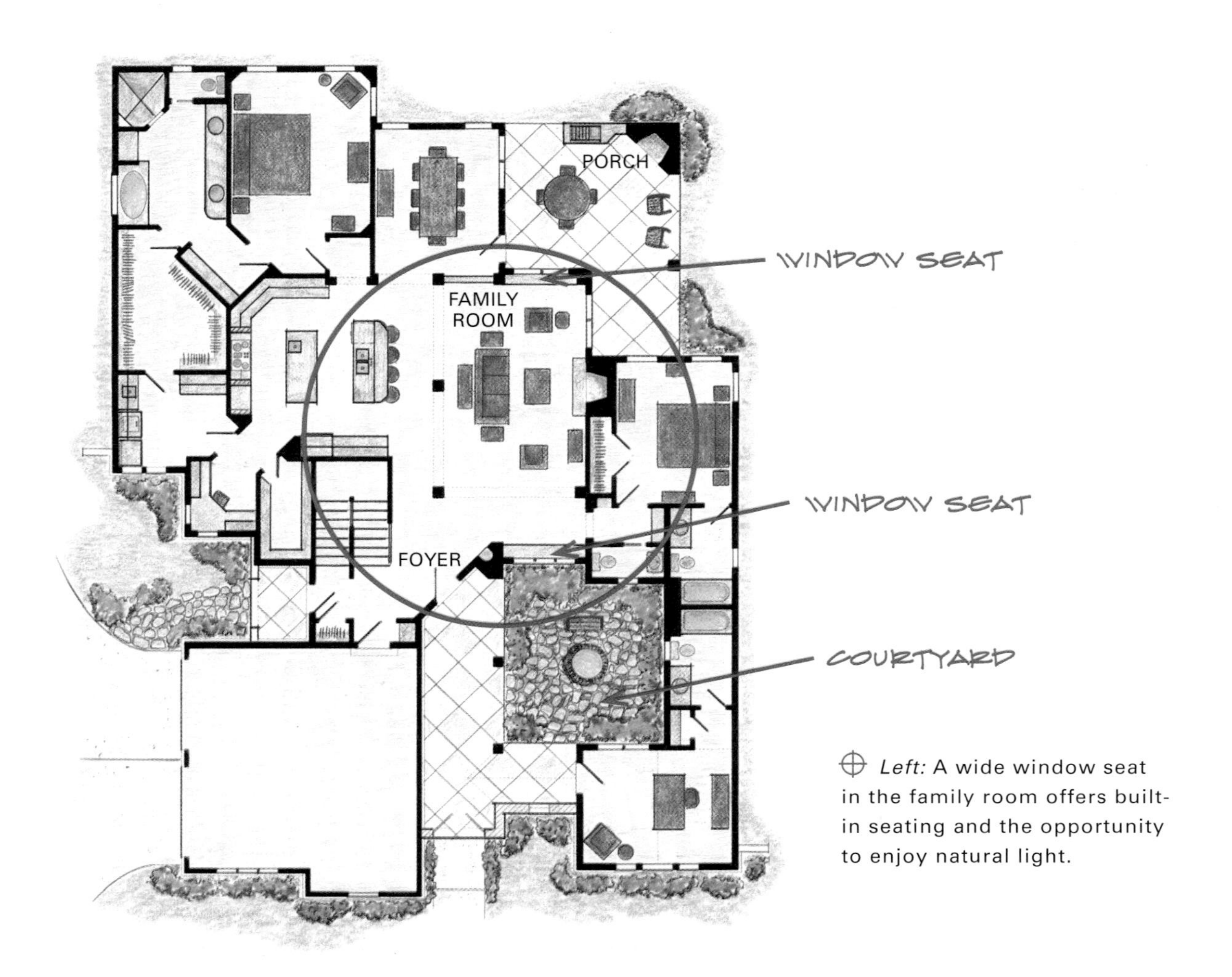

Left: A wide window seat in the family room offers built-in seating and the opportunity to enjoy natural light.

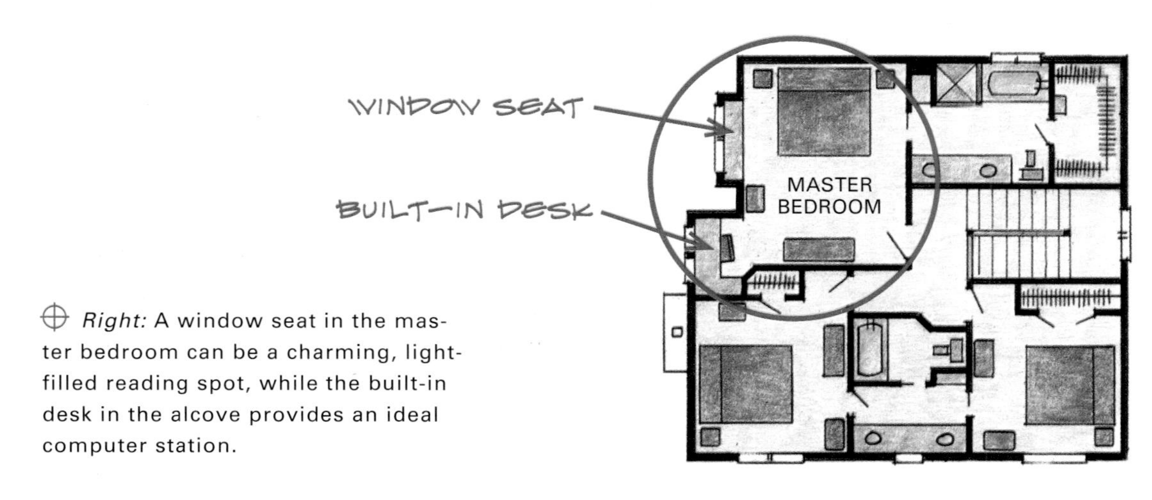

Right: A window seat in the master bedroom can be a charming, light-filled reading spot, while the built-in desk in the alcove provides an ideal computer station.

Over the years I've tried to remain acutely aware of each client's uniqueness. I recall working with one of my very first clients, who insisted on an elegant foyer with two circular staircases and an enormous living room that featured 20-foot ceilings. These areas appeared so overwhelming that your initial response was to simply say, "Wow!" Thus, I began to label such spaces as *wow!* rooms. I also designed for these clients a wonderful kitchen and family area with finely detailed trim and expansive windows overlooking their pool. They later told me that this room, just large enough for a sofa and two comfortable chairs, became the area where they spent most of their time. However, they promptly also related how much they enjoyed their magnificent living room, as they hosted frequent dinner parties and social gatherings. This became a valuable lesson for me as a designer: listen very carefully to how clients live and take the amount of time required to understand their personal tastes and needs.

Obviously, what one family considers inviting and functional may be overwhelming and wasteful to another. This diversity of personal preferences explains why many people, after searching through hundreds of predrawn plans, ultimately turn to a design professional to create their home. Regardless of the path you take to find home plans, carefully consider the lifestyle of your family.

Spend as much time as possible contemplating your daily routines. Ask yourself not only which individual room features will make areas appealing to you, but also what details might enhance their functionality.

Understanding Floor Plans

Design professionals often forget that their clients may never have faced the challenge of trying to read and understand the sketches and drawings they present. Like any information we face for the first time, house plans can be confusing and even intimidating. So, if you have difficulty understanding floor plans, you're certainly not alone! Few individuals can look at a floor plan and understand just how the completed home will look. Take a look at this basic floor plan and see what some of the various symbols mean.

The designer is probably the only person who can really visualize the unbuilt home, but you can use the steps outlined on the next page to help you get a sense of it. Remember, there are no right or wrong answers here. Your responses will simply help determine whether the plan seems right for your family.

① Start with the foyer. What is the ceiling height? Try to relate this height to a room in your present home.
② Imagine entering through the front door and looking into the adjoining rooms. Scanning left to right, what would you see? Are you looking directly into the family room? Are there windows in the family room that open to the backyard or pool?
③ Can you see the kitchen from the foyer? While some plans (especially those with smaller square footage) intentionally place the kitchen with a line of sight to the entry area, this may not suite your tastes.
④ Imagine what you will see if you step from the foyer into the family room. If you were sitting on the sofa, could you see the front door? Can you look into the kitchen?
⑤ If you're sitting in the family room, can you view the door of a bedroom? Does this detract from the feeling of privacy you'd want for a bedroom?
⑥ How big is the family room? Will it accommodate the furniture you want to place in it? Room sizes are usually labeled on plans. Try comparing the size of the family room on the plan to that of a room in your present home. This may help you understand the actual size of the area.
⑦ Proceed through the plan in this manner, room by room, imagining how the windows, doors, ceilings, and lines of sight will appear. By analyzing one room at a time, you should be able to formulate a greater understanding and visualization of the plan. This procedure will take some time, but it will help you decide whether the plan is right for you.

Room Sizes and Furniture Placement

Room dimensions can be quite deceptive when seen on paper. The best way to make sure a particular room will accommodate your furniture and the activities you plan to have in it is to map it out in ¼-inch scale. In this system, each ¼-inch square equals 1 foot, and 1 inch equals 4 feet. Most office supply stores will have an inexpensive ¼-inch scale paper made specifically for this use, or pads of graph paper with a ¼-inch grid. To download a ¼-inch scale grid, go to www.homeplandoctor.com. As a last resort, you can create your own grid by drawing horizontal and vertical lines at ¼-inch increments.

Technically the grid doesn't have to be ¼ inch as long as your scale is consistent (just make sure that each square represents a foot). However, using ¼ inch will keep your plans and drawings in sync with those of your architect and builders, for whom the ¼-inch scale is the industry standard.

UNDERSTANDING FLOOR PLANS

Typical symbols

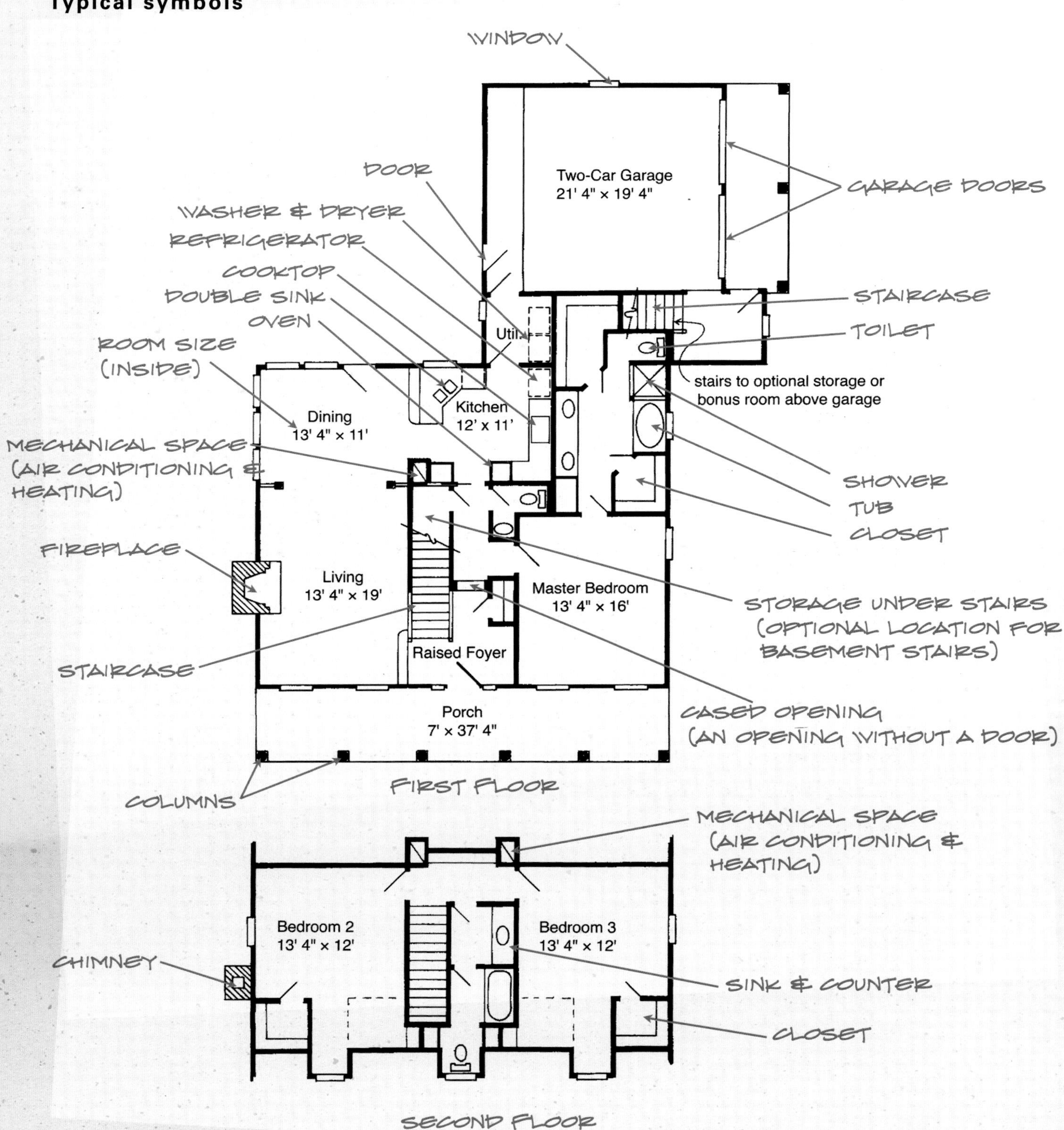

Understanding Room Sizes

Use graph paper with a grid of ¼-inch squares to map out the rooms of a plan you're considering. In this grid, 1 inch is made up of four squares, and each square represents 1 foot. Room dimensions should match the inside dimensions of a room. (In this example, the master bedroom is 13 feet wide and 18 feet deep.) Here's what you do:

Step 1

Sketch the room you're examining on ¼-inch scale graph paper.

Step 2

Measure your existing furniture.

Step 3

On a separate sheet of graph paper, sketch your furniture to scale.

Step 4

Cut out each piece of furniture and place it on the room you've sketched.

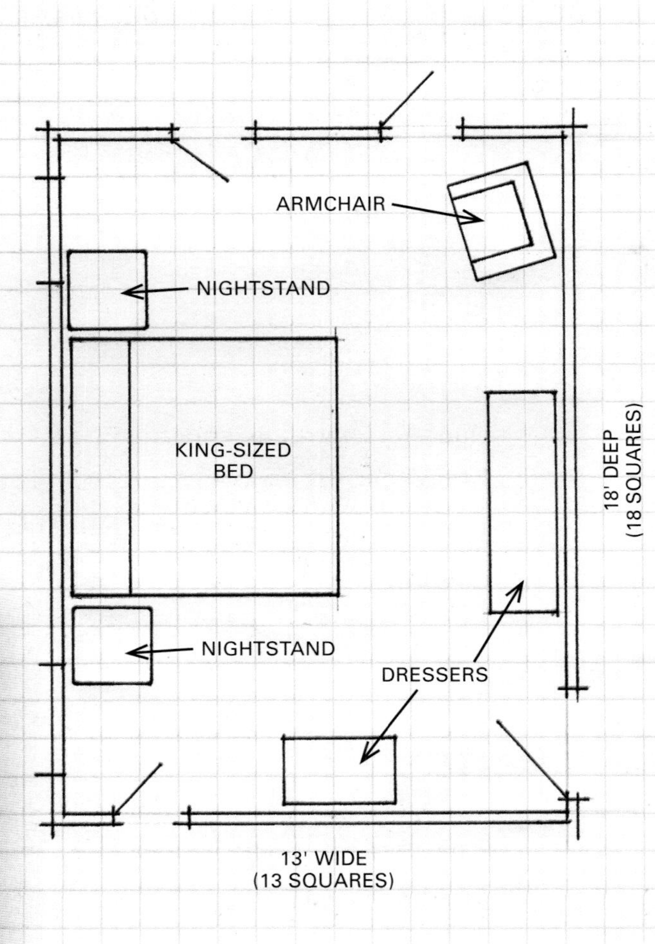

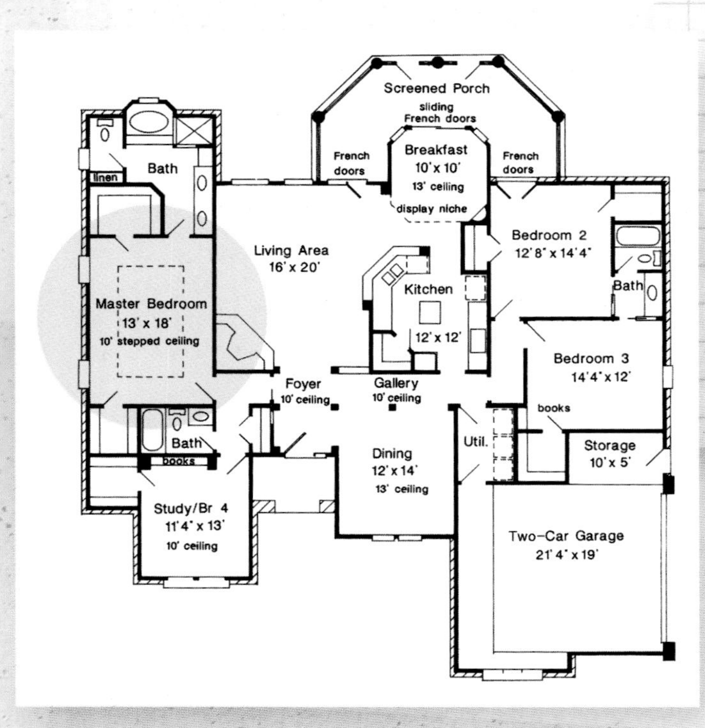

Once you've mapped out a room, measure each piece of furniture, draw it to the same ¼-inch scale on paper, and cut it out. By placing the cutouts on the floor plan, you'll have an accurate idea of how well your furniture will fit. These cutouts will also come in handy when you're evaluating the electrical plan for your new home; you can place the cutouts on the plan to make sure you will have electrical outlets where you need them.

Square Footage Defined

One of your first considerations when selecting a plan for your new home is its size. While the overall dimensions of the house determine its square footage, what's the difference between *living* area and *total* area? How about *framing* area and *slab* or *foundation* area? As you can see, the discussion of size and square footage can get rather complicated. Unfortunately, there is not a great deal of consistency when it comes to calculating square footages.

Living area is typically defined as the space that is heated and cooled. It does not include garages, porches, or storage areas (unless they are heated or cooled). Although that sounds simple enough, several variations exist. Some living-area calculations include not only the exterior framing walls but also stone or brick veneer walls. Some calculations don't include any walls! As a point of reference, most tax authorities will figure the size of your home based on the outside wall dimensions, thus including both the framing walls and any brick or stone veneer walls.

Floor plans published in magazines or on the Internet usually state the room dimensions. While it is helpful to know the exact size of each room, these measurements often lead to a great deal of confusion about the home's square footage. If you calculate the areas of each room using these interior dimensions, the grand total will often be several hundred square feet *less* than the published total living area. The reason is simple: When you merely figure the inside areas of individual rooms, you haven't included the square footage of the walls themselves, not to mention the hallways and closets. This is a very common misunderstanding.

Area is a two-dimensional calculation, measuring width times depth and not including height. In other words, the area of a room does not change whether it has a one-story-high or a two-story-high ceiling.

How can you identify the method used to calculate the area of a particular plan? Footage calculations are often defined on plans. Sometimes the living area is calculated with two separate methods: one for the framing area and one including the brick or stone veneer. This is an advantage if you decide to either add more brick or eliminate the brick altogether.

How Important Is Square Footage?

Square footage is always important, since the cost of a home directly relates to its size. Or does it? Unfortunately, the answer is not simple. I often refer to square footage calculations as a "game" those of us in the building profession play. Yes, virtually everyone involved in the construction of your new home (including the designer) will base his or her fees on a price per square foot. However, the actual cost of each square foot proves much more complicated.

For instance, the cost for every square foot of kitchen or bath space will be many times that of the bedroom closets. If you add an additional bathroom, the cost will be substantial. However, adding an extra foot to the length of a bedroom often costs very little. In fact, simply adding length to various rooms can prove to be an economical way to increase your home's size. After all, the additional material is often negligible. In the illustrated example on page 116, adding an extra 2 feet of length (30 square feet of area) to the bedroom required only the following additional material:

- Four 2×4 wall studs (two on each side wall)
- One sheet of drywall for the new walls
- One sheet of drywall for the ceiling
- A minimal amount of material for the extra foundation
- No additional electrical or plumbing materials

On the other hand, if you wanted to add another bathroom (50 square feet of area), the cost would be substantial, primarily due to the cost of plumbing and fixtures. So, we might say that although square footage directly affects the ultimate cost of a home, all square footage is *not* created equal! As you consider various changes to a plan, this realization can be extremely important.

Square Footage Tips

When looking into square footage, here are the main points to remember:

- *Living area* refers to the area where you *live* — all the enclosed spaces that are heated and air-conditioned. Garages, porches, and storage areas are not included.
- *Total area* is just what it says: the total of all areas, including the living area plus any other enclosed areas, regardless of whether they are heated and air-conditioned.
- The area of a staircase is typically counted only on the main floor.
- The *price per square foot* generally refers to the living area only.

Price per Square Foot

When attempting to estimate the construction cost of your new home, make sure you understand the typical procedure in your local area. Square footage calculation methods vary from one region to another, as does the formula for arriving at a price per square foot.

Generally the price per square foot refers to the *living area* of the house. For example, your builder may tell you that a 2,000-square-foot house will run $125 per foot, or $250,000 (2,000 × $125). So, what happened to the 500-square-foot garage and the 200 feet of porches? Don't worry; you're still paying for them! However, the cost for both the garage and the porches has been amortized and included in that $125-per-foot cost. In reality, the $125 figure is an amount the builder has arrived at by first determining the costs of the living area, the garage, and the porches and then averaging the totals. If you decided to change the two-car garage to a three-car garage, that $125 figure would increase accordingly.

Some builders present estimated costs in a format that itemizes the costs per square foot of each of the various areas of the home. This allows you to understand exactly what you're paying for the living area, the garage, and the porches.

Obviously, you must have an idea of the size you want your home to be before you begin searching for a plan or visiting with a local design professional. In order to begin with realistic expectations based on your budget, you must first discover the price-per-square-foot ranges in your local area. The best way to do this is to visit several home builders and real estate agents and ask to see examples of recently built homes at various prices per square foot. Keep in mind that the cost for an identical 2,000-square-foot plan can vary dramatically depending on the finish materials selected and the building site. This way, you will begin to see the relationship between the level of finish and the corresponding cost.

Since my home designs have been published in magazines over the years, I've had the opportunity to see many of them built. I never cease to be amazed at the often drastic differences in homes built from *identical* plans. Variations in materials, site conditions, and geographical location result in a dramatic range of prices.

One final word: Consider offering a set of plans to your local tax authority after your home has been built. Since tax authorities are forced to make their measurements without actually entering homes, sometimes their calculations are not very accurate. For example, if you have a vaulted ceiling in the foyer or family room, they may assume that volume space includes a second-floor room above. Viewing the house only from the outside doesn't allow them to accurately understand the plan. Therefore, you may be taxed on more square footage than you actually have.

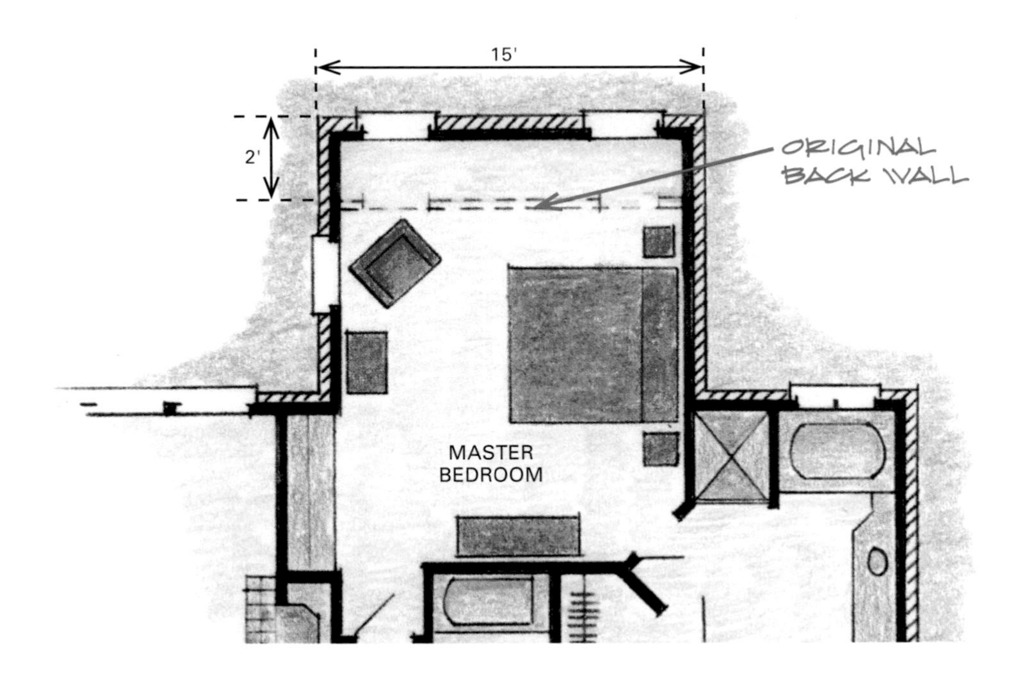

Adding square footage. Adding 2 feet to the length of this bedroom increases the living area by 30 square feet (calculated from the outside wall) while requiring a negligible amount of additional construction material.

Reducing Costs per Square Foot

Reducing the square footage of a house is one way to lower building costs. However, dealing with square footage is like managing your body weight — it increases easily and, once gained, is difficult to lose! If you trim 1 foot off the width of a bedroom, you might save as little as 15 square feet. Recalling that all square footage is not created equal, you'll find that eliminating a 50-square-foot bathroom will offer a much greater savings than reducing the family room by the same 50 square feet. Of course, that extra bathroom may be one of the reasons you wanted to build a new home in the first place!

Let's look at some other options, starting with some basic information about the costs associated with various elements of construction. First, consider this: A 2,000-square-foot house will not cost double that of a house with 1,000 square feet. Nor will 4,000 square feet cost twice as much as 2,000. In fact, the cost per square foot should be reduced as the footage increases!

The explanation for this is simple when you consider three of the primary expenses involved in building a house: the costs of the kitchen, the bathrooms, and the electrical wiring. These will be almost identical for any three-bedroom home, whether the home is 1,000 or 2,000 square feet.

The larger home simply has increased room sizes and theoretically is considerably less expensive *per square foot* to build. Quite frankly, this explains why many builders hesitate to construct smaller houses. The challenge of creating economical housing directly relates to this issue.

Nevertheless, square footage will always have a significant impact on the costs of construction. Throughout this book you'll find suggestions on how to utilize the overall area of your home efficiently. This includes ideas such as eliminating seldom-used formal dining and living rooms and creating careful traffic flow patterns that allow some rooms to function better with less square footage.

Other Ways to Cut Costs

Rather than focus entirely on the square footage of the plan you're considering, look closely at the complexity of the design. Theoretically, any variation from the basic shape begins to add costs. In other words, the additional walls required to create offsets add to the expense. Excessively high ceilings also add to the costs per square foot. Although the upper levels of two-story rooms do not factor into the square footage calculations, they often double the cost of the room. After all, a two-story family room measuring 18 feet by 20 feet only needs a floor installed to create an identical-size room above!

The use of standard-size windows will offer substantial savings over specially sized or shaped windows. As a strong proponent of quality windows, I always attempt to convince my clients of the value of using readily available window sizes and avoiding (or at least minimizing) the use of arches and other custom shapes so that they can afford to buy the best-quality windows available.

Of course, any discussion of costs invariably ends up with the considerations of quality. Every homeowner, no matter how large or small the budget, will struggle with the ultimate conflict of cost versus quality. The various materials you select, from granite countertops to high-end kitchen appliances, will dramatically impact the final dollars you spend. For some people larger square footage is more important than the quality of the materials used. Others believe that it's essential to carefully select the proper materials and create a plan that accurately addresses their lifestyle. As always, there's no definitive right or wrong here. Since we spend such a considerable portion of our lives in our home, we would be wise to give very careful consideration to exactly what matters to us as we design and build.

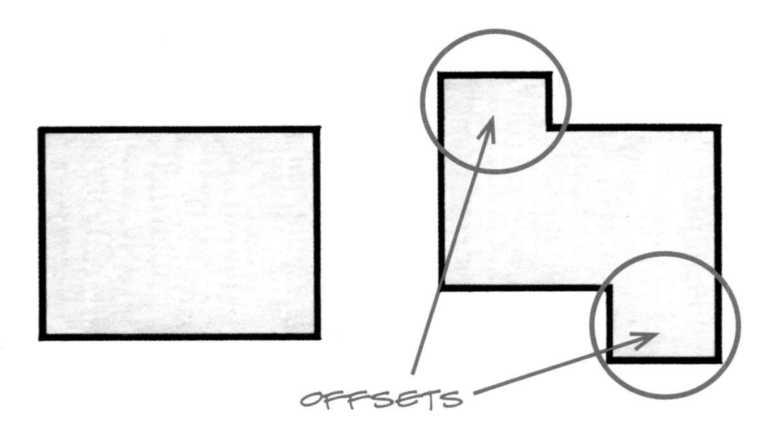

Offsets cost extra. Offsets, or walls that protrude from the basic rectangular shape of the house, increase the cost of construction. In these examples the total area (or square footage) of each space is identical. However, the offsets increase the total length of the walls.

9

Practical Considerations

One of the most critical elements of a floor plan is the traffic pattern — in other words, how you travel from one room to another. Other practical considerations include designing for privacy and planning for the future. Thinking in terms of universal design can enable you and your family to live comfortably in your home for many years. All of these topics are covered in this chapter.

Directing Traffic

The best way to determine whether a plan has a logical traffic pattern is to imagine living in the house and think about how you might walk from one area to another. For example, as you enter the home from either the front door or the side entrance, how will you reach the kitchen? Do you have to pass through the family room first? What if you want to move from the living area to your master bedroom?

A home's rooms should be arranged so that the flow of traffic throughout the house is logical. Ideally you will be able to move from one area to another without crossing *through* any room. Recent designs seem to show an ever-increasing awareness of proper

DESIGN DIAGNOSIS

Improving traffic patterns. By slightly revising a floor plan, traffic flow can be redirected to avoid walking through one room to get to another. The addition of the gallery defines the areas and directs traffic. The kitchen and dining areas have been modified to improve traffic and create a more open space.

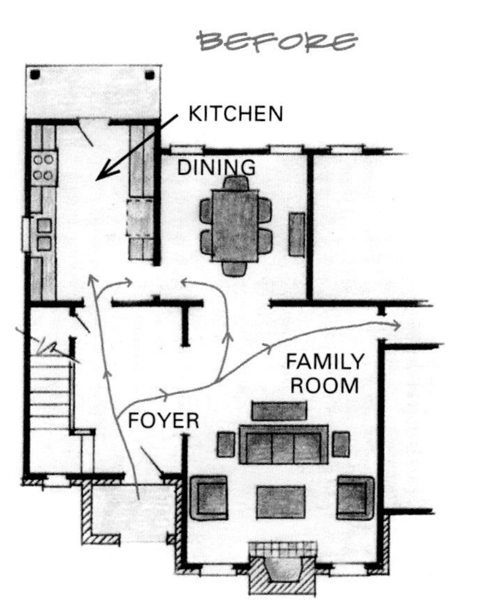

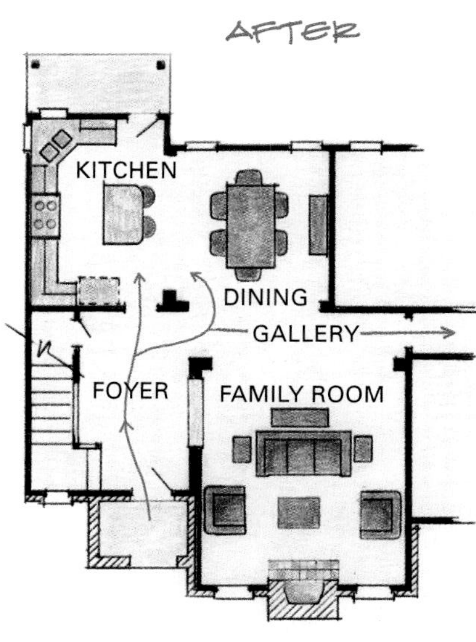

Terms to Know

Gallery. This area functions as a hallway in that it offers a passageway from one part of the home to another, but typically it has no walls (though sometimes it contains columns).

Clerestory windows. These are small windows located high on a wall to allow light into a room while protecting privacy.

traffic patterns. You'll find that it's not necessary to walk through the family room to reach the other side of the home. Instead, designated hallways or *galleries* direct traffic.

Eliminating crisscross traffic through the family room offers better options for furniture arrangements. No longer must the seating be situated to allow enough space for people to walk through the area. In addition, a plan with logical traffic patterns can allow some rooms to be smaller, thus achieving a reduction in square footage without any compromises.

Some plans may not use the term *gallery* to designate a major traffic path. Depending on the actual floor plan, such a defined area might not be appropriate. However, the logical movement from one room to another should still be evident. Functional paths not only serve as walkways from one area to the next but also become areas that visually belong to each adjacent room, creating an illusion of greater space for these rooms.

Are Hallways Necessary?

Over the past ten years or so residential designers have made tremendous progress in offering open floor plans. By eliminating long hallways and unnecessary walls and expanding ceiling heights, we have created much more exciting living spaces. However, this openness is sometimes carried to the extreme. The huge great rooms popular in the 1970s and early 1980s, for example, eliminated hallways in order to add this so-called wasted space to the family room. These designs destroyed any semblance of privacy for the master bedroom and often created great rooms so massive that furniture arrangement became an impossible task.

We've all been in homes like this. The great room is so enormous that two separate seating groups must be used. One focuses on the television and fireplace, where everyone wants to be, and the other seating group at the opposite end of the room has no real function other than to look nice. Unfortunately, many plans of this type are still in circulation today.

HEALTHY EXAMPLES

Directing traffic

Example 1

With a gallery. A central gallery provides a logical path from one side of the home to the other. Even the traffic from the gallery to the rear door moves between the family room and the kitchen.

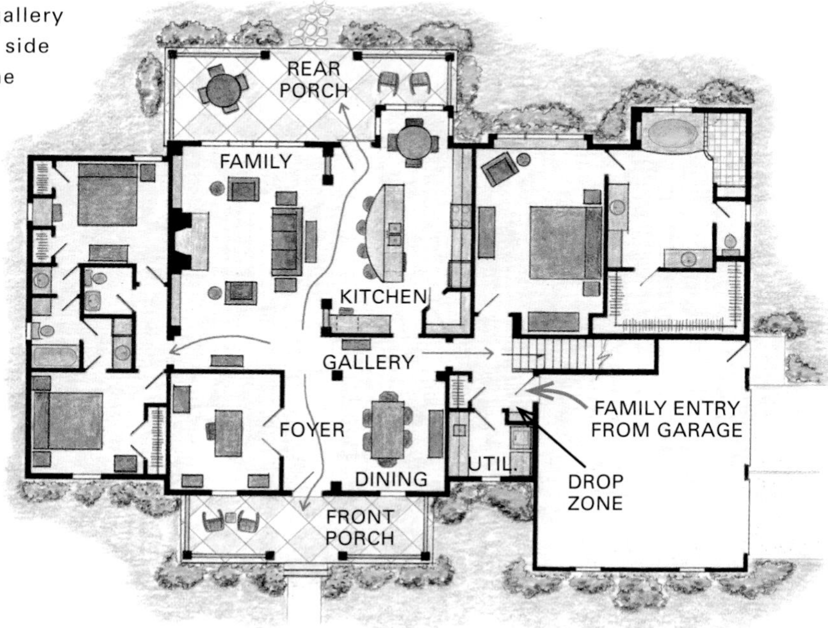

Example 2

Without a gallery. Although this plan has no designated gallery, it's easy to see that you can travel from one part of the home to another without being forced through a room. Walking from the foyer to the dining area or master bedroom takes you *between* the kitchen and family room. This path visually belongs to both the kitchen and the family room, making each seem more spacious.

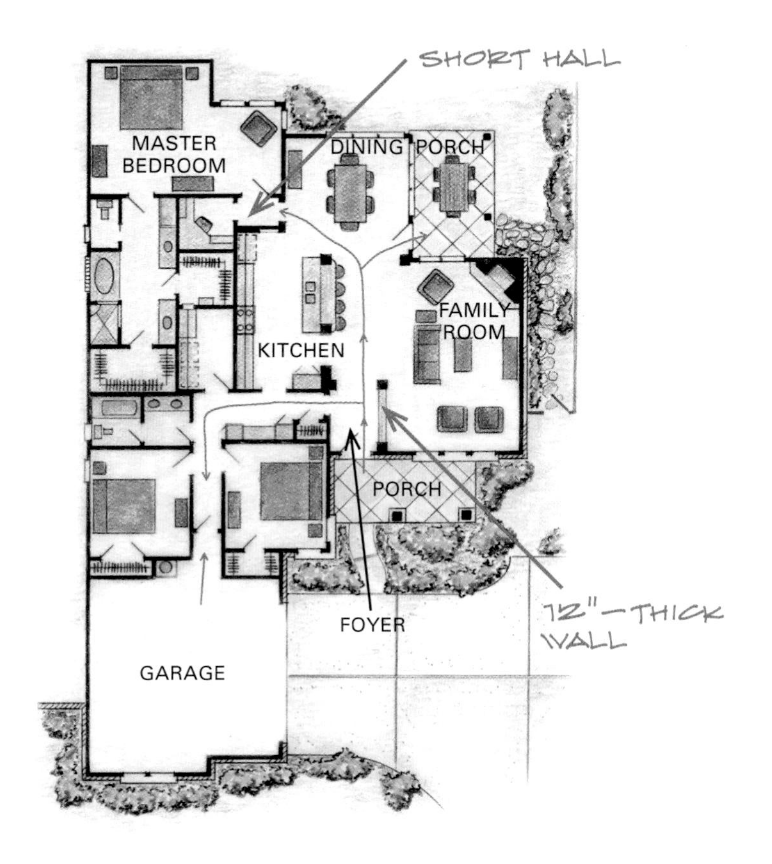

While openness is desirable, bedrooms and bathrooms still need hallways that offer privacy from the main part of the house. In particular, avoid selecting a plan that saves hallway square footage by opening the bedroom directly off the family room. Even a very small hallway can create a sense of privacy for a bedroom.

Each of us has our own ideas regarding good design. To some, this emphasis on logical traffic flow throughout the home may not seem important. Nevertheless, a little extra time spent analyzing a floor plan can prevent some unpleasant surprises when you actually move into your new home. Imagine relaxing in your new family room for the first time and realizing you have an amazing view of the big-screen television — and the bed in your master suite.

Design Diagnosis

Using headers and columns to define traffic

Left: A view from the family room towards the gallery and foyer illustrates the use of columns and dropped headers to define the areas. *Right:* A central gallery directs traffic from the formal front entry and the family entry. Travel between spaces follows a logical path without passing *through* any room.

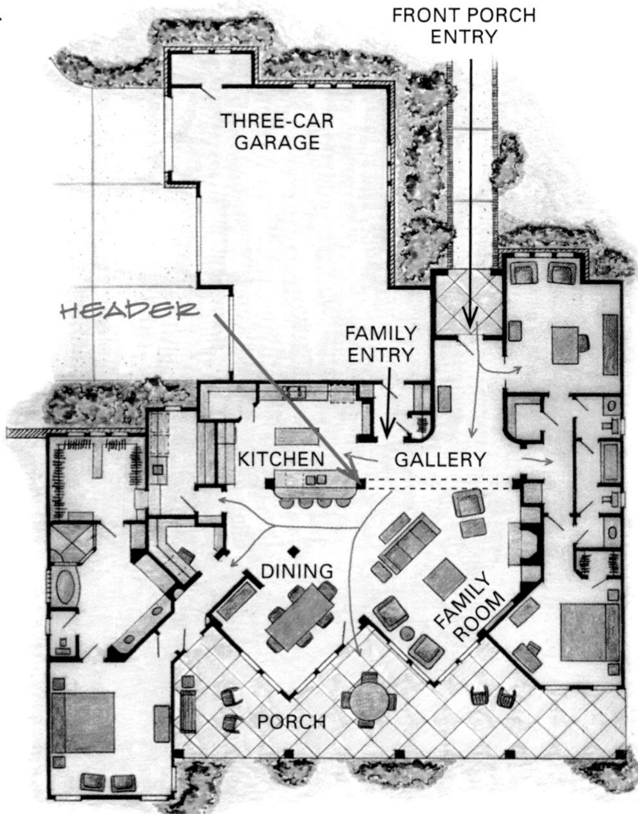

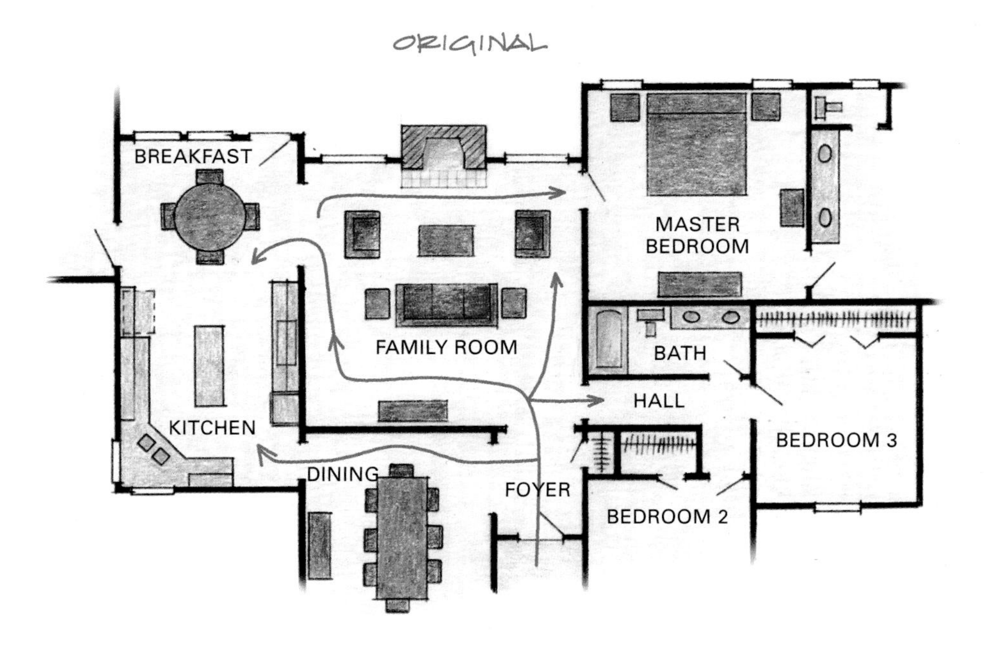

DESIGN DIAGNOSIS

Redirecting a floor plan

The rooms in these two floor plans are essentially in the same locations. However, in the revised plan below, the addition of a gallery and a short hall provides improved traffic patterns. The master bedroom has not only more privacy but also a much better door location. Traveling from the foyer or bedrooms towards the kitchen no longer requires crossing diagonally through the family room. Better traffic circulation often leads to other design improvements. In this case, the formal dining room and foyer have become much more open, and the revised kitchen layout features a snack bar that opens to the family room.

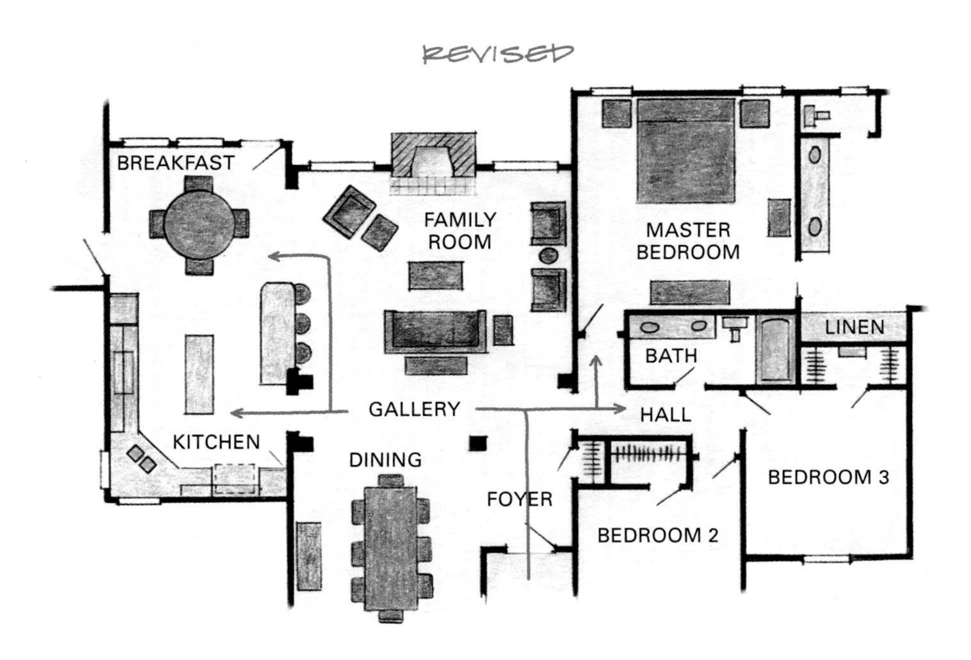

Designing for Privacy

Most of us appreciate the opportunity to find a place where we can enjoy some time to ourselves. Adults may seek peace and quiet, while teenagers may want privacy in their bedrooms or a game room in which to hang out with friends. Unfortunately, as we open up our floor plans, these private areas become more and more difficult to find. The solution does not involve building more walls and returning to long hallways. Simple design decisions can yield a variety of private areas even in an open floor plan.

Privacy within the Home

Adding a few square feet to a hallway can transform the space into a photo gallery or a library with built-in bookcases. Placing a window seat in the hall makes the area a cozy place to relax with a good book. The extra width and windows transform the hall from a dark corridor to an inviting, quiet space filled with natural light.

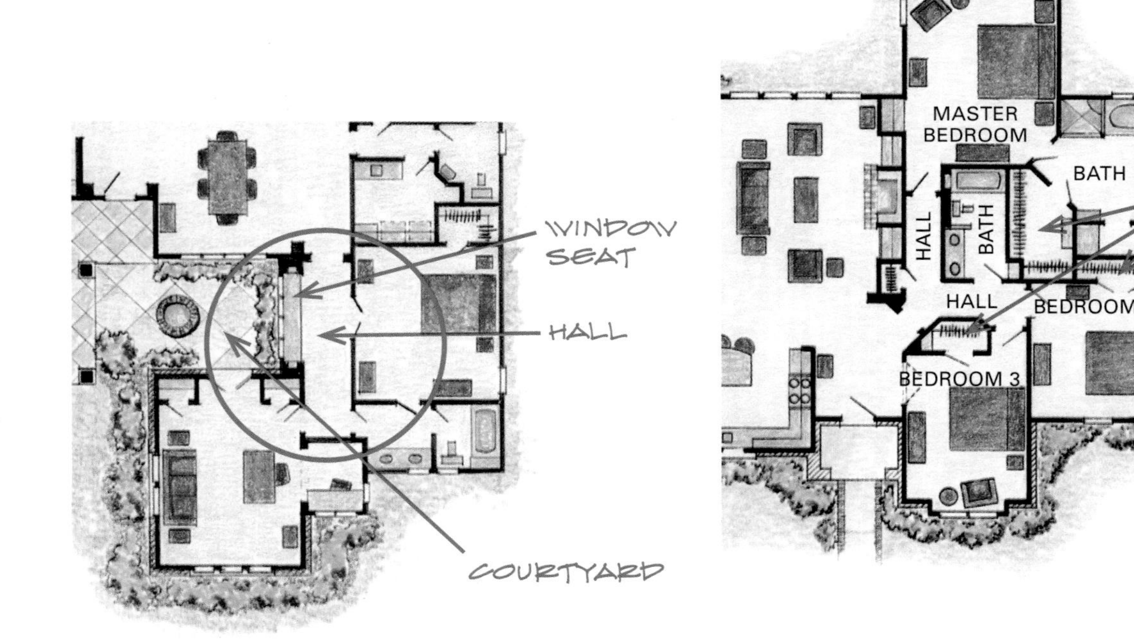

A private sanctuary. A typical hallway can be easily transformed into a cozy reading retreat with the addition of a light-filled window seat.

Sound buffers. Parents may want to have their bedroom close to the younger children's rooms. Privacy can still be maintained by careful door placement and the use of multiple walls of closets and bathrooms that serve as sound buffers.

As we've discussed, the master bedroom will benefit from having a short hallway or buffer zone between it and the more public areas of the home. Secondary bedrooms also require a certain amount of seclusion. For parents with young children, isolating the master bedroom from the children's rooms may not be desirable. However, congregating all of the bedrooms in one area of the house doesn't necessarily result in a total loss of privacy. Avoiding common walls between secondary bedrooms and the master bedroom will offer more privacy to both. Having the bedroom doors open off a short hallway allows them to be located far enough from one another to create a sense of privacy; placing the master bedroom entry beyond the sight of the other bedroom doors adds to this perception.

DESIGN DIAGNOSIS

Detached guest quarters

In this plan a casita, detached from the house and adjacent to the garage, offers complete privacy to its inhabitants. With a full bath and closet it is ideal as guest quarters, and with the door opening to the entry porch, it could double as a home office that allows clients to visit without entering the main home. *(For more on casitas, see chapter 13.)*

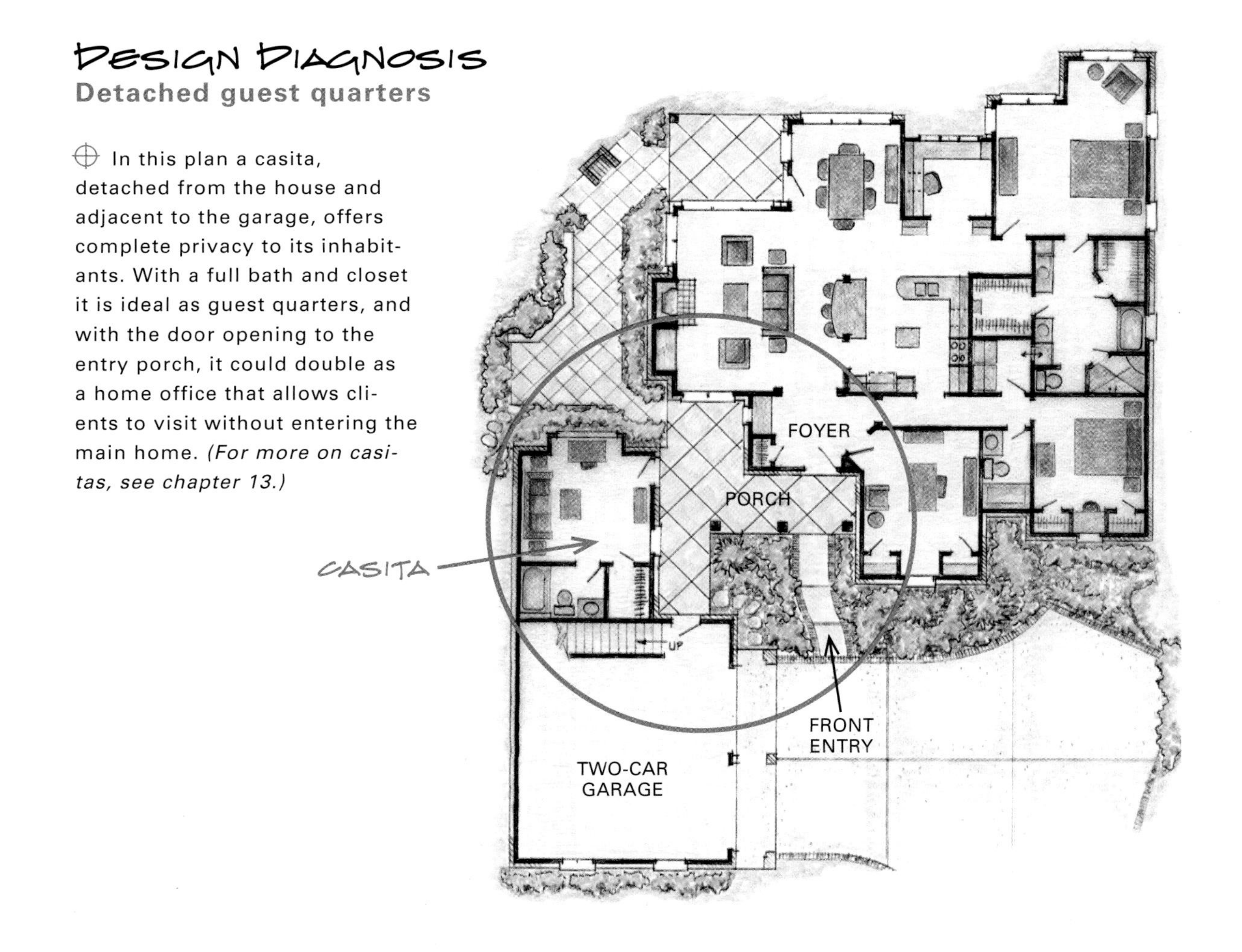

In addition to visual privacy, sound can be a critical issue. After all, your teenager's current music tastes probably differ from your own! Even if they're similar, you may not appreciate the decibel level when you're attempting to sleep. The two elements that control the transmission of sound are insulating materials and buffer zones between the bedrooms. Insulating interior walls offers an easy and fairly economical way to minimize the transfer of sound. You could also have a second layer of drywall placed on selected walls to deaden noise. (Since nails transmit the sound, using glue to apply this extra layer is essential.)

Locating a closet or bathroom between the master bedroom and the other bedrooms creates an important sound buffer.

Many homeowners want rooms to accommodate guests but express concern about the costs involved in building and maintaining seldom-used bedrooms. As a result, some have an interest in building separate guest quarters. Not only are these detached areas more efficient to heat and cool, but the privacy they give to both guests and homeowners is quite appealing. These separate areas, often called *casitas* (Spanish for "little house"),

A second-floor game room. A game room often becomes a teenager's favorite area, particularly if it's on the second floor and offers at least a semblance of privacy.

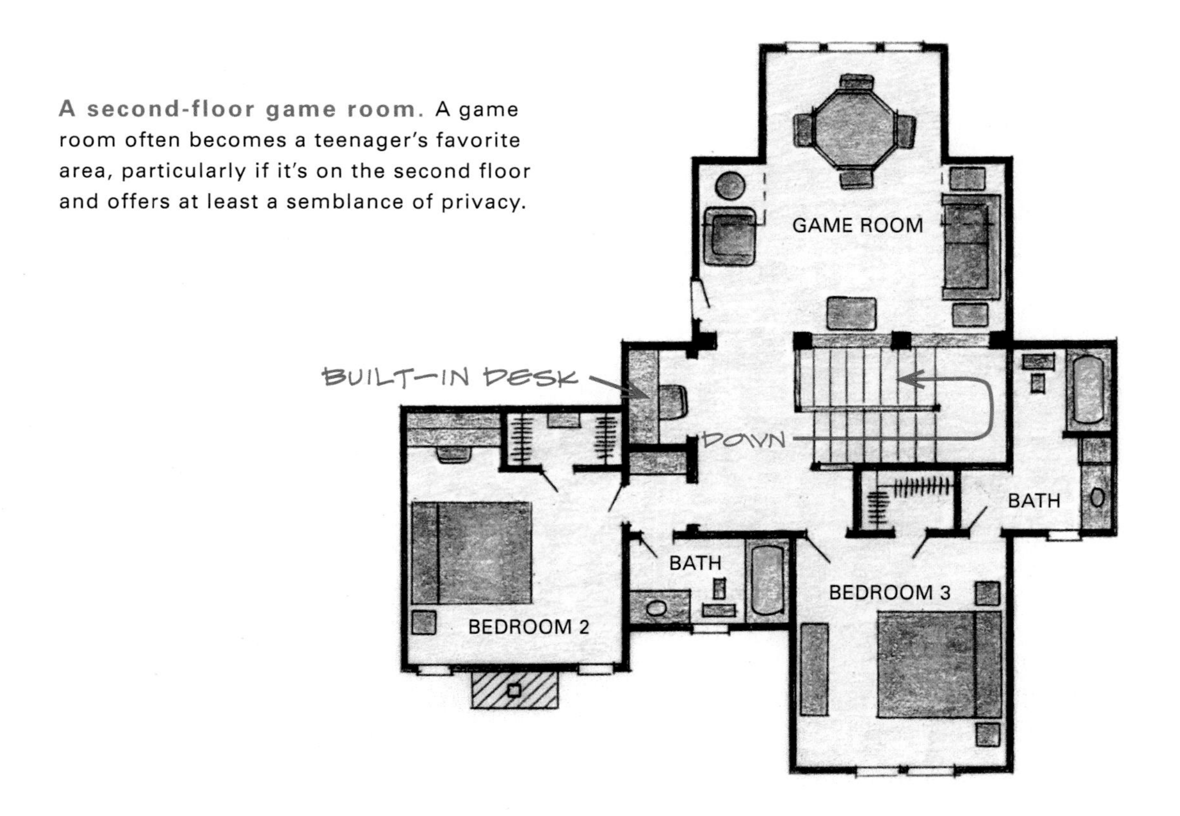

have grown in popularity over the past few years. We'll discuss them in more detail in chapter 13.

While game rooms have been popular for years, their location depends on the homeowner's anticipated use. Families with younger children may want a game room close to the family room or kitchen, so that parents can monitor the activities in it. Older children usually want more privacy. Perhaps teenagers need even *more* monitoring than younger children, but if they think adults are near, they may not use the room at all. You know the theory: better to have them in *your* home, even if it's in a game room on the second floor away from the family.

A home theater also requires some serious consideration. With surround-sound and subwoofer speakers that shake walls, this room can easily compromise the privacy of the entire house. One of the best locations might be in a bonus room above the garage. In this location, with the walls insulated, the home theater is unlikely to disturb those not interested in hearing the all-too-real sounds of jet airplanes landing and battles being fought.

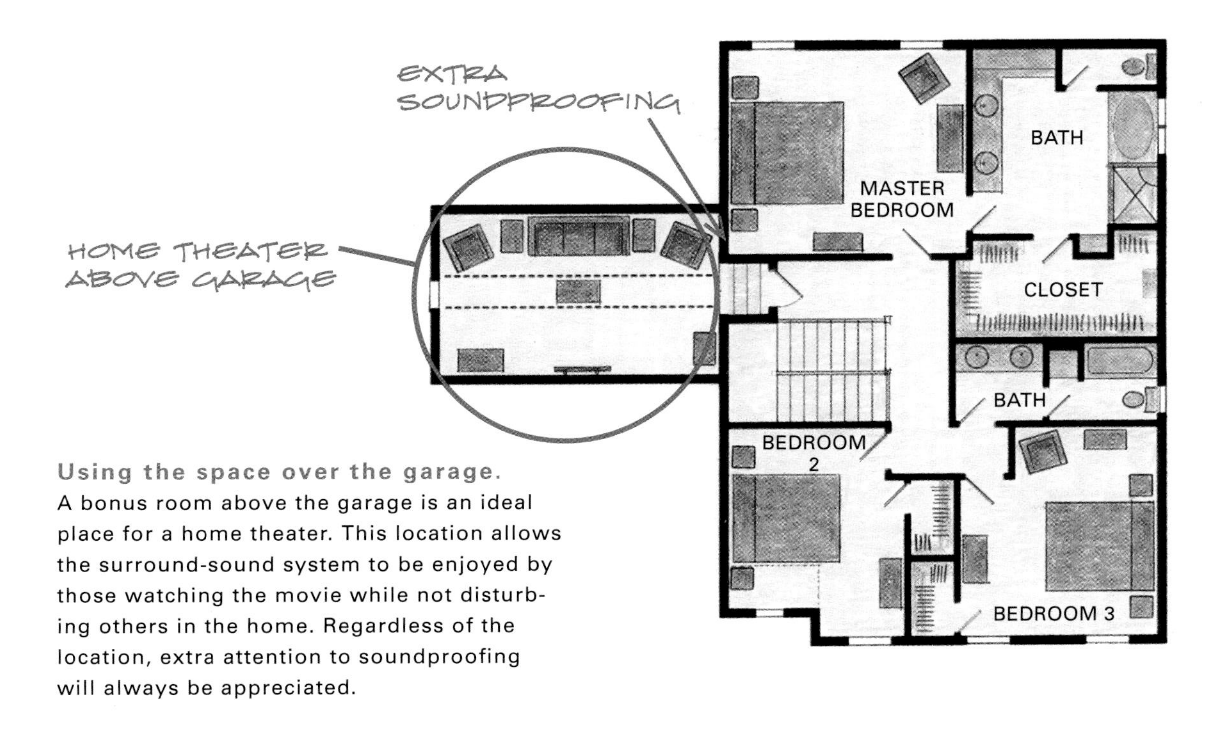

Using the space over the garage. A bonus room above the garage is an ideal place for a home theater. This location allows the surround-sound system to be enjoyed by those watching the movie while not disturbing others in the home. Regardless of the location, extra attention to soundproofing will always be appreciated.

Privacy from the Neighbors

While designing homes with interior privacy requires a logical yet critical analysis of the floor plan, maintaining a sense of privacy from neighboring houses involves careful consideration of the immediate surroundings. Each building site offers unique challenges. The proximity of roads and adjacent homes should influence the overall design of the floor plan and the placement of windows. If you're building on several acres, this may not be an issue. However, in most new planned developments, maintaining a sense of privacy and seclusion can be a challenge.

Narrow lots present the greatest challenges to privacy. Room orientation and window placement are critical. For example, the master bedroom or bathroom should be situated to overlook the most private area of the property, and your home plan should minimize window exposure to neighboring homes.

Privacy can be maintained even in high-density developments as long as careful attention is paid to each home. Each home should be designed to complement its neighbors, providing everyone with a sense of seclusion on their own property. When building codes for high-density developments give extra attention to window placement, landscaping, and other privacy concerns, these developments can feature more privacy than traditional larger-lot subdivisions with no such rules.

Always spend the necessary time to investigate the overall site design of any planned development. Talk with the architectural control committee and your designer to ensure that the privacy of your home will not be compromised by an ill-conceived design of an adjacent house. If no design guidelines and restrictions exist, you'll find it almost impossible to anticipate how your neighbor's design might impact your home. Essentially, narrow lot developments must have rigid design guidelines regarding such issues. If they're not adequate, give some serious consideration to whether this is where you want to build.

DESIGN DIAGNOSIS
A creative use of windows

Sometimes a design minimizes window exposure at the front of the home while placing expansive glass toward the private rear yard. Small clerestory windows allow light into the garage and master closet while eliminating the need for draperies.

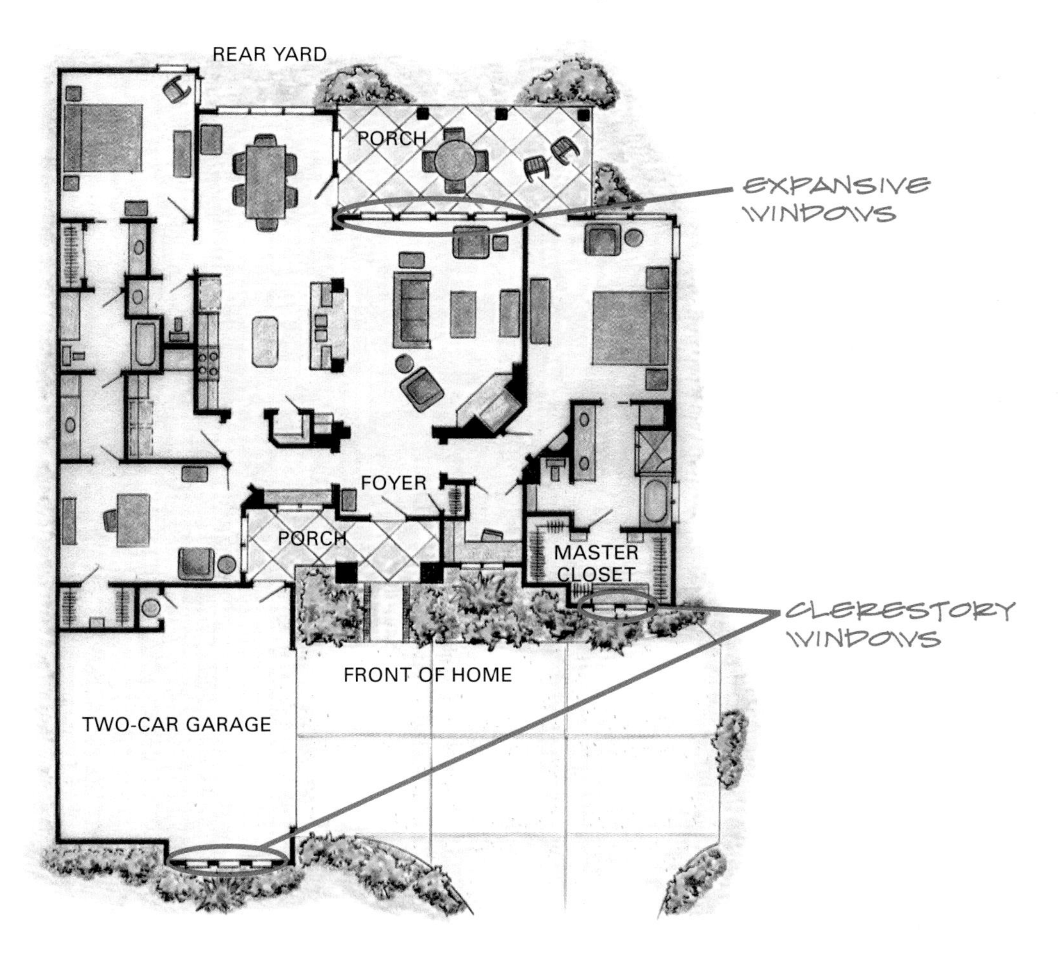

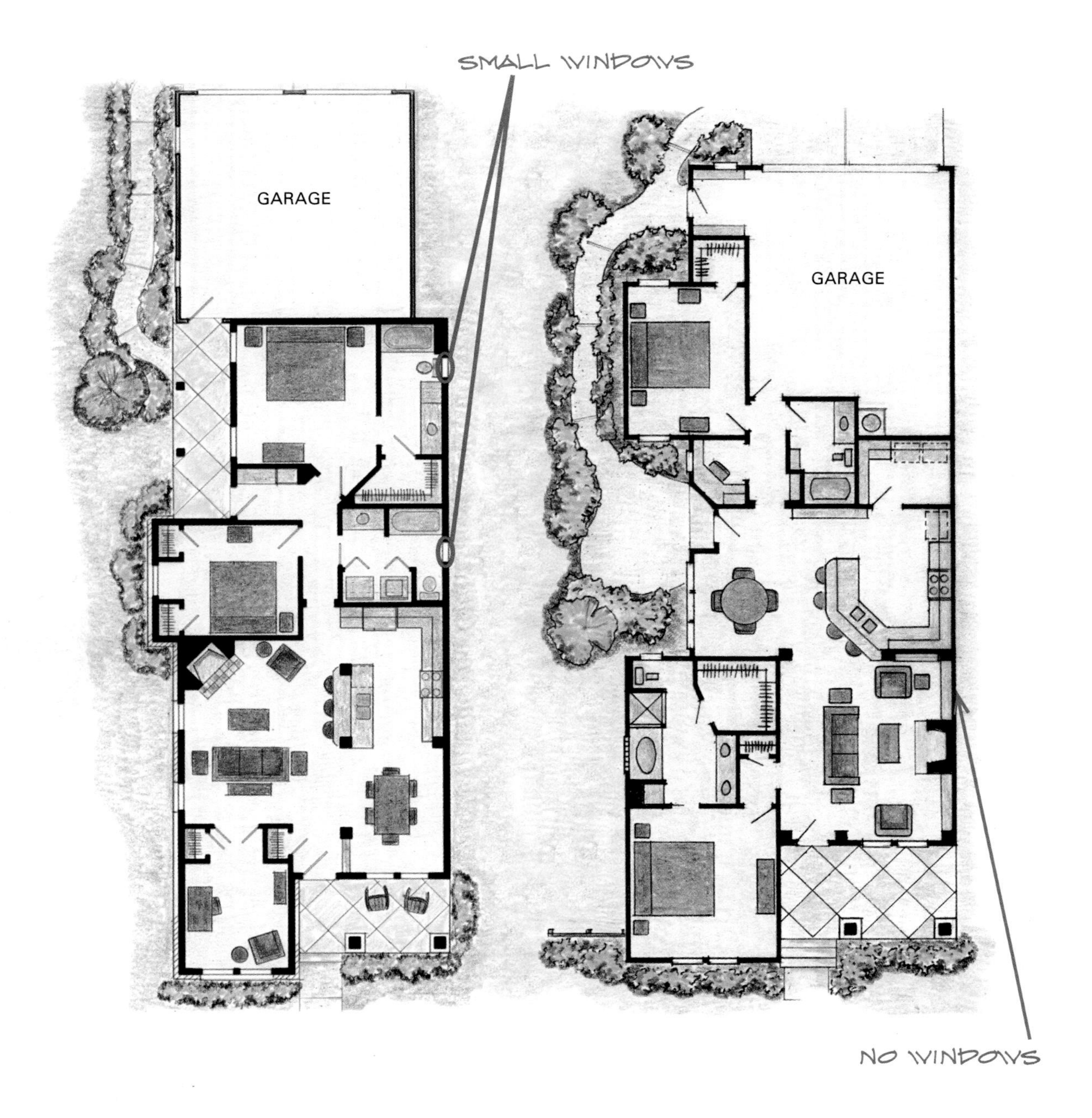

Design Diagnosis

Privacy on narrow lots

Narrow-lot developments should have strict design guidelines to maximize privacy for each home. For example, window exposure to neighbors should be minimized (as in the plan on the left, which features only small bathroom windows on the side) or prohibited (as in the plan on the right).

Universal Design

Though we may find luxurious features appealing, many of us have come to realize that at some point in the future practicality will be even more important than aesthetics. Will our family and friends always be comfortable in this environment we call home? For many people "aging in place" seems like a great idea; in other words, we wish to create a home that we and our families will be able to live in now and as we age. Of course it's impossible to predict what life holds for each of us. Nevertheless, by paying attention to some practical details, we can increase the chances we'll be able to remain in our home for all the years to come.

Simply stated, *universal design* refers to design principles that promote comfortable and equitable living for everyone, regardless of physical ability. Universal design can be applied not just to home design but also to everything from cooking utensils to telephones, public transportation, and all other aspects of daily life. Universal design evolved from the idea of *barrier-free* design, which sought accessibility for those with disabilities.

Unfortunately, barrier-free design often means "separate but equal" installations, such as a back entry with a ramp for wheelchair users. Universal design, on the other hand, is intended to be not only better design for those with physical challenges but just *better design*.

While universal design comprises many specific standards for home interiors and exteriors, it essentially strives to achieve two things: First, all persons, regardless of their abilities, should be able to use every aspect of the home. Second, the design should not direct special attention to any of the details or construction required to make the home universally accessible. In other words, the design should be universally functional *and* appealing. Many of these details just make sense:

- Hallways and doorways are slightly wider than normal. (Standard doors are 32 inches wide. Increasing their width to 36 inches usually involves only a few dollars apiece if specified on the plans.)
- Electrical switches and outlets are at heights that are easy to reach; in most cases this means switches are lower and outlets are higher.
- Large push-button switches are used, rather than small toggles.
- Cabinetry is designed with easy-open latches and slide-out shelving, so that it's easily accessible for everyone.

DESIGN DIAGNOSIS

Universal design principles

⊕ Homes designed according to the principles of universal design feature wide hallways and doorways, walk-in showers, and many other features that add not only to the home's functionality but also to its feeling of spaciousness and its aesthetic appeal.

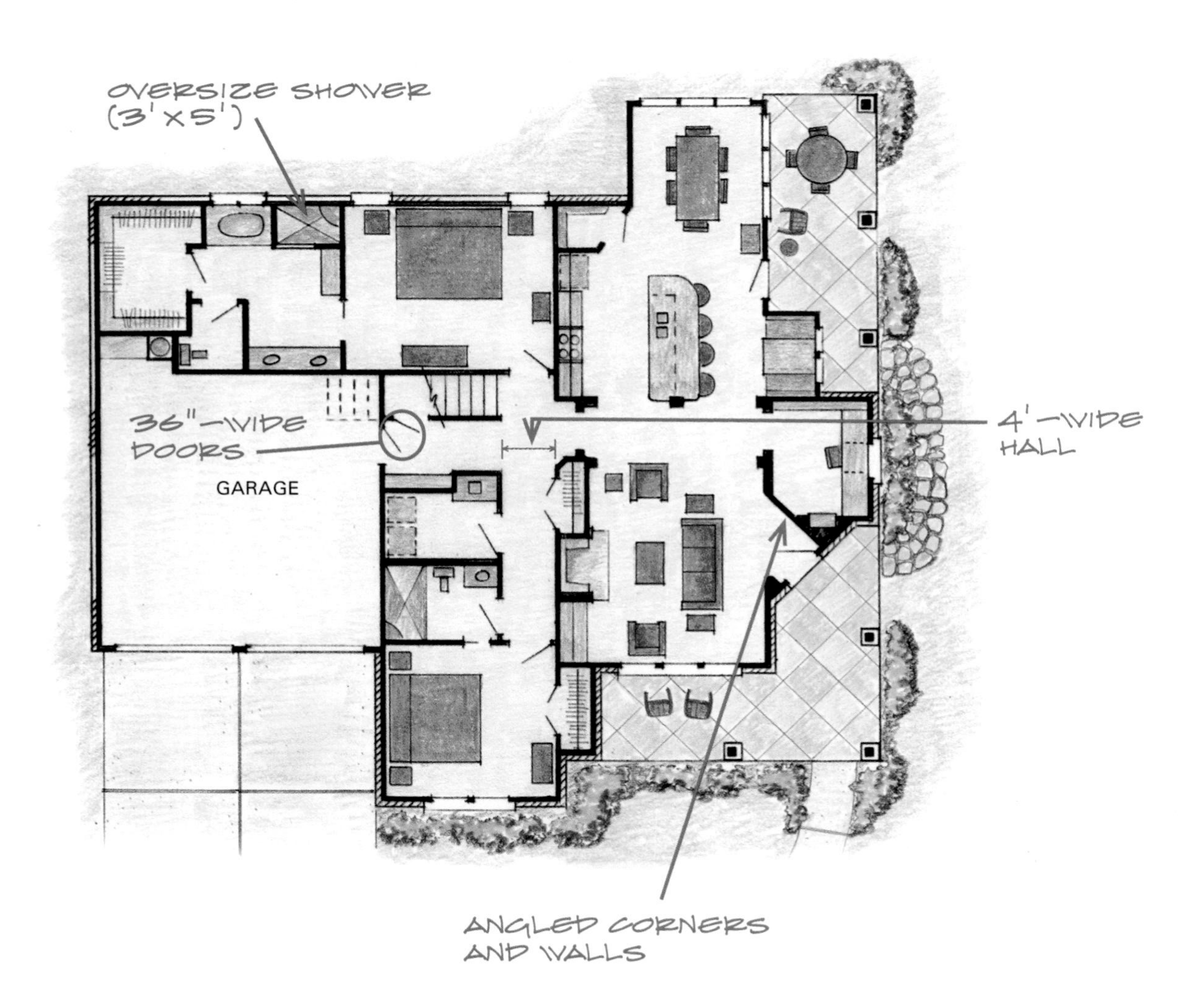

- Bathroom and kitchen countertops are constructed at an accessible and comfortable height.
- Typical doorknobs are replaced by lever handles that are easy to operate.
- Appliances are operated with buttons that can be distinguished by touch.
- Showers are doorless and do not have a raised threshold.

These are just some of the details considered as part of universal design. Almost every one of them can enhance not only the functionality but also the overall appearance of a home. And they help ensure that the home you build now will comfortably house you and your family through all the phases of life.

Many universal design details can be incorporated into a home plan for little or no cost, provided they are specified before construction begins. Making these changes later, after the home has been built, can be expensive, if not completely impractical. Increasing the width of a hallway, for example, may not be possible; adding structural framing behind a wall to accommodate a grab bar in the bathroom may be an expensive proposition. So if you're interested in designing a home for "aging in place," be sure to discuss universal design with the design professional you are working with.

If you'd like more information about universal design, look up the Center for Universal Design, a research and development center for this field, and The Design Linc, a clearinghouse for design ideas and products for creating accessible environments. *(See* Resources *for Web site addresses.)*

10

Come Inside

Since the foyer offers the first (and often last) impression of a home, it is a vitally important design element. Realizing this, builders and design professionals have gradually increased the amount of square footage allotted to the foyer. It's not unusual to enter a recently constructed home and find yourself standing in an entry of at least 150 square feet with a 20-foot ceiling. Impressive? You bet! In fact, it's often the perfect example of a *wow!* room *(see page 109)*.

As with any architectural detail, defining good or bad design for the foyer is inevitably subjective. For some homeowners, a *wow!* foyer with soaring ceilings may be a necessity. Others might prefer an entry that seems less elaborate and more functional. Regardless of how grand the foyer might be, certain aspects of the design should always be considered.

A Well-Designed Foyer

To begin, the entry must be an inviting space to welcome guests. A coat closet should be easily accessible. While many recent designs feature foyers that open directly to the living area, you may still prefer some degree of separation so that the front door can be opened without a visitor immediately having a view directly into the family room. Even if the entry area does offer a view of the family area, under no circumstances should it offer any view of the bedrooms.

Of equal importance is how the area functions on a day-to-day basis for the homeowner. Ideally the foyer not only will provide a dedicated entry to the home but also will act as a traffic hub that directs you to various other areas and rooms. The foyer should, in conjunction with a gallery, offer logical paths to bedrooms and the kitchen that do not pass through the family room. (*For more on galleries, see pages 120 to 123.*)

Just how large does a foyer need to be? The answer relates to the size and proportions of the home itself. A 6,000-square-foot home naturally demands that more area be allotted to the foyer than in a 1,200-square-foot cottage.

Decorating a staircase area. The simple addition of a 1×12 trim board along the tall wall in a staircase can eliminate the feeling of an overwhelming expanse of blank wall space.

Since a staircase can potentially be one of the strongest architectural elements of a home, we often place it prominently in the entry area. This allows the grandeur of the staircase to be displayed. An entry with a staircase certainly requires considerable space. But having stairs in the foyer can often be somewhat inconvenient. For example, children typically travel between their bedrooms and the kitchen and family room on a daily basis. If their bedrooms are upstairs, they are forced to pass through the foyer, which may not be the best solution.

For many families, locating the stairs adjacent to the kitchen and family area proves to be much more practical. A so-called main staircase in the foyer might then be rarely used and become merely an expensive decoration.

Family Entry

For years we've placed tremendous emphasis on the design and construction of front entries. From richly detailed doors to elaborate foyers with vaulted ceilings and multiple layers of crown molding, formal entryways all contribute to the initial impression of a home. That is, they do if your guests enter through the front of the home. All too often guests end up maneuvering through a cluttered garage or laundry area.

Terms to Know

Family entry. A convenient, less formal entry to the house designed to help organize the comings and goings of a busy family.

Family room. This is the room where the family spends much of its time. I use this term instead of *living room,* which implies a more formal guest entertainment area that is rarely used.

Flush Hearth. This term refers to a hearth (the area of a fireplace that extends into the room) that is at the same level as the floor of the fireplace.

Foyer. This area serves as an entry or entrance hall to the rest of the home. Typically it is a formal space, often used only by our guests.

Landing. The landing is a resting spot that serves as a break in climbing stairs. It's usually placed at the midpoint of the climb where the stairs change direction, especially in homes with high first-floor ceilings.

Straight-run stairs. In contrast to stairs with a landing, a straight run is a stair design that places all of the steps in a long, straight line.

You'll still find many house plans that direct traffic from the garage or side entry directly into the utility room. I imagine the logic behind such designs was based on having the laundry area also function as a mudroom. In most cases, though, this utility entry becomes the family's main entrance, and guests follow suit.

For many families the front door remains the least-used door in the home, opening only on those occasions when a new guest visits for the first time. Those who appreciate a more functional approach to design may find a plan that has both the family entry and the front door opening into the foyer quite appealing, as it allows them to enjoy the foyer on a daily basis.

While this shared family/formal arrangement may not be possible with every plan, an appealing and functional family entry should always be considered. Typically we enter our homes through a side or back door, with our first stop being the kitchen. Here we deposit the mail, keys, and cell phones. The kitchen island becomes a constant reminder of our disorganized and often hectic lives.

A family entry provides an easy and practical solution. It should, of course, be located at the side or rear door where family members normally enter the home. Essentially a transition space, the family entry should include a drop zone, which could consist simply of a built-in cabinet and counter with dedicated places for mail and keys, in addition to electrical outlets for charging cell phones. (How many times have you walked out the door and realized your cell battery had no power? That is, if you can *find* your phone in the first place.)

HEALTHY EXAMPLES

Impressive Foyers

Example 1

⊕ **Harmonize open spaces.** In addition to providing an attractive entry, the foyer should offer logical paths to bedrooms and the kitchen that don't pass through the family room. In this plan, 12-inch-thick columns and archways define the foyer and gallery. Notice that the wood floor continues throughout the entire area, allowing the spaces to "borrow" from each other and appear more spacious.

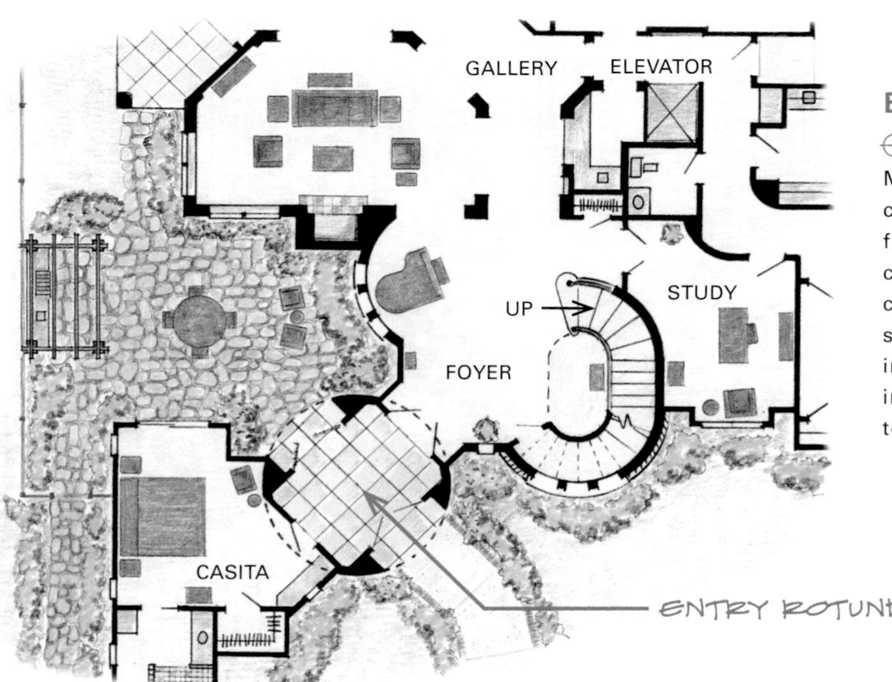

Example 2

⊕ **Keep a *wow!* room functional.** Massive ceilings and 20-foot-tall walls can make foyers overwhelming and difficult to decorate. In order to maintain a comfortable scale, this plan uses 10-foot ceilings that open up to a two-story-tall staircase with rounded walls. Although impressive, the area is not overwhelming. Rather, it serves as an introduction to the rest of the home.

HEALTHY EXAMPLES

Functional foyers

Example 1

Strategic placement. This U-shaped staircase is conveniently located adjacent to the kitchen and family entry. Note the landing located halfway up the stairs. The functional foyer offers a welcoming entrance to the home with a handy coat closet and a cozy window seat that provides plenty of natural light.

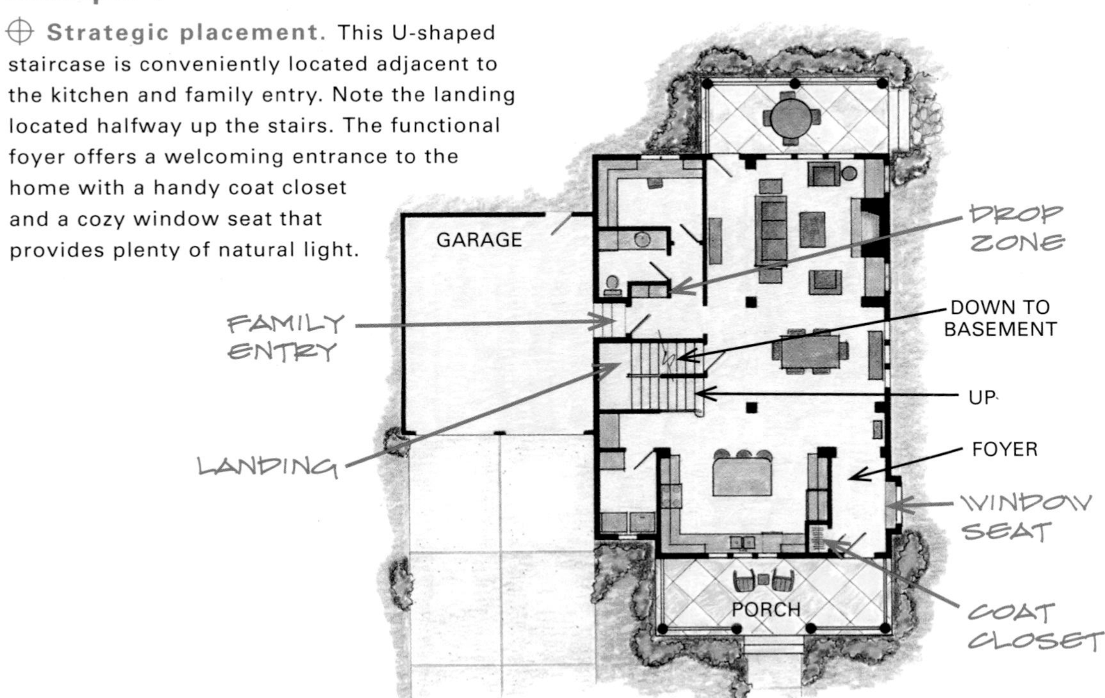

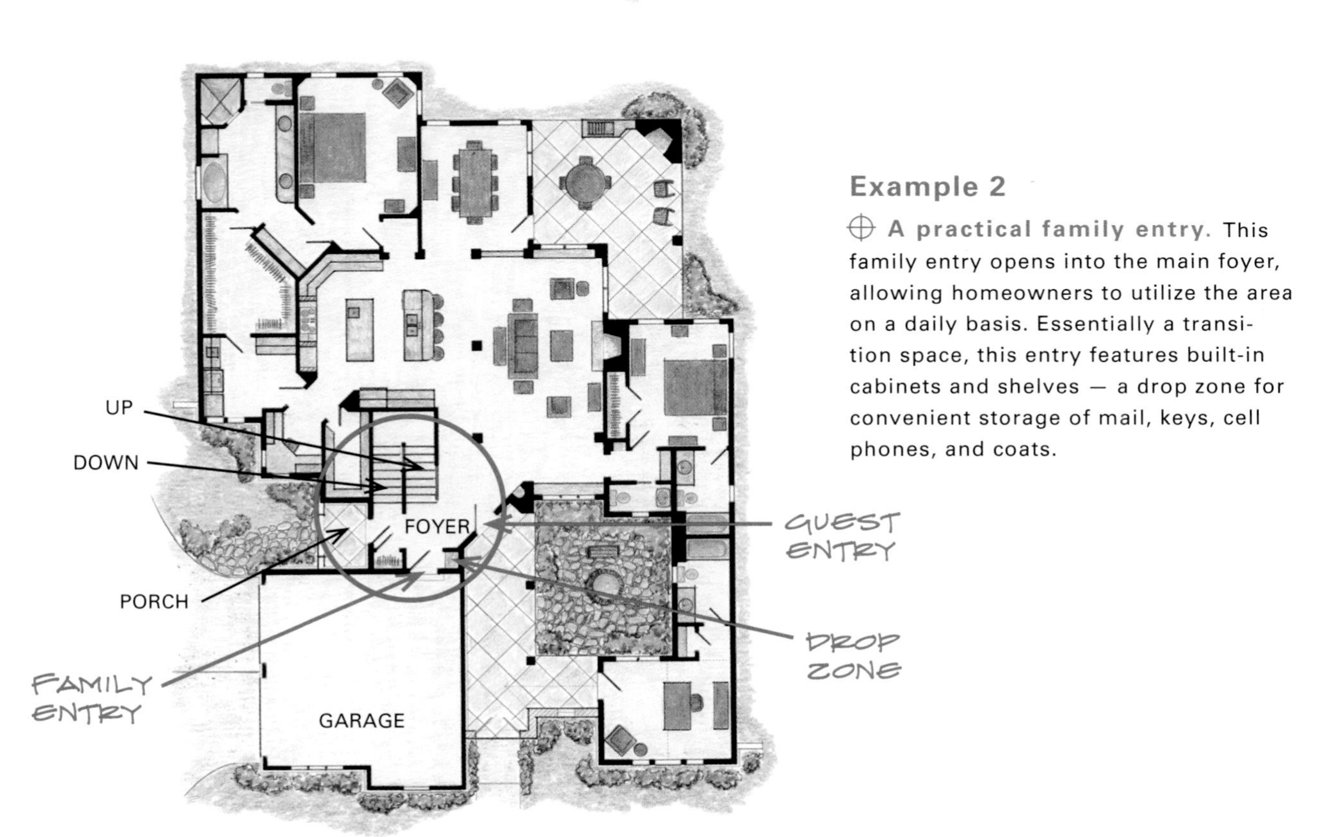

Example 2

A practical family entry. This family entry opens into the main foyer, allowing homeowners to utilize the area on a daily basis. Essentially a transition space, this entry features built-in cabinets and shelves — a drop zone for convenient storage of mail, keys, cell phones, and coats.

If square footage allows, a more spacious design might also include a mail sorting area where bills, personal mail, and catalogs can be filed. You might even locate a paper shredder here to immediately dispose of the junk mail we all receive. A locker for each member of the family gives everyone his or her own storage for shoes, coats, and sports equipment. While you might think such "cubbies" are only for the children, parents will also appreciate having their own private storage space.

A bulletin board in the entry provides a place to post important events and family photos.

The real measure of a home's lasting appeal and satisfaction probably has more to do with how we as individual homeowners enjoy the day-to-day experience of living in our home than with how impressed our guests are with our formal foyers. Sure, everyone derives satisfaction from the aesthetic qualities of a home, but we also appreciate the practical aspects of the design. There's a lot to be said for being able to find your keys each morning and having the cell phone charged and ready!

Design Diagnosis

Plan for convenience

For a family entry to function on a daily basis, it must be conveniently located. With this plan, entering from the garage or the front door allows easy access to the drop zone and other family entry storage solutions.

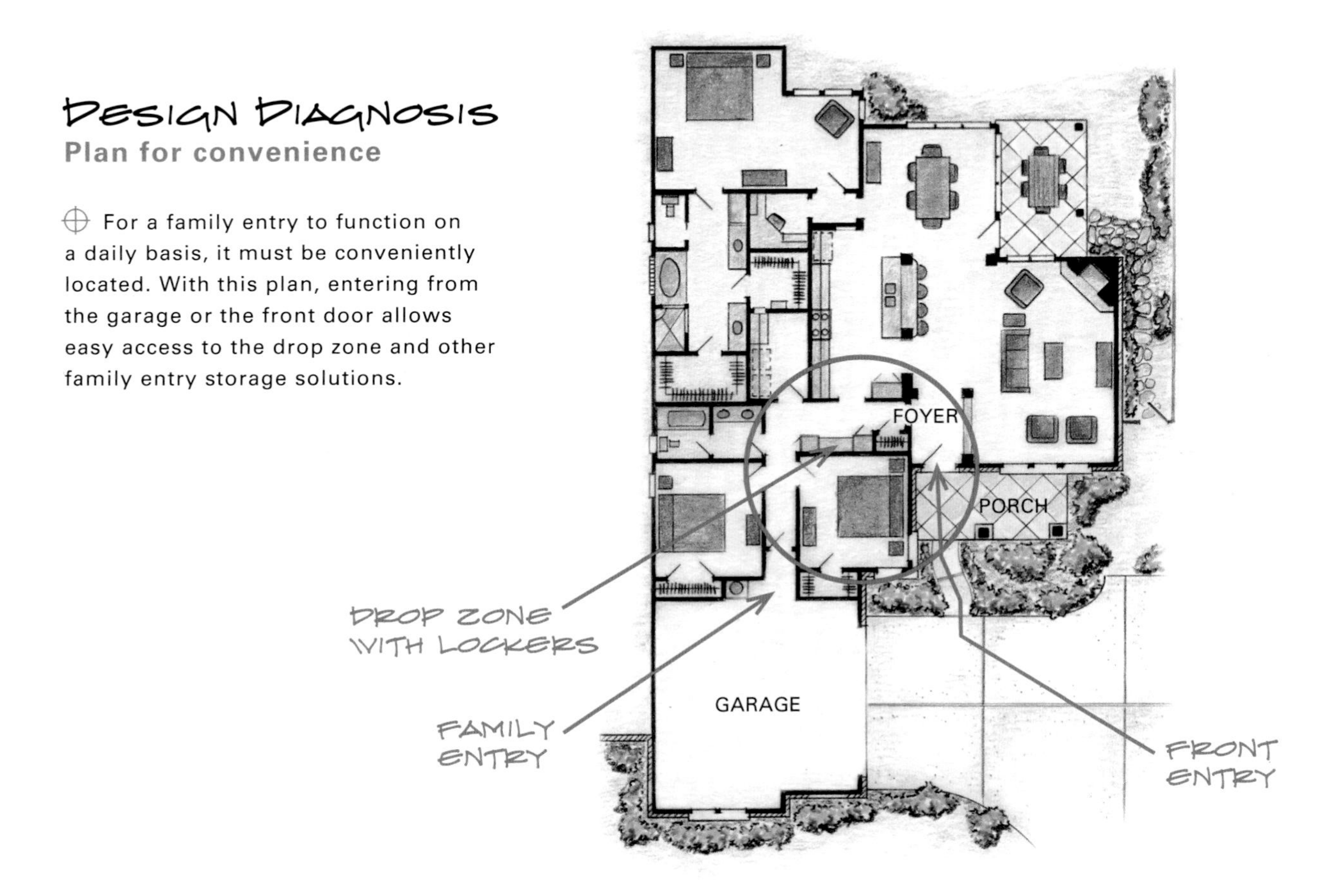

HEALTHY EXAMPLES

Family entry way features

Example 1

Getting organized. This drop zone at the family entry has a place for sorting mail, drawers for keys, a cell phone charger, and a coat closet.

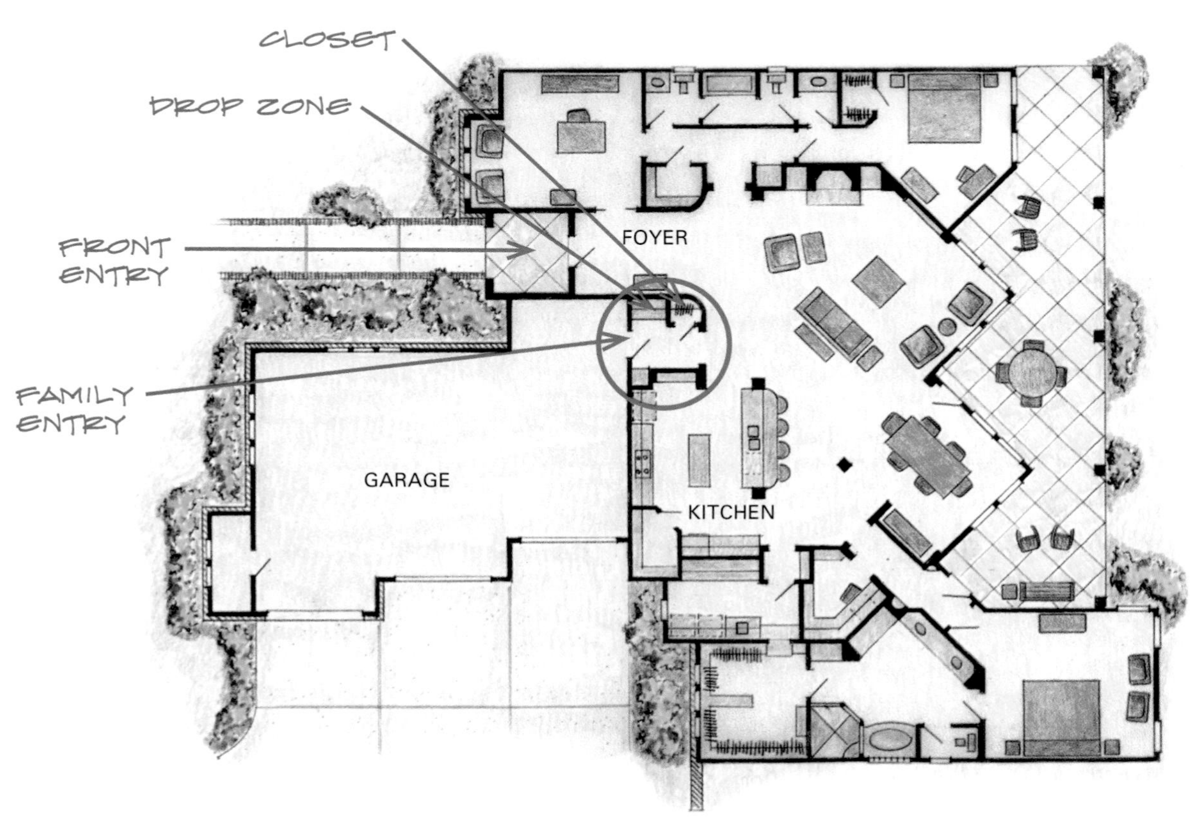

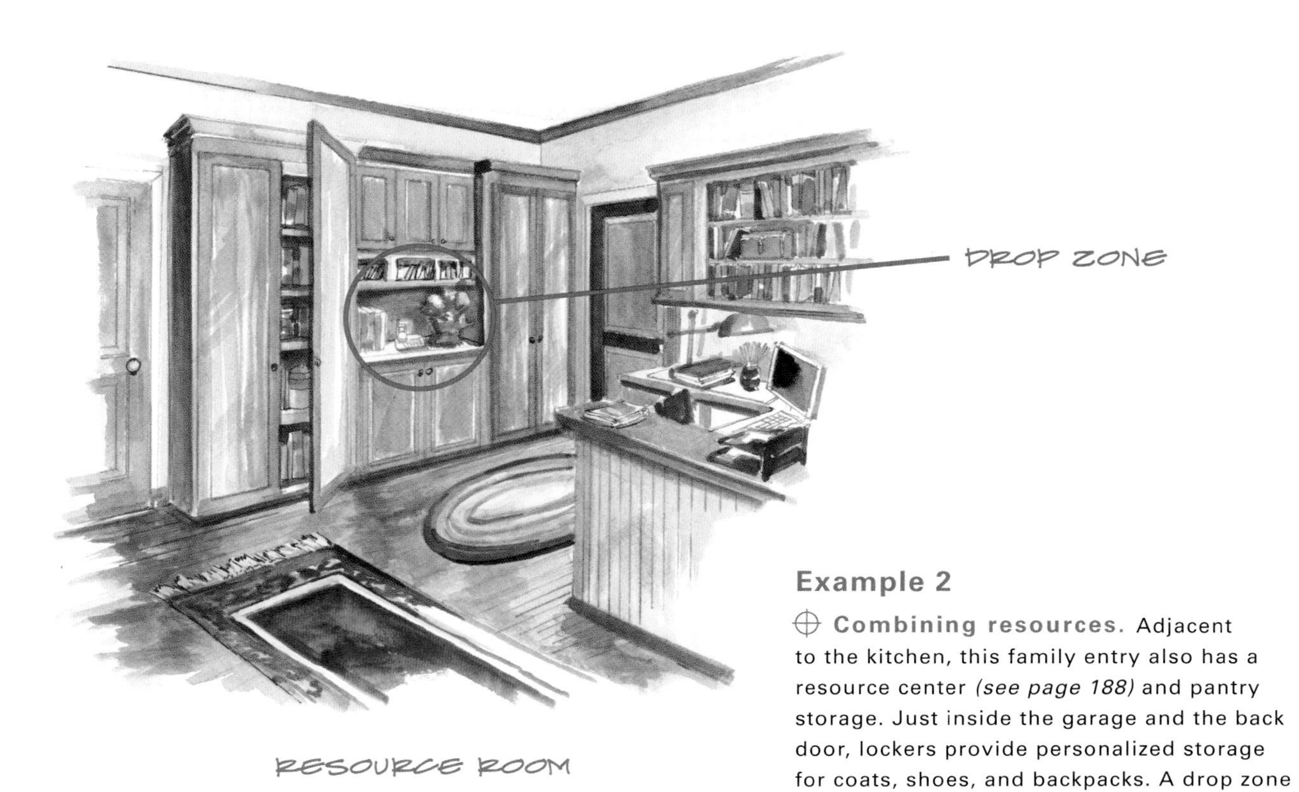

Example 2

⊕ **Combining resources.** Adjacent to the kitchen, this family entry also has a resource center *(see page 188)* and pantry storage. Just inside the garage and the back door, lockers provide personalized storage for coats, shoes, and backpacks. A drop zone has a place for sorting mail and storage for keys and cell phones.

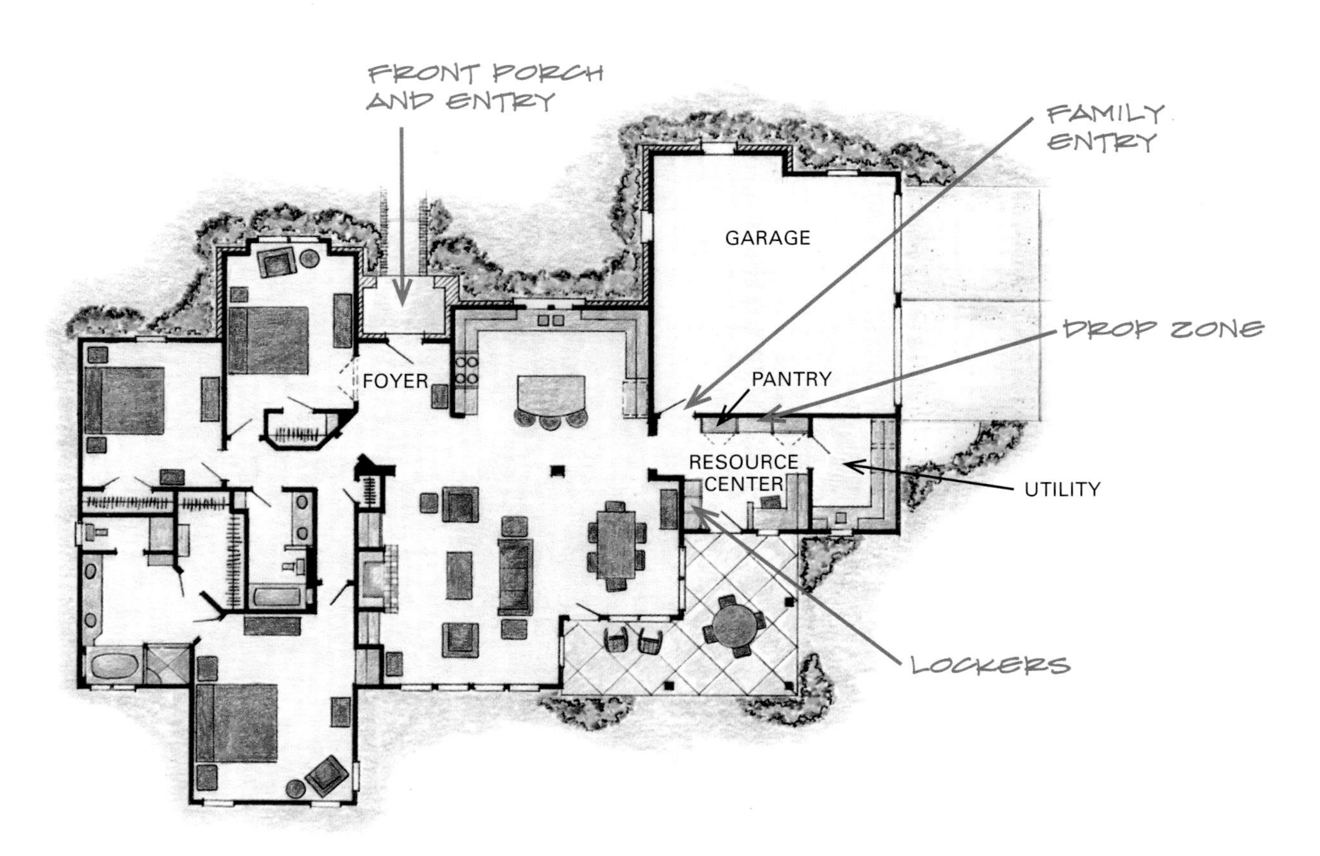

What's in a Name?

The family room has evolved over the years, both in use and in name. I recall as a child my family having a living room furnished in a manner that made it off-limits for daily use. I remember thinking that the name *living room* was strange, since we actually *lived* in another room near the kitchen that we called the *den*. At some point in design history the term *den* logically evolved into *family room*. As the living room gradually disappeared from most home plans and hallway space was incorporated into family rooms, the larger space often became known as the *great room*. I suppose this ominous-sounding name might have been considered more descriptive of the one large room that combined the family *and* living rooms.

When browsing plan collections on the Internet or working with a local design professional, you'll likely see all of these terms used as labels for the area where you and your family will spend a great deal of time. Over the years I myself have utilized all of these names at one time or another in my designs. I now prefer to call this living area the family room, possibly because of my difficulty with the off-limits aura of the term *living room*, but also because it better describes the focus of the living area: family time.

Family Room

The family room is designed to be the space where the family spends most of its time in the house. As with the design of other areas in the home, many options exist, there are no definite right or wrong decisions, and the ultimate design must be determined by your personal tastes and your family's lifestyle.

For many homeowners, a living area open to the kitchen and dining space seems to function quite comfortably as a family room on a day-to-day basis. When fast-paced lives limit the amount of family time available, combining the kitchen, dining, and family living spaces gives us more opportunity to spend time together. The person preparing the meal can still be involved in a conversation (or television program) taking place in the family room. One child can work on a school project at the dining table while another plays a video game in the family room, and a parent can stay involved as he or she prepares dinner.

For many homeowners, the question of whether they want an open plan often becomes a question of just how open the floor plan will be. Some current plans feature a single large room with a kitchen at one end and the living area at the other, with a dining table in between. Often, a large room such as this becomes difficult to furnish and offers virtually no distinction among the various activities. Many early designs that explored the open concept gave little thought to traffic flow, sometimes even forcing residents to walk around the seating area to reach a bedroom or hall.

HEALTHY EXAMPLES

Using ceiling height effectively

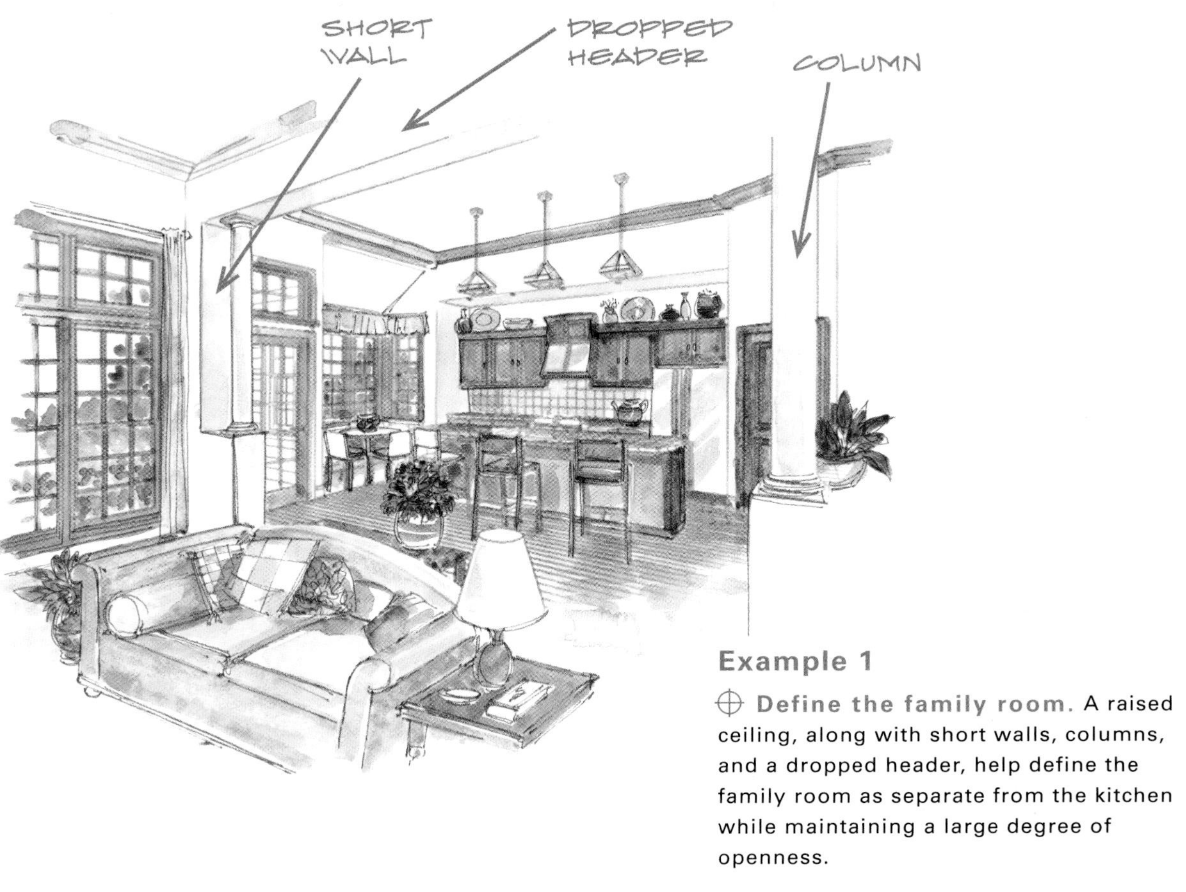

Example 1

⊕ **Define the family room.** A raised ceiling, along with short walls, columns, and a dropped header, help define the family room as separate from the kitchen while maintaining a large degree of openness.

Example 2

⊕ **Design a kitchen alcove.** Locating the kitchen in an alcove adjacent to the family room and dining area retains the feeling of openness but adds a degree of separation. Although no one can watch the television from this kitchen, the potential for distracting kitchen noise is minimized.

In order to keep an open concept from becoming just one huge room, you may want to consider some means of defining each part:

- Use single or doubled columns, in place of solid walls, to define areas.
- Use a dropped header or an arch to separate two spaces; either will keep the spaces open to each other while also distinguishing them from each other.
- Change the ceiling height or treatment from one space to the next in the open area. For example, raising the ceiling in the living area can create a spacious feeling, while simultaneously providing a sense of enclosure for the kitchen with its lower ceiling.

In general, the floor covering should be as consistent as possible throughout the main living area. Maintaining the same floor through the kitchen, the dining room, and the family room allows each area to "borrow" visual space from the others, making each seem larger than it is.

Locating the kitchen in an alcove adjacent to the dining and family area is a middle ground between an open and a closed plan. While the kitchen has some seclusion both visually and from a noise and clutter standpoint, it still has a strong sense of connection to the family area.

Ceiling Height

In addition to defining and separating areas, the living area ceiling has an enormous impact on the overall perception of spaciousness. The house plans should spell out the height and the shape of the ceiling. Dashed lines indicate some type of exposed beam or decorative truss; if the plan simply notes the ceiling height, you probably can assume the ceiling to be flat. In other cases the ceiling shape may be referred to as one of the types shown on this page.

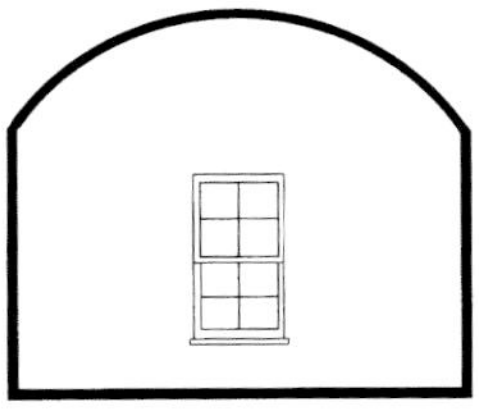

VAULTED CEILING

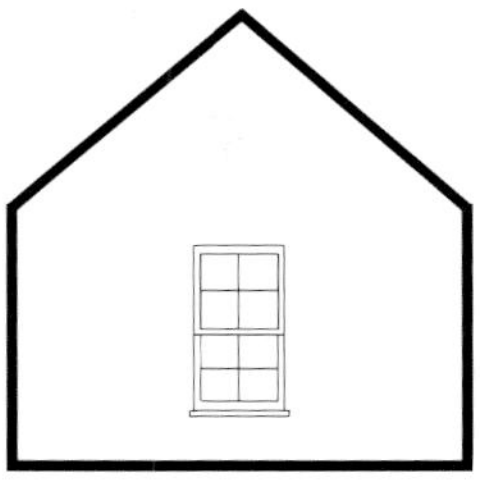

CATHEDRAL CEILING

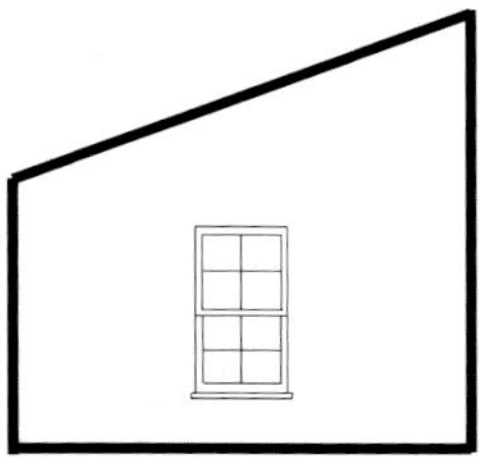

SLOPED CEILING

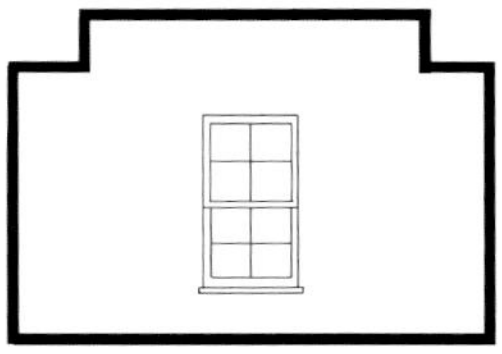

TRAY CEILING

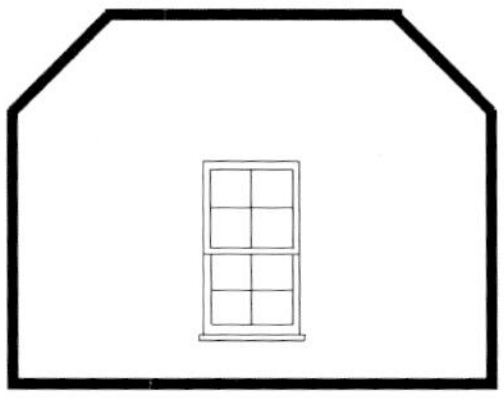

GAMBREL CEILING

Once you determine the type of ceiling called for, you must carefully consider the overall height. Most people assume that high ceilings always make a room seem larger and more spacious. Not so! In fact, the exact opposite can occur: instead of enhancing a room's perceived size, an excessively high ceiling can cause the room to feel much smaller. This all has to do with the proportions of the room *(see page 105)*. Although other variables such as window size and finish materials have an impact, the length and width of a room have a direct relationship to the proper height of the ceiling.

Although I can't give you a specific formula for proper ceiling height, here are a few considerations. A 9-foot ceiling has been standard for the last few years, though we now see many larger homes with minimum ceiling heights of 10 feet. In general, smaller rooms should have lower ceilings, while higher ceilings should be reserved for larger

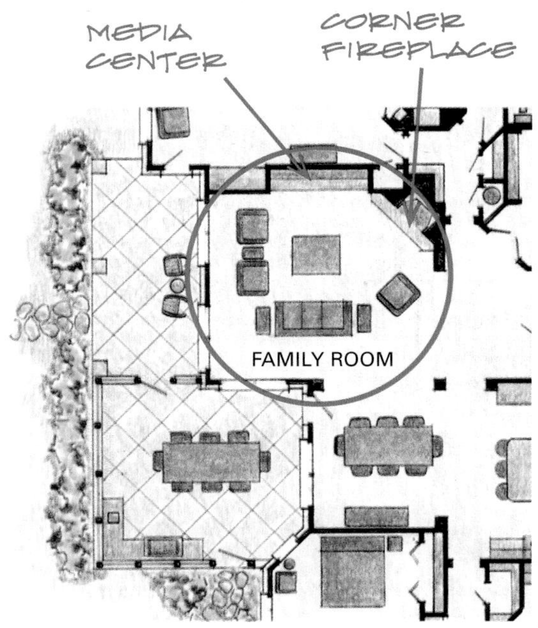

Combining style and function. An impressive high ceiling is counterbalanced by a cozy corner fireplace and a media center along an adjacent wall.

rooms. For instance, a 3½-foot-wide hall will seem smaller with a 10-foot ceiling than with a 9-foot ceiling.

Since family rooms usually are the largest areas in a home, they're the perfect place for a higher ceiling. A 16-foot by 20-foot family area might feature a ceiling up to 12 feet in height. Any dimension greater than 12 feet may cause you to feel that the room is closing in on you.

As always, such design decisions are a matter of personal taste. For instance, a living area with a 20-foot-high ceiling opening to a balcony above will surely become one of those *wow!* rooms discussed earlier. Your friends might be impressed, and so might you! Just carefully consider not only the *initial* impact on you and your guests but also the *long-term* impact on the daily life of your family. Often these *wow!* spaces become overwhelming and difficult to furnish.

A living area, or any room for that matter, will ideally provide a welcoming and functional environment where you feel comfortable doing the things for which the room was designed. For the living area, that means enjoying conversation with friends and family, watching television or listening to music, and perhaps simply reading a good book. Will the *wow!* effect of a high ceiling compromise the comfort and coziness you desire as your family watches television, plays games, or enjoys relaxed conversation? Again, while my personal aversion to exceptionally high ceilings may appear obvious, the ultimate answer relates to how you and your family envision this living area being used.

Fireplace vs. Media Equipment

Another important consideration for the family room is the placement of the television and other entertainment or media equipment. I recall in years past when clients seemed reluctant to talk about television placement. Many almost felt a sense of guilt if they admitted their enjoyment of watching TV. As a result, many family rooms designed in the past offered no place for what was then a large, bulky piece of furniture. Obviously, much has changed since then. Designs for living areas in recent years tend to feature media centers with space for large-screen televisions and speakers strategically placed for surround sound.

Fireplaces were an essential element in homes until central heat became prevalent. Today, in most cases, the fireplace has become more of a decorative element. When homeowners want to use wood for heating, a woodstove is usually a much more efficient and functional choice. As a result, some new homes are being built without fireplaces.

DESIGN DIAGNOSIS

Combine the television and fireplace

⊕ *Left:* With new flat-screen televisions, the dilemma of fireplace and television placement has a new solution: combine the two! This not only allows the seating arrangement to focus on one area but also frees up the adjacent wall for windows.

⊕ *Below:* When placing your television above the fireplace, make sure the firebox and mantel design allow for the TV to be located low enough for a comfortable viewing angle. The exact location will depend on the room size and viewing angle from the seating arrangement.

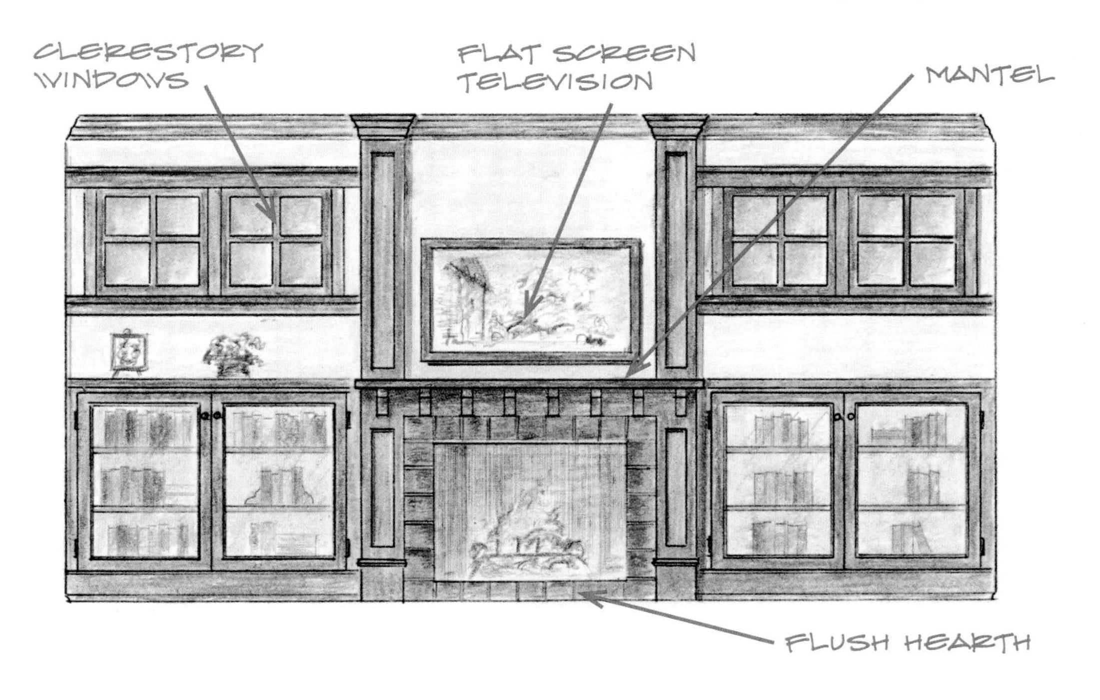

Design Diagnosis

Planning a television wall recess

When placed in a recessed area in the wall, the flat-screen television can become a significant part of the interior design. This offers a viable option for those who resist the idea of placing the screen above the fireplace.

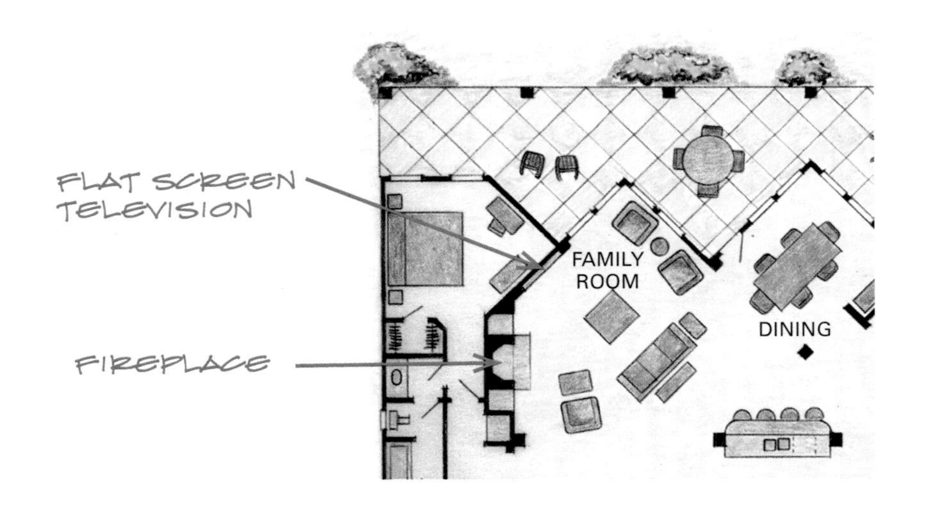

Homeowners who want both a fireplace and a media center can present a challenge for designers. The goal is to place the television in a location that allows for comfortable viewing while keeping the fireplace as the traditional focal point of the room.

One of the most functional designs situates the fireplace at a corner, with the TV located along an adjacent wall. With this layout, the fireplace remains the focus of the room while allowing perfect viewing angles for the television.

Of course, as large flat-screen televisions rapidly decline in price, another option now exists. The once obtrusive TV can be mounted directly above the fireplace. The remaining audio-video equipment can be located in a rather small cabinet. In fact, with on-demand movies and miniaturized sound systems, it won't be long before a small remote control device will be the only auxiliary equipment needed. It seems as though the massive media center will have experienced a very short life!

Even though the placement of the TV and fireplace have become flexible, keep a couple of details in mind: make sure the design of your fireplace places the firebox low enough for the TV above it to be mounted at a reasonably low height. With some fireplace designs, especially those with raised hearths, the flat-screen televisions must be placed at an uncomfortably high location. Also, check with the television and fireplace manufacturers to make sure the heat will not present a problem for the electronics.

For those who just can't agree that the television should be placed above the fireplace (after all, that's where the family portrait should go!), new technology offers still more options. When set in a slight recess in the wall (approximately 2 inches deep), the large flat screen becomes an impressive part of the interior design. Placement of the fireplace on an adjacent wall still allows for sensible furniture arrangements.

As discussed in chapter 9, traffic patterns are of great importance in family room design. For the most functional and comfortable furniture arrangements in your family room, avoid floor plans that force you to walk across the living area to reach the entry, kitchen, or bedroom area. Not only does this become extremely distracting for people in the family room, but the plan requires a much larger area to be devoted to the family room, one that usually results in wasted space around the furniture arrangement to allow for this traffic path.

Frequently Asked Questions

Ⓠ *We have U-shaped stairs with extremely tall walls from the first to the second floor. How do we decorate the area?*

Ⓐ Staircases present a unique challenge. Vast expanses of white walls can become a decorating nightmare. Try defining tall walls with a simple horizontal band of wood trim, placing either a 1×12 trim board or a smaller chair rail molding approximately 9 feet from the first floor. This will essentially define the first and second floors and make easier the installation of artwork at an appropriate height. You might also consider installing a recessed display area at the landing, which can transform the space into an art gallery or family photo display. If possible, add some windows for natural light. *(See page 135.)*

Ⓠ *We have a plan we like, but we'd like to move the stairs from the foyer to a location closer to the kitchen. Is this a major change?*

Ⓐ Because the staircase is critical in the design of a multilevel home, its location must be of primary consideration from the very beginning of the design process. In many cases the floor plan is actually designed around the stairs, down to such details as the roof slope. As a result, stair placement on an existing design might be difficult to change.

Ⓠ *What's the best layout for stairs?*

Ⓐ Any design that varies from the *straight run* provides stairs that are much easier to climb. Particularly with 9- and 10-foot-high ceilings, climbing a straight run can be quite an effort. The L or U shape is probably the most practical, while curved staircases are the most dramatic — and expensive! Spiral stairs work well in small areas, but they make it difficult, if not impossible, to transport furniture upstairs.

Ⓠ *I don't want a huge foyer, but it seems like all the new homes have one. Is it a mistake to build a home without a grand entry?*

Ⓐ Resisting the urge to follow a current trend can be difficult. While you need to keep an eye on the resale value of your home, I firmly believe that your first priority is to create a home that addresses your family's needs and desires. We all tend to think our tastes are unique. In reality, if you create a functional entryway, many other people will also find it appealing. On the other hand, there will always be those who appreciate large and elaborate foyers.

Ⓠ *A real estate agent told me that it would be a mistake to locate the stairs any place except the foyer. Is that true?*

Ⓐ The housing market is simply too diverse to make any absolute statements. Trust your own judgment. A functional, well-designed home will always have appeal. While many potential buyers will insist on having a formal staircase in the foyer, there are many others who believe just as you do.

11

Kitchen and Dining

If there's one lesson we all should have learned by now, it's that the kitchen functions as the hub of the home. Yet we continue to see homes built with small kitchens separated from the family room and dining area. The next time you entertain guests, notice what happens. Even if you place food in a formal dining room, people will fill their plates and then naturally gravitate back to the crowded kitchen. As more and more homeowners decide to eliminate the formal living room *and* the formal dining room, the kitchen truly becomes the center for entertaining.

If you question the necessity of a large, open kitchen, just observe what happens the next time you entertain at home. Invariably everyone will insist on gathering in the kitchen!

Accessible Kitchens

If you want the kitchen to serve as the home's focal point, you must carefully analyze any floor plan you intend to build. While guests enjoy being in the kitchen socializing, the area must still function for food preparation.

If space allows, a center island provides an additional working surface. Make sure you have at least 40 inches (preferably 48 inches) between each side of the island and opposing cabinets. In some cases the island can double as an eating area. Larger kitchens may have space for a separate dining counter with chairs or stools; this allows people to either sit or stand at the "snack bar" while food continues to be prepared or served. If the dining counter surface is at the same height as the rest of the countertops, it also functions as a kitchen workstation.

Traditionally kitchen design dictated that the sink must be located beneath a window. In recent years, as floor plans have become more open, the sink often can be found in an island that overlooks the family room and breakfast area. Any natural light at the sink must then be "borrowed" from the windows in the family and breakfast rooms. While this layout often is appealing, it puts the kitchen work area at risk of reduced natural light — a serious drawback for those who like a bright, light-filled kitchen. Here are three things to watch for:

- Determine the ceiling heights in the kitchen and adjacent areas (usually the family room and dining area). Higher ceilings in these areas will allow you to increase the overall height of the windows, thus introducing more natural light.
- Take a close look at any porches off the kitchen and adjacent areas. Depending on the orientation of the home and the porch depth, any natural light from windows opening onto a porch may be dramatically subdued. As a general rule, if the porch depth exceeds 10 feet, the light that filters in will be insufficient.
- Notice how far away the porch-facing windows are from the kitchen. Generally a distance of 10 to 15 feet will allow sufficient light. Windows located further than that from the kitchen will probably not offer much natural light. Obviously, the quantity, size, and orientation (direction they face) of the windows must also be considered.

Kitchen island seating. A center island can be used as an informal snack area. In homes with a single dining area, this snack bar essentially replaces the breakfast room. This kitchen layout features triple windows above the sink, allowing plenty of natural light and a view of the front yard.

HEALTHY EXAMPLES

Stylish and functional kitchens

Example 1

⊕ **An island for food prep.** An additional sink and food prep area is located in a separate island, with views toward the family room and dining areas. Expansive glass provides a view of the rear yard.

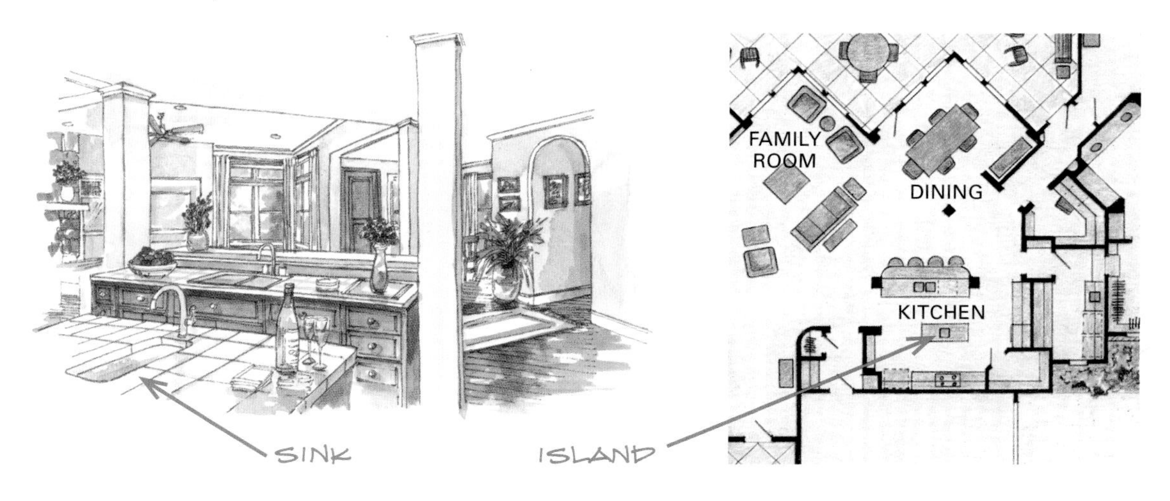

Example 2

⊕ **Bringing light into the kitchen.** Triple windows directly above the sink offer plenty of natural light and a view to the front yard. Note that the windows in the dining area allow a view of the rear porch.

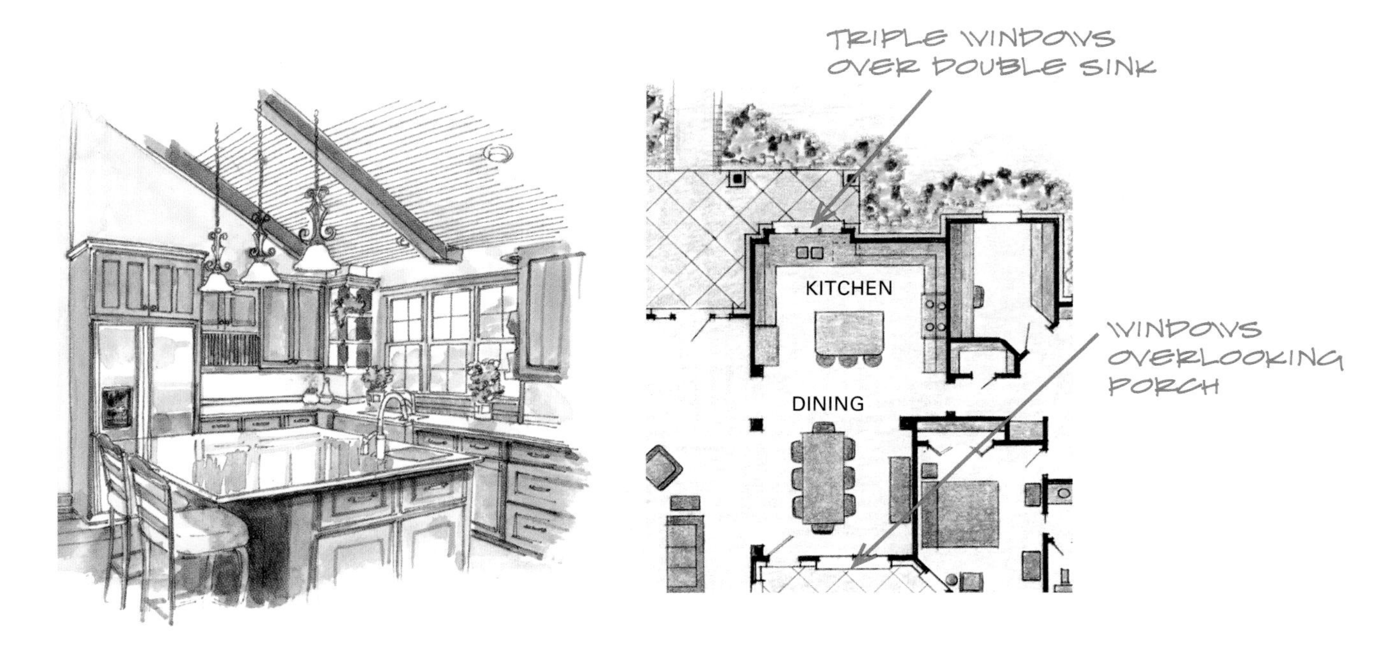

With home plans featuring one large dining area as opposed to a formal dining room and small breakfast room, some other opportunities for kitchen light become available. For instance, in a home with a formal dining room at the front of the house and a breakfast room overlooking the backyard, the kitchen is usually sandwiched in between with no opportunity for a window. If the formal dining room disappears, the kitchen suddenly gains a wall along the front of the house where a window can be added. Now we potentially have the best of both worlds: an open kitchen that overlooks the family and dining areas, with the traditional window above the sink.

Design Diagnosis

Save space and add light

⊕ *Left:* This kitchen is sandwiched between two dining areas, with no opportunity for windows. *Right:* When the formal dining room disappears, the kitchen gains a wall along the front of the house. Now the kitchen can overlook the family and dining areas, with the traditional window above the sink.

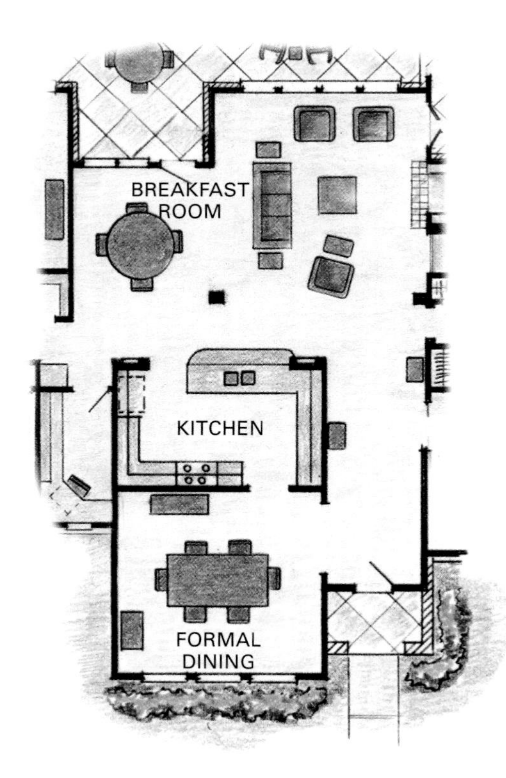

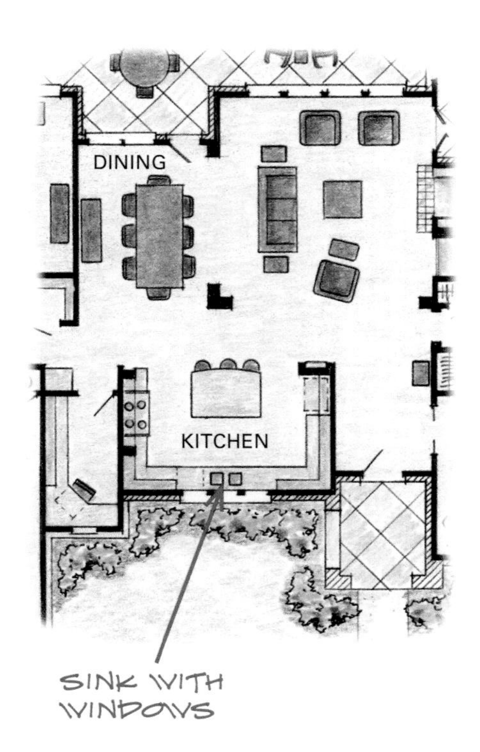

Traffic patterns, can be one of the most critical elements of a successful floor plan. *(See chapter 9.)* Avoid plans that force traffic through the kitchen. Instead, select a design that directs people around the area, thereby reducing congestion within the kitchen. Make sure that your plan provides convenient and logical passage from the kitchen to the garage or family entrance for ease of unloading groceries. Somewhere along this family entrance passage, plan for a drop zone designing practical storage for keys, cell phones, and the like makes them less likely to end up on the kitchen counter. *(See chapter 10.)*

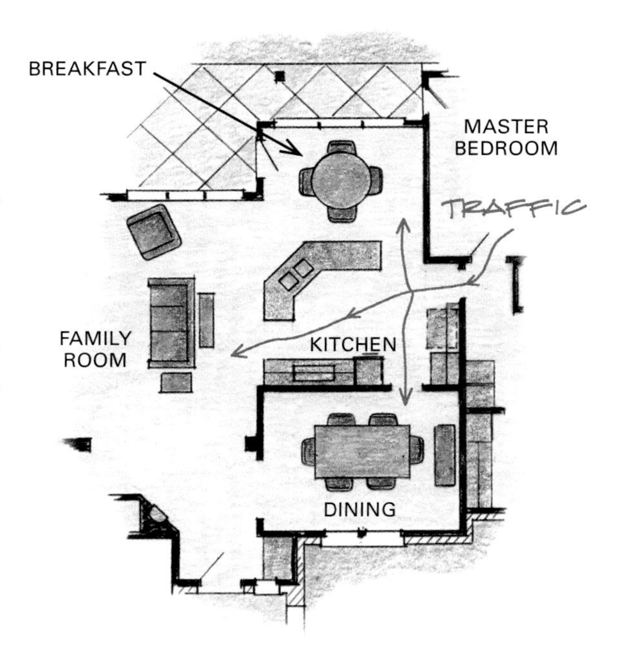

Don't do it this way! Avoid plans that, like this one, force traffic directly through the kitchen.

Pantry Solutions

Of course, any mention of storage space in regard to kitchen design immediately brings up the idea of a large pantry. In fact, a walk-in pantry consistently remains one of the top items requested in a new home. And there's no doubt that, if the square footage allows, a walk-in pantry will be appreciated.

However, keep in mind that a large closet may not be the most efficient place to store food and kitchen supplies. In fact, a large pantry with deep shelves can easily become a cluttered collection of canned goods impossible to organize. I recall the story of friends attempting to organize and clean their large pantry one day. Their 10-inch-deep shelves could store three rows of cans. Unfortunately, a few cans in that last row never made it to the front, resulting in the discovery of green beans about four years beyond their expiration date. I imagine this to be a rather common occurrence.

Some of the new full-height cabinet-style pantries prove to be efficient and easy storage spaces. Consisting of several layers of narrow shelving units, they provide an amazing amount of storage space in a very small area. Their adjustable shelves, deep enough to display only one row of cans, allow everything to be always visible. This eliminates those last-minute trips to the grocery store for an item that hides in the back row waiting to expire!

HEALTHY EXAMPLES

A well-organized kitchen

Example 1

⊕ **Plan for work and storage.** A walk-in pantry and center work island remain two of the most requested kitchen features. This kitchen also offers a handy message board and telephone center adjacent to the refrigerator. Notice also how the different heights of the upper cabinets add to the overall appearance.

Example 2

⊕ **Build a cabinet-style pantry.** This kitchen design, though on the smaller side, offers plenty of storage with an entire wall of cabinet-depth pantry and display shelves.

The walk-in pantry can be quite handy for larger items, such as canned drinks and bottled water. Keep in mind, though, that 6-inch-deep shelves will still offer better organization than deeper shelves for many supplies. Deeper shelves should be placed at the lower levels and used for larger items. If your kitchen has enough space, you might consider including both types of pantry storage. If you're building in a rural area, this might be one of the best decisions you make. With an abundance of storage space, you'll be able to buy groceries in bulk, eliminating those frequent long trips to town.

Other Strategies

Many homeowners want kitchens that open to the family room and dining areas. Such openness allows people to feel as though they are involved with the activities in the kitchen, even though they remain in the family room or dining area. Additionally, the person preparing meals does not feel isolated and can take part in the family room conversations and activities.

Although this kitchen/family room combination appeals to most households, some critical concerns should be addressed. To begin, the different areas should be defined from each other, to prevent them from merging into a single cavernous room. The design ideas described for defining the family room *(see page 142)* can be applied here.

The noise and clutter involved in food preparation and cleanup should be considered, as they can be distracting for those in adjacent areas. Consider the process of preparing the meal and cleaning up afterward. Does the operation of the dishwasher or garbage disposal conflict with the performance of other kitchen chores or family room activities?

Many dishwashers now on the market are "whisper" quiet and can barely be heard. While more costly, a quiet dishwasher usually ends up being a small price to pay for the convenience of opening up the central living areas of the home. Another option is to raise the snack bar 6 inches above the kitchen counter height. This will buffer some of the kitchen noise and provide a visual barrier to the dishes that might remain in the kitchen following a meal.

HEALTHY EXAMPLES

Combining rooms

Example 1

⊕ **Kitchen and dining areas.** In this living area, the openness and continuous flooring allow each space to borrow visually from the others, making them all seem larger than they are. The kitchen area is defined by 12"-square columns. The single dining area with two large windows facing a front porch offers plenty of room for family meals and formal entertaining.

Example 2

⊕ **Dining and family areas.** A single dining area and family room can borrow visual space from one another. Columns and dropped headers define each area, while consistent flooring adds to the continuity of design.

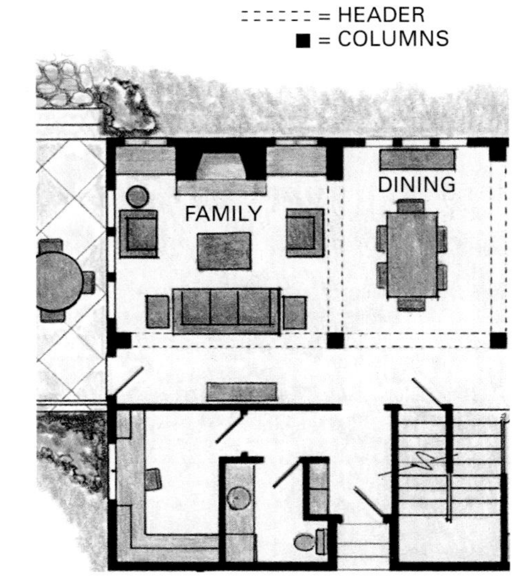

Dining Areas

First, a disclaimer: I don't consider formal dining areas to be very practical. Having admitted my biased opinion, it seems as though I'm not entirely alone. More and more homeowners are deciding to forgo the expense of building square footage they use only a few times each year. Even on those rare occasions when the room is used, there never seems to be enough space to accommodate the entire dinner party. Do you recall the Thanksgiving gatherings when the children were forced to eat at a card table in the foyer while the adults squeezed into the undersize formal dining room?

The average formal dining room consumes about 175 square feet of living space. That's valuable area that could be added to the family room or bedrooms — it's even enough area for an additional bedroom. Or, depending on the cost per square foot, the homeowner could save approximately $15,000 to $20,000 by doing away with this seldom-used area.

While escalating construction costs certainly offer an incentive to eliminate the area required for a formal dining room, many people simply prefer a more casual and functional kitchen and dining arrangement. A centrally located family dining area, open to both the kitchen and the family room, will likely be used more on a day-to-day basis than an enclosed formal room separated from all the activity. As with all spaces in open plans, however, the dining area will be most comfortable and aesthetically pleasing if it is defined in some manner from the adjacent spaces. *(See page 144 for tips on defining open spaces.)*

The creation of a single dining area involves more than just enlarging the traditional breakfast room. Special lighting can be installed to transform the space into a more formal setting for special dining occasions. Although many homeowners will give up their formal dining table, they draw the line when asked to scrap their grandmother's hutch or china cabinet! A designated wall with enough space for such furniture often becomes a critical feature.

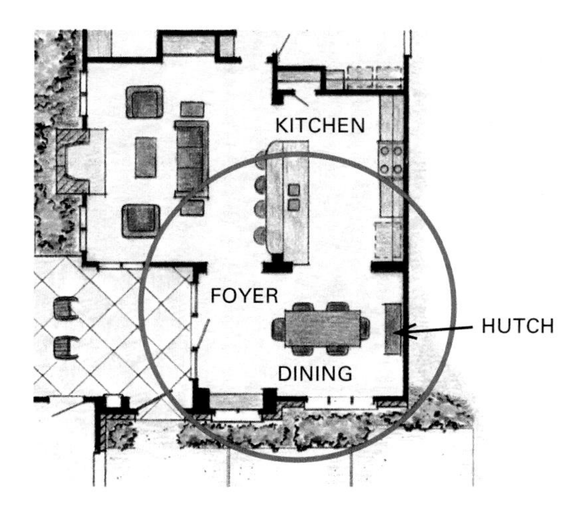

Formal dining. Locating a dining area next to the foyer allows the opportunity to furnish the room in a more formal and elegant manner. This might be the perfect compromise for those reluctant to completely eliminate the formal dining room.

Design Diagnosis

Planning for special dining room furniture

This single dining area is more than just an enlarged breakfast room. A designated wall large enough for a hutch or china cabinet is a key feature.

The location of the dining area can help define just how formal it will be. Placing it adjacent to the foyer provides the opportunity to furnish the room in a more elegant and formal manner. This might be an excellent compromise for those reluctant to completely do away with a formal dining room.

How Important Is Size?

How large should the family dining area be? Obviously its size will vary with the overall size and design of the home. The space should be large enough to accommodate a long table that seats six to ten. While the exact furniture selection depends on personal tastes, look for comfortable seating that will be inviting to use on a daily basis. Ideally the area will allow the flexibility of adding extensions for the table to expand toward the family room. Even if everyone cannot be seated at the table, an adjacent kitchen snack bar can provide additional seating within the same area. In this way all the guests feel as though they are part of the dinner party.

If situated properly the dining area functions as a multipurpose space, ideal for working on large projects or hobbies and with additional seating that can easily expand toward the family room for conversation or television viewing. Recently I designed a

Design Diagnosis

A special plan for book lovers

This preliminary sketch shows a dining room that was custom-designed for clients with an enormous book collection. Bookcases are built in below expansive windows. Thick columns and a change in ceiling height define the area while still maintaining an open relationship to the family room. Although an inviting and unique place for meals, the room is used daily for reading and writing.

new home for a retired couple who expressed a strong desire for an extremely efficient and flexible floor plan. They simply didn't want to build and maintain rooms that would seldom be used. Since both were avid readers, they had an enormous collection of books. In fact, I quickly realized that even though their study called for floor-to-ceiling bookcases, adequate book storage would still be lacking. Having already decided to eliminate the formal dining room, we began to discuss the possibility of creating a dining area that would do double duty as a library.

When we finished the design, we actually ended up with a *library* that doubled as a *dining area*. The space, still very open to the family room, had two exterior walls that featured expansive windows with built-in bookcases below. The kitchen snack bar accommodates informal meals on a daily basis, while the dining area is a unique location for dinner parties and family gatherings. However, it's used daily as the couple's library, with plenty of space for reading the newspaper and spending time reviewing an ever-expanding collection of books.

So, will we see the formal dining room disappear from new homes just as the formal living room has? Not likely. There will always be homeowners who place great emphasis on having formal areas for dining. Particularly in the higher-end custom market, where additional square footage ceases to be an issue, the formal dining room offers an opportunity to create an elaborately finished room, complete with multiple layers of crown molding, ornate ceiling detail, and magnificent chandeliers.

Typically those clients who are attracted to impressive foyers will also insist on a formal dining room. And there will always be the client who simply cannot part with his or her formal dining furniture for sentimental reasons.

Such diversity presents a challenge for both the homeowner and the designer as we consider eliminating a formal dining room. The real estate profession probably dictates what we design more than we care to admit. Homeowners become nervous when told that they must consider the resale implications of building a home that deviates from the typical floor plan. However, there certainly appears to be a large and expanding group of homeowners who no longer consider the formal dining room necessary. As with many decisions you'll be forced to make in the process of designing your home, place a great deal of trust in your own thoughts and feelings. We all tend to believe that our requirements must be unique, when, to the contrary, most often the feelings we have about "good design" are not so dissimilar from those of other people.

FREQUENTLY ASKED QUESTIONS

Q *My husband and I both enjoy cooking. Is there anything special we should consider in planning our new kitchen?*

Ⓐ For two (or more) people working in a kitchen, ample counter space and adequate room to maneuver are the primary concerns. Here are some ideas:

- A center island with a vegetable sink will definitely be an asset. While 36 inches is the minimum distance to maintain between counters and an island, try to expand this to at least 42 to 48 inches. This will allow for two people to move about without stepping on each other.
- A kitchen that opens to a dining area and family room seems to work for most families. If both husband and wife remain in the kitchen cooking, this open design will prevent guests from feeling ignored by their hosts.
- Some cooks find an additional water faucet located at the cooktop quite handy. This saves steps to the sink when filling pots with water.

Q *I've heard about a "work triangle" in the kitchen. What exactly is this, and why is it important?*

Ⓐ This imaginary triangle connecting the cooktop, sink, and refrigerator has been a formula used in kitchen design for years. Think of each of these three areas as a point on a triangle. Traditionally, the ideal total length of all three sides of this triangle is 21 feet or less. While there certainly is some merit to this design theory, many newer kitchens have become too large to precisely follow such a formula. With work islands that include an additional sink, multiple dishwashers, and the possibility of several people working in the kitchen at once, the triangle has grown in size.

Nevertheless, it's important that these three main areas be close to and easily accessible from each other so that the kitchen functions efficiently. When studying a plan, pay close attention to the location of these three areas. Try to imagine yourself in that kitchen as you prepare a meal. Is the refrigerator convenient to a countertop? Can you open the oven without backing into the sink area? Some logical thinking while reviewing a plan can help you choose a kitchen that functions properly for your family.

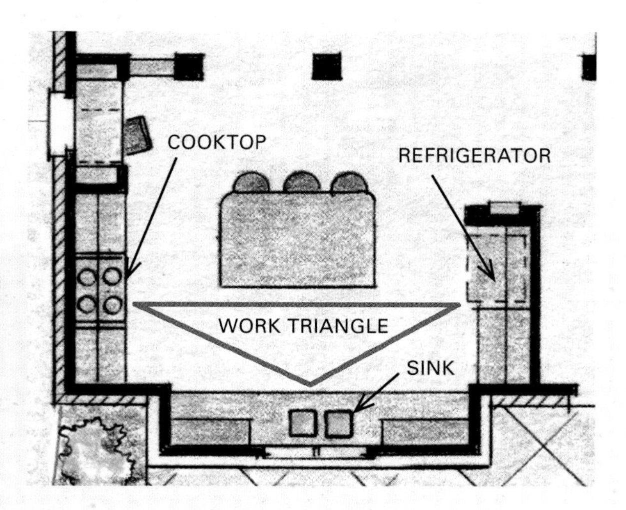

Plotting a work triangle. The kitchen work triangle is based on three areas: the cooktop, the sink, and the refrigerator. Traditionally, an efficient triangle is considered to be 21 feet in total distance.

12

Bed and Bath

Along with the emergence of open floor plans, the most dramatic change in home design over the past few years relates to the master bedroom. Not only have the overall dimensions of the room almost doubled, but we now find it featuring fireplaces, sitting areas, and adjacent exercise rooms. Add to this an enormous bathroom and the term *master suite* certainly seems an appropriate label.

Spacious or Overwhelming?

Before you become emotionally attached to such an expansive room, carefully consider how functional the overall layout will be for your lifestyle. By analyzing your requirements and desires, you can create a master retreat that you'll find *spacious* without being *overwhelming.*

First, ask yourself whether you or your spouse will actually use a sitting area. For some, such an alcove serves as a cozy retreat for reading a book or for relaxing away from the other activities of the home.

As the formal living room has disappeared, many homeowners find a private sitting area becomes their only refuge. Add a fireplace, and the master sitting area might end up being one of your favorite parts of the home.

On the other hand, some people discover that they simply never use this area and wish they had placed the square footage elsewhere. For them it ends up being not only a waste of valuable square footage but often a too-convenient place to drop clothes, the laundry basket, and other clutter.

Instead of a sitting area, you might consider placing a window seat on a wall with indirect sunlight. This cozy alcove can provide a great place to read a book and might be all the sitting area you need! Also, the *illusion* of space created by the extended windows makes the master bedroom seem more spacious.

Another critical element is the actual dimensions of the master bedroom. I always tell clients, "A room needs to be *only* as big as it needs to be!" Then I explain what I mean.

The master bedroom (or any room, for that matter) should be large enough to accommodate the required furniture and provide comfortable circulation throughout the space. The key word here is *comfortable.* A room with too many pieces of furniture or furniture that is massive in scale will feel crowded and restricted. On the other hand, if the room is too large, the sense of coziness and comfort disappears.

So, what's the magic formula for setting appropriate dimensions for a master bedroom? The answer relates to the furniture you plan to place in the room. By measuring your existing furniture (or finding the exact dimensions of the furniture you intend to purchase), you can experiment with different arrangements and determine how large your bedroom should be. *(See pages 110–113 for mapping room sizes and furniture placement.)*

A charming window seat. A window seat not only offers a cozy place to relax and perhaps read a book but also makes the room appear more spacious.

As you map the master bedroom, be sure to leave adequate space between the various pieces of furniture. For example, the distance between the foot of the bed and the wall or dresser opposite it should be a minimum of 36 inches, and ideally about 48 inches. You've most likely been in a bedroom where you can barely walk between the bed and the dresser or wall; the room feels cramped. However, you've probably also seen bedrooms with 8 to 10 feet between the bed and the dresser or wall; such a large expanse results in a room that goes beyond feeling spacious and seems, instead, uninviting.

If you decide to include a sitting area, its overall dimensions play a critical role. An area just large enough to accommodate two comfortable chairs and a small table can offer a sense of privacy. Increase the area by as little as 2 to 3 feet and you might lose that feeling of coziness.

As you map the furniture placement in the master bedroom of any floor plan you're considering, make sure there is a wall where your bed can be placed. Believe it or not, too often we find designs for master bedrooms with so many extra features such as fireplaces, expansive windows, and sitting alcoves that there's simply no wall space remaining for a bed!

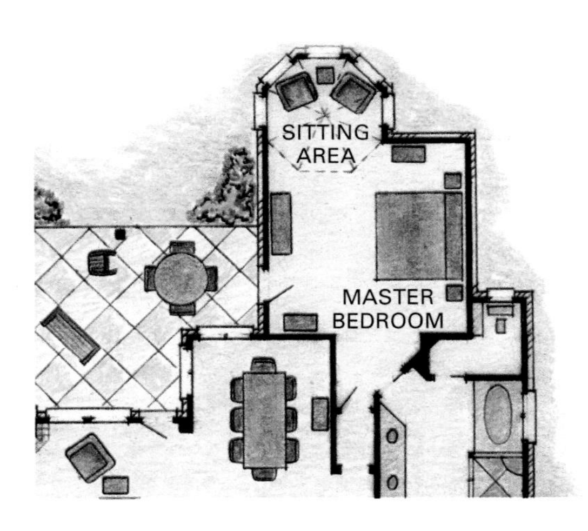

Create a cozy corner. A sitting area in the master bedroom can be a welcome refuge. An area just large enough for a couple of comfortable chairs and a small table offers a sense of seclusion and coziness.

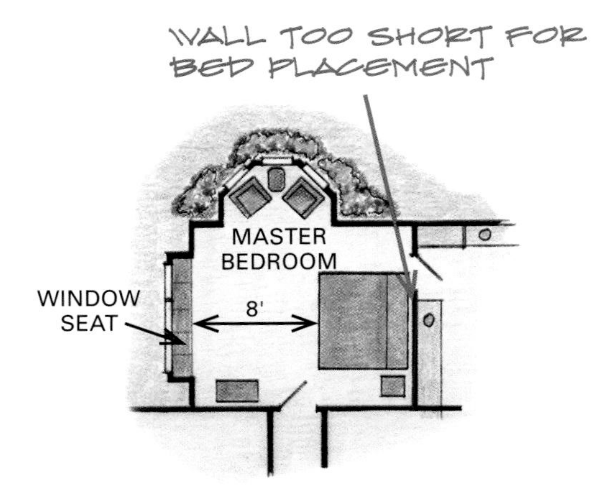

Pay attention to wall space. This design seems fine until you discover that your king-size bed will obstruct the bathroom door. Also, note the excessive distance between the bed and the window seat. Time spent critically analyzing a plan can help avoid such problems.

Windows and Privacy

Window size and placement play an equally important role in the ultimate success of a master bedroom design. Bringing natural light into any room obviously has a big impact. However, as with any sleeping area, you must give careful thought to the effect this light will have on your ability to sleep in the master bedroom.

Realistically, the orientation of your home in relation to the sun may be dictated by the constraints of your property location, especially if you're building in a subdivision.

While room-darkening shades can offer a satisfactory solution to intrusive sunlight, intrusive neighbors can be an entirely different situation. Bedroom windows facing your rear yard will usually offer an adequate degree of privacy. Those facing the side yard may very likely become an issue. First, consider reducing the size of these side-facing windows, possibly using transoms (smaller windows approximately 2 feet tall and placed at a height of about 8 feet) that will allow light to enter without compromising your privacy. Next, try to place your bed so that the windows are to its sides and not on the opposing wall. This will prevent the neighbors having a view directly toward your bed.

Plan strategic hallways. Even a very short hall can create a sense of privacy for a bedroom. Note the large built-in clothes storage just inside the bathroom. With sufficient drawers and cabinets for clothes in the master bath, there's no need for dressers and chests in the bedroom.

The issue of privacy extends to your own household. Earlier in the book I mentioned a master bedroom that could be viewed from the foyer. Fortunately, that's a rare occurrence. However, I continue to see floor plans that place the master bedroom entrance directly off the family room. This practice began several years ago when the design community suddenly began to think of hallways as wasted space. Eliminating the hall passage to the master bedroom saves from 25 to 30 square feet, but at what price? In most cases the price is the complete loss of privacy! Homes designed in this manner offer anyone sitting in the family room an unobstructed view to the one room that really should enjoy the most secluded spot in the entire home.

First or Second Floor?

The discussion of just where the master bedroom should be placed is an ongoing one. If you're building a two-story home, should the master bedroom be on the first or second floor? What about its location in relation to the other bedrooms? Certainly privacy is a concern; the master bedroom should be insulated both visually and in terms of noise from other bedrooms. *(See page 125.)*

From an energy standpoint, keeping all the bedrooms together allows the use of a *zoned* heating and cooling system, in which the temperature of the bedrooms' zone is controlled separately from that of the rest of the house. Such a setup tends to be more efficient. During the day the sleeping zone can be set for reduced heating or cooling, since the family will spend most of its time in the living zone. At night you have the opportunity to save energy by limiting the heating and cooling required for the unused living zone.

The question of whether a master bedroom is best situated on the first or second floor requires some consideration. If your building site offers spectacular views, you may want the master bedroom on the second floor to take advantage of them. On the other hand, if you're thinking of growing old in this home, you may prefer a first-floor master bedroom, which is more easily accessible. Will you be able (or willing!) to climb the stairs to a second-floor bedroom? Perhaps that climb will end up being part of your daily exercise!

Secondary Bedrooms

The total number of bedrooms you require obviously depends on your family circumstances and lifestyle. As you consider just how large or small a bedroom should be, remember: the room needs to be *only* as big as it needs to be.

The dramatic increase in square footage devoted to the master bedroom and bath is sometime achieved by decreasing the square footage in the secondary bedrooms (although the average home size has also increased). Typical secondary bedrooms have dimensions of approximately 11 to 12 feet in width and 12 to 13 feet in length. It's not unusual to find them as small as 10 feet by 10 feet.

Let's investigate just how you plan to furnish a secondary bedroom. First, every bedroom requires a bed. But will it be a twin bed for a child or a queen bed for guests? Does the room need to have space for a desk or a comfortable reading chair? Once you begin to answer these questions, spend some time mapping furniture locations with cutouts *(see pages 110–113)*. There really is no better way to make sure you have adequate room sizes. Remember, more than 36 inches between pieces of furniture will be an added luxury, while less than that may cause the room to feel cramped and uncomfortable.

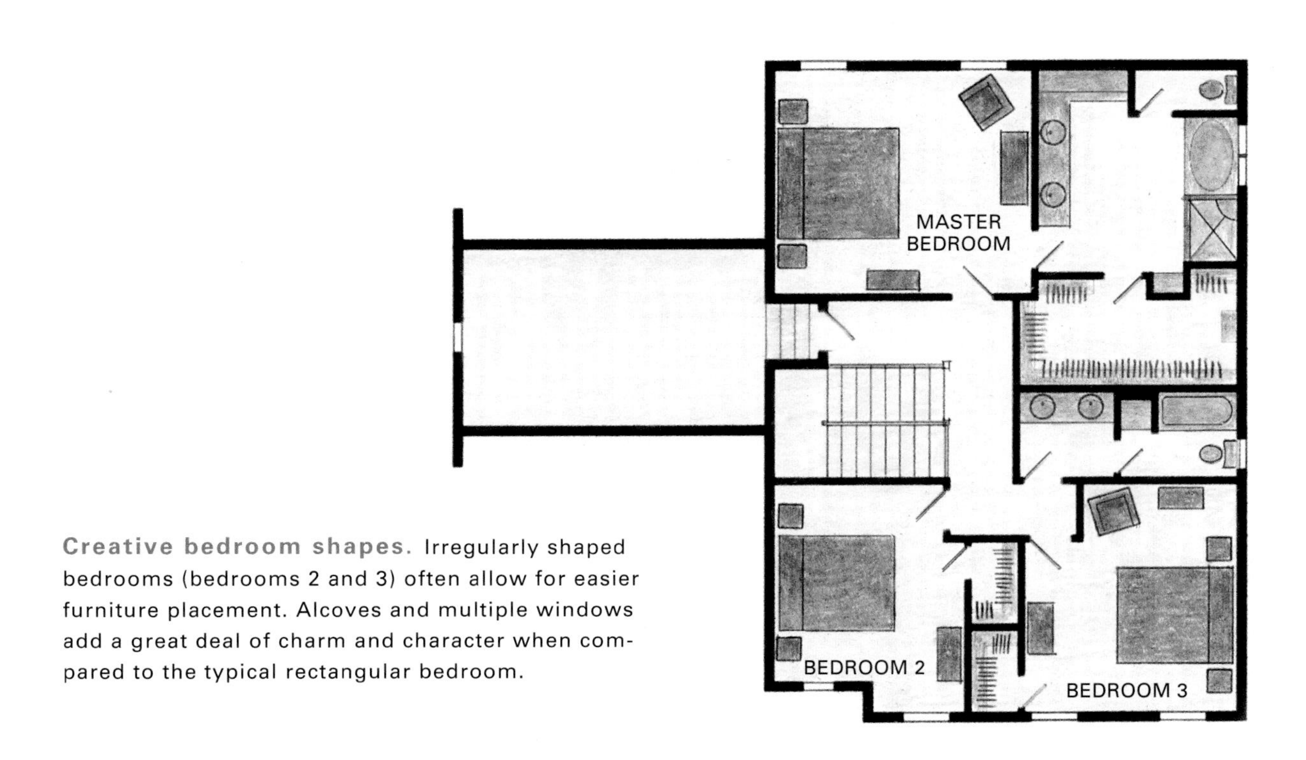

Creative bedroom shapes. Irregularly shaped bedrooms (bedrooms 2 and 3) often allow for easier furniture placement. Alcoves and multiple windows add a great deal of charm and character when compared to the typical rectangular bedroom.

Planning for Computers

Over the past few years, as computers have become more of a necessity than a luxury, some people began planning a specific area in their children's room for this equipment. However, with the unknowns related to the Internet, many parents have now decided that computers should be located in a more public area of the home, such as a resource center *(see page 188)*, where they can monitor their children's Internet activity. This fact, combined with the growing use of notebook computers, probably eliminates the need for additional bedroom area to accommodate a computer center.

As a side benefit, when you include a resource center and/or game areas in your home, your children's bedrooms may not need to be as large as you once thought. In the past, houses featuring large secondary bedrooms most likely didn't include other spaces to play and study. Another way to potentially reduce the size of bedrooms involves the use of built-in furniture and storage. Built-in bookcases, cabinets, and desks will utilize the space more efficiently than freestanding structures. In most cases these features can be built for less money than you would have to spend to buy similar furniture.

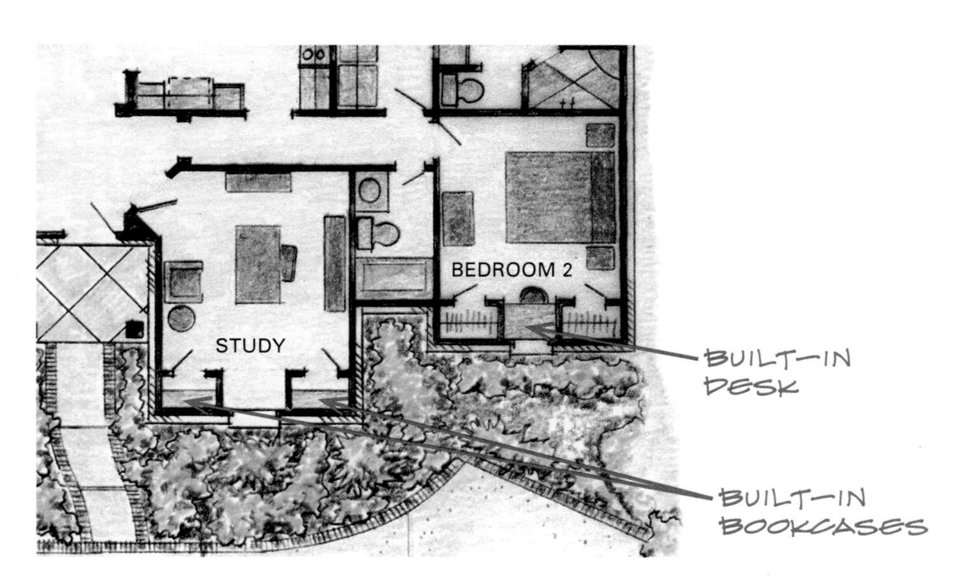

Built-in furniture. Planning for built-in furniture, along with logical window and door placement, allows even relatively small bedrooms to function quite well.

CLOSET STRATEGIES

Depending on who will use it, closet space can be either minimal or rather large. The typical single hanging rod encourages clutter in most closets. Most hanging clothes don't require the full length provided by a single rod. Adding a second rod at a lower height doubles the linear footage of any closet; the lower rod also allows young children (and those in wheelchairs) easier access to their clothing. Add some shelving and you have quickly increased the closet's efficiency and storage capacity.

Many options exist for efficient closet organization. In fact, several companies offer specialized closet organization systems. In addition, you can find an abundance of ideas for closet design in decorating magazines.

Master Bath

The master bath has been the focus of attention for a number of years. In fact, it's not unusual to allot more square footage to the bath than to the bedroom itself. Those involved with the custom home business for the past fifteen years undoubtedly have seen and built extravagant master bathrooms that included see-through fireplaces, marble walls, and whirlpool tubs large enough to accommodate the entire family!

There's no question that these elaborately designed and decorated baths draw a great deal of attention — they're another example of *wow!* rooms. But just how functional are they? Do they satisfy the homeowner's requirements day in and day out? Although it is difficult to answer these questions precisely, we do know this: an increasing number of individuals who have lived in a home with one of these ultra-extravagant baths specifically request a more functional design for their next master bath.

While you may not want a bath that's "over the top," the master bath should still have visual and emotional impact. How can you determine whether a master bath design will be functional on a daily basis while still possessing a certain amount of elegance and excitement? First, carefully consider the location of the bath and its window selection and placement. Next, analyze each of the major components — shower, tub, vanity, water closet, and storage — for proper placement, size, and aesthetics.

Maintaining Privacy

The location of the bath can be influenced by several factors. For instance, a location offering spectacular views may call for the bath to have expansive glass walls located to take advantage of the view. However, the placement of the bath should not compromise the opportunity for the master bedroom itself to take advantage of these views.

On the other hand, a large number of windows may compromise the overall feeling of privacy and seclusion in your bath, particularly in a higher-density development. If neighboring homes present a privacy challenge, the master bath may need to direct views toward the rear yard. Another option is to use glass block to provide natural light in the bath without compromising privacy.

While a floor plan featuring expansive glass in the master bath overlooking a courtyard may be tempting, such a concept can greatly compromise the overall privacy of the bath on a day-to-day basis. Although a courtyard will offer privacy to your home from neighboring houses, it's unlikely to provide the seclusion you probably want in your bathroom. Master baths are unique in regard to window design and placement; often the feeling of seclusion has more to do with *perceived* privacy than *actual* privacy.

If a large window above the tub faces toward a large window of a room across the courtyard, or even toward the activity of the courtyard, your sense of security and comfort might be completely disrupted.

Of course a similar situation may arise with bathroom windows on the side of your home that face your neighbor. However, a 6-foot-tall privacy fence can usually solve this situation. Bathrooms located on the second floor present an additional challenge. If it's unknown when you're building exactly what a bathroom window may be facing, glass block or some other obscured glass (possibly art glass) might be a wise choice in place of typical windows.

These are examples of the value of visualizing a plan before it's built. Time spent imagining each and every view from within a room can help avoid some unpleasant surprises, such as relaxing in your new tub for the first time only to see your new neighbor enjoying his coffee — and the view from his breakfast room bay window!

A Floor Plan for Different Schedules

Another important master bath consideration involves your family's lifestyle. Many couples express concerns about their different work schedules. One may be required to leave for work quite early each morning, potentially disturbing the other as he or she moves in and out of the bath area. Locating the bath entrance next to the bedroom entrance allows access to and from the bath area without disturbing someone in the master bedroom.

HEALTHY EXAMPLES

Plan for privacy

Example 1

The glass block solution. To provide plenty of natural light in the bath without compromising privacy, consider using glass block instead of windows at the tub and shower.

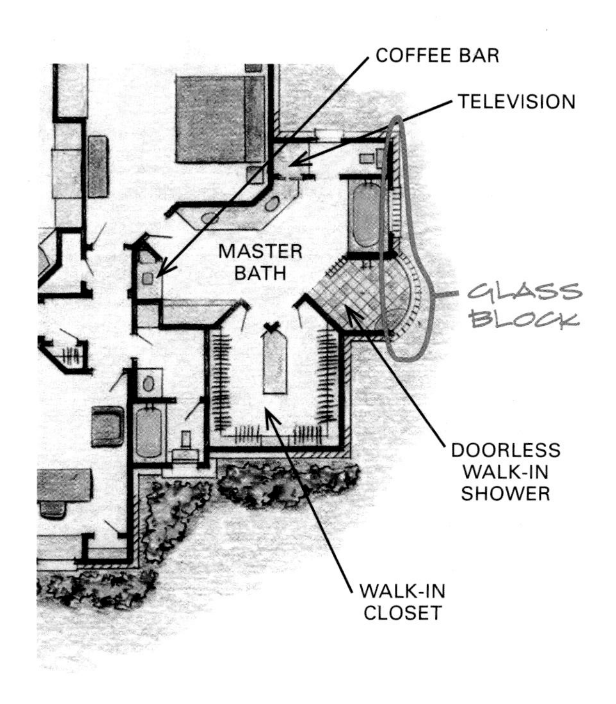

Example 2

Place windows with care. While it might be tempting to place large windows overlooking a pool and courtyard in the master bathroom, this can create a serious privacy issue. Instead, direct a view of the courtyard from the master bedroom by including a window seat.

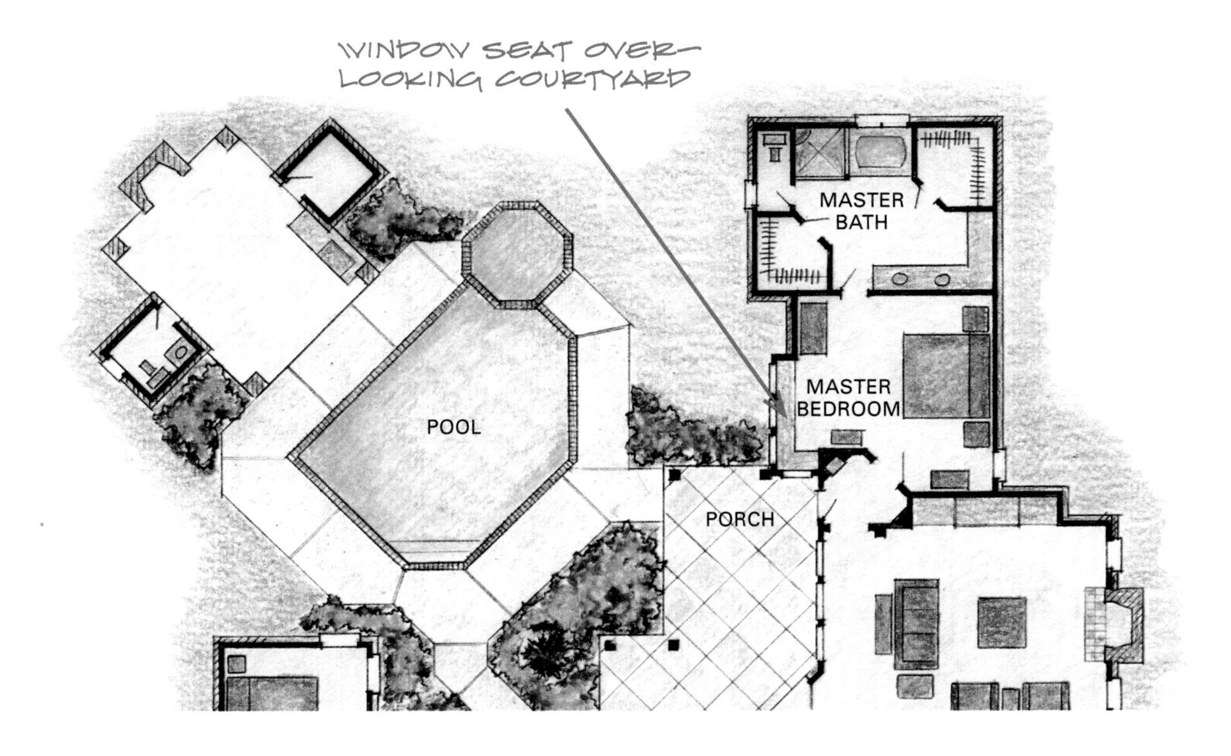

HEALTHY EXAMPLES
Accommodate his-and-her schedules

Example 1

⊕ **Separate entrance to bed and bath.** Locating the master bath and bedroom entrances next to each other allows access to and from the bathroom without disturbing someone in the bedroom. *His*-and-*her* vanities, dressers, and closets provide an extremely functional dressing area.

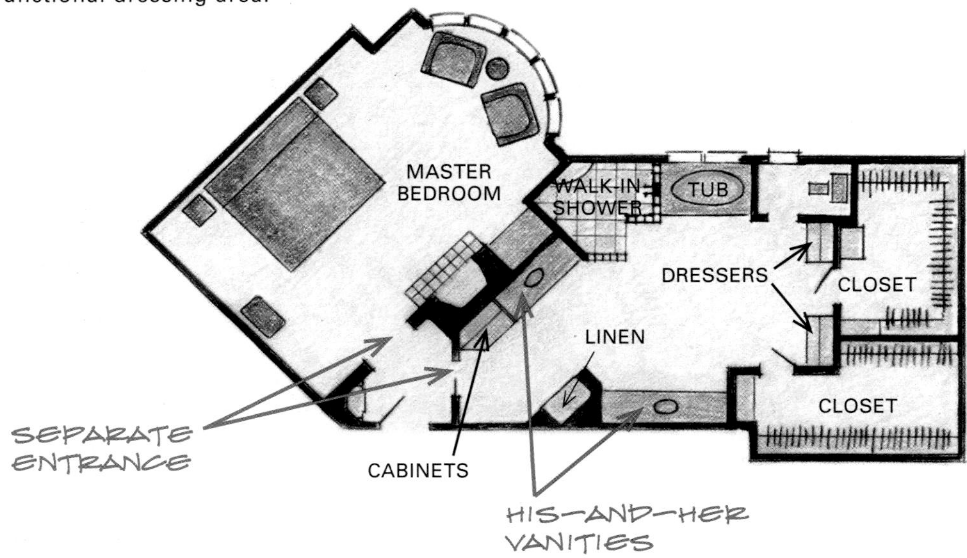

Example 2

⊕ **Separate closet and dressing area.** This secluded master suite allows separate access to the bath, a practical arrangement for spouses on drastically different schedules. Note the *his*-and-*her* vanities and the built-in drawers and linen storage. The dressing area also can be entered without disturbing someone in the bedroom.

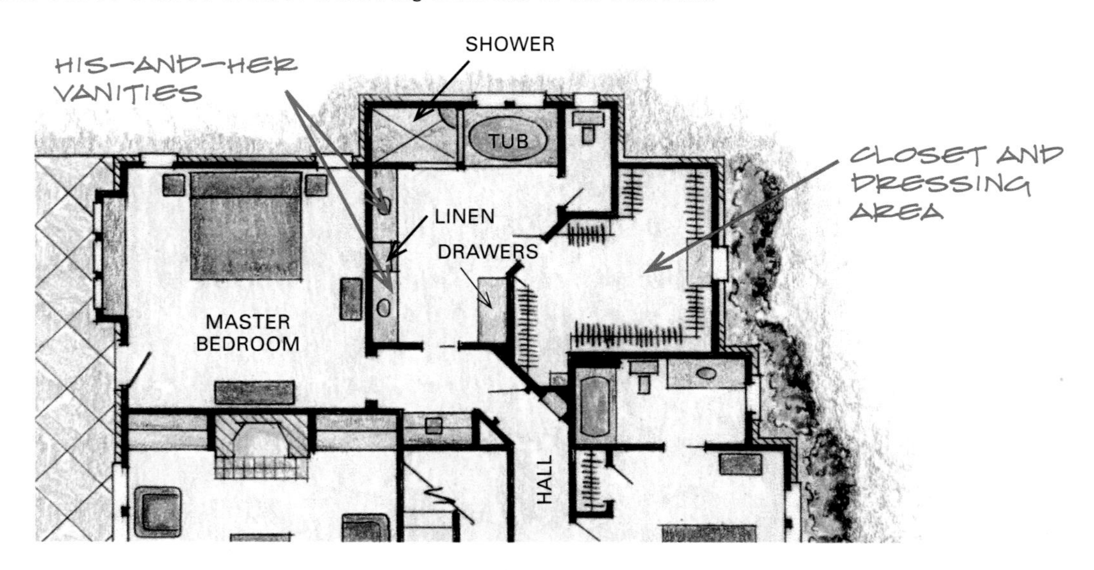

Bathtubs and Showers

For the past few years tubs have been the focal point of bath design. They have grown to be as large as small swimming pools, with jets, swirling action, and more, and have been adorned with everything from Roman columns to extravagant marble finishes. In general, today's homeowners seem to prefer a more reasonably sized tub, but many still enjoy the whirlpool option. Rather than allocating the area and expense for a large tub, they appreciate the functionality of a spacious shower.

In fact, one of the most requested items today is a large, doorless shower. The addition of multiple shower heads and a built-in seat offers a luxurious yet functional bathing environment. The considerable cost of such an expansive shower might be offset by reducing the size of the tub. In fact, many bathtub manufacturers now offer extremely appealing smaller tubs you may want to consider. Take a close look at any tub design in regard to the ease of climbing in and out. Tubs sunk below floor level or requiring steps may prove quite difficult to access in years to come.

A master bath is truly functional when it can be utilized as a dressing area, with ample storage space for clothing, including dressers with multiple drawers. This eliminates the need for clothes storage in the bedroom itself. Essentially a homeowner can enter the bath and not return to the bedroom until completely dressed. Even a relatively small master bath can be designed with ample clothing and linen storage.

A full-service bathroom. Adequate built-in drawers and cabinets in your master bath will eliminate the need for clothing storage in your bedroom. In other words, you should be able to enter the bath each morning and not return to the bedroom until completely dressed.

Evolving Ideas

Tradition plays a large role in all aspects of home design. So much of what we design and build could be described by the simple statement, "That's the way it's always been done." The height of bathroom countertops is a prime example. A height of 32 inches is generally the unquestioned standard. Of course, this height was based on the average human height in the mid-1900s. While this dimension still works for many people, for others a height closer to 36 inches (the height of a kitchen counter) is more convenient. In fact, it's not at all unusual to have both heights in the same bath, in custom *his*-and-*her* areas.

Another remnant of traditional design is door sizes. Typically bathroom and closet doors are only 24 inches wide. Although smaller secondary baths may not have room to accommodate a wider door, the master bath usually has enough existing space for the door width to be enlarged. While 32- to 36-inch doors are ideal, since they offer easier accessibility, even a 30-inch door will be appreciated.

An enclosed area for the commode may also present a challenge for increasing door size. Such enclosures are commonly designed with dimensions of 32 to 36 inches in width and 60 inches in depth, with a 24-inch door. If space allows, consider increasing

A design for today's needs. In this bathroom, the counter height is raised from the traditional 32 inches to 36 inches. Glass block offers natural light to the tub and shower area without compromising privacy. Note the large doorless shower and the attractive antique tub.

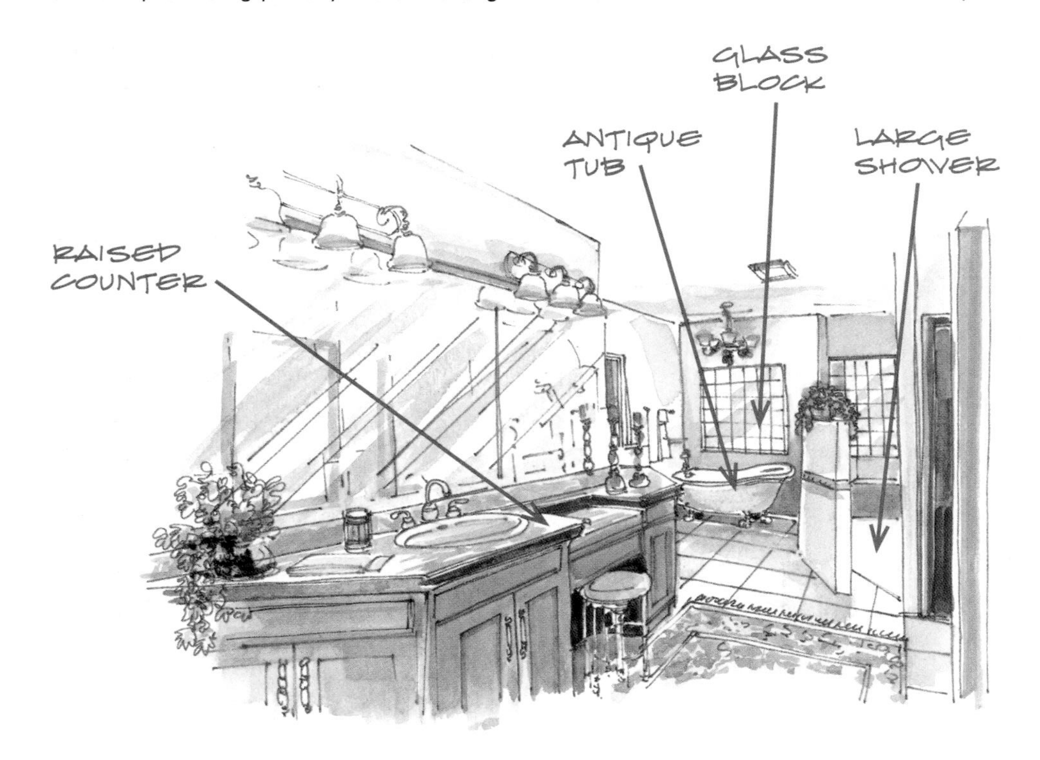

these dimensions to allow for at least a 32-inch door. If the additional area simply can't be found, you might want to just eliminate the door and frame a 36-inch-wide opening. A 48-inch-high wall can also offer a sense of separation without enclosing the area completely. In any event, placing the commode along an outside wall will allow for a window. If your bath design doesn't show such a window, a slight revision might provide the opportunity for it.

While functional layouts and a practical dressing area form the basic elements of exceptional bath design, even the most thoughtful creation will be incomplete without careful attention to the materials, products, and colors used. Quite often the services of a qualified interior design professional will determine the ultimate success of a master bath.

An operating window obviously offers a source of ventilation. Additionally, be sure you have an electric exhaust fan. These fans sometimes include a small heater that you'll appreciate on those chilly mornings. You might also want to consider adding a ceiling fan for those muggy summer days when the steam from your shower makes it difficult to cool the bathroom.

In recent years the trend has been to design *his*-and-*her* walk-in closets accessible from inside the master bath. This coordinates with the concept of having all of the clothes stored and available in the bath area instead of the bedroom. Walk-in closets certainly are a luxury. However, as with the other rooms we've discussed, some critical dimensions should be considered. Any walk-in closet needs to be at least 68 to 72 inches wide in order to allow hanging space on each side and room to walk through the middle. While extra width can be a luxury, additional hanging space is achieved only by increasing the length. For example, a closet that is 68 inches wide and 72 inches in length will have the same hanging space as one that is 80 inches wide by 72 inches in length. In other words, simply increasing the width of your closet will usually result in no additional hanging space.

A few years ago I designed a home that placed the master walk-in closet towards the front of the home. In order to complete the exterior design, we decided to place a small window in the master closet. To everyone's surprise, the window became a delightful addition to the large closet by allowing plenty of natural light and an increased sense of spaciousness. With a bench and storage beneath the window, the closet became a wonderful dressing area. Once again, I realized that just because we *traditionally* avoided windows in closets certainly doesn't mean we must never place them there!

DESIGN DIAGNOSIS

Plenty of bathrooms

Ideally each bedroom will connect to a private bath. A powder room for your guests can be conveniently located just off the foyer. A separate half bath can become part of an outdoor pavilion adjacent to the swimming pool.

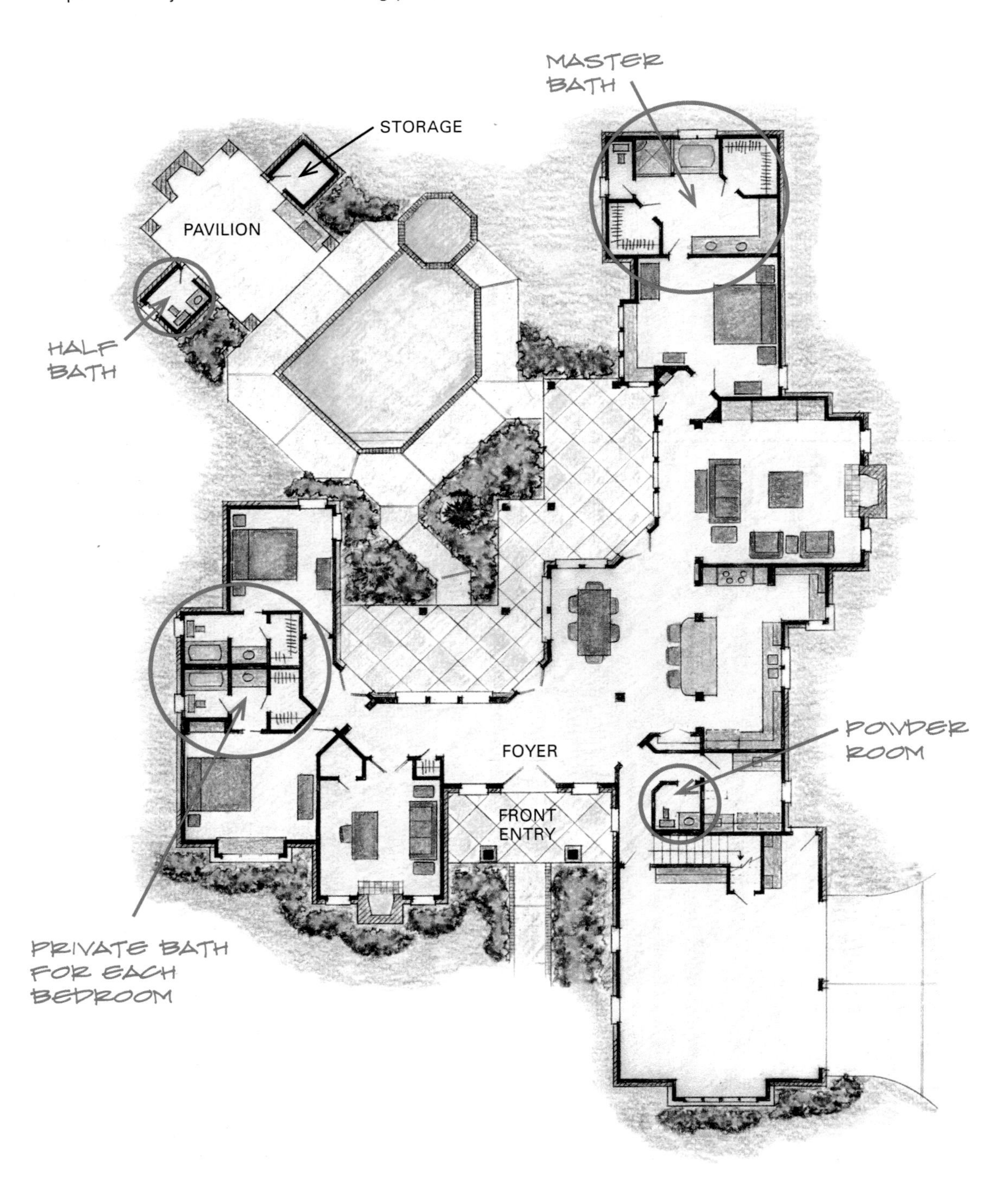

Secondary Baths

Since we've already discussed the master bath, you may be tempted to skip this section. If so, you wouldn't be the only one to ignore secondary bathrooms. Browse through most home magazines and you'll find the bathroom features often focus only on the master area. However, regardless of the size of home you're considering, these "other" bathrooms are much more important than you might initially believe.

Consider two facts: First, based on costs per square foot, bathrooms are the most expensive area in the home. Second, dissatisfaction with current bathrooms typically is one of the main reasons people want to build a new home.

Let's start with the *half bath* and *powder room.* While often considered the same, there's actually a difference between them. Technically, both have only a lavatory and toilet, with no tub or shower. Powder rooms (so called after the ladies' practice of powdering the nose) were once found only in larger, more expensive homes; they provided convenient facilities for guests and allowed the homeowner's bathroom to remain private. With that in mind, I usually consider a half bath located especially for guests to be a powder room. Typically it is an elaborate area with expensive fixtures, wallpaper, and an ornate mirror. A half bath, in contrast, is a more casual and functional facility that might be located near a back door or garage and intended for use by family and friends. Of course, these are just labels, and you'll find different opinions regarding their use.

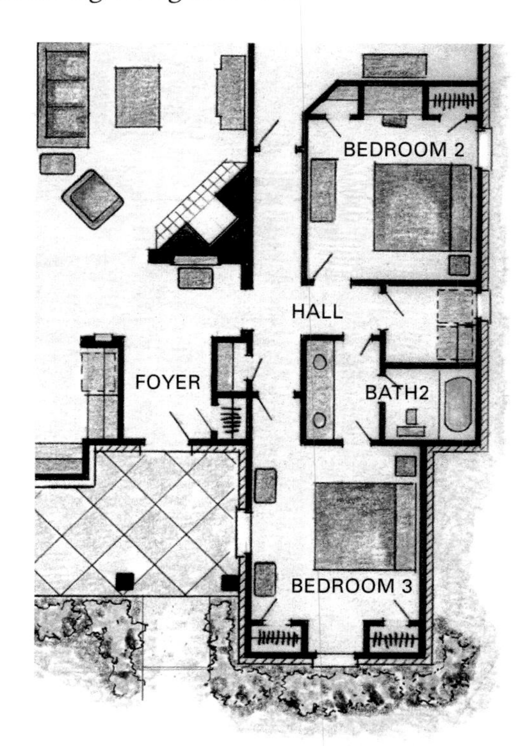

Sharing a bath. A door separating the lavatory from the tub and toilet allows at least two people to share a bath with a certain amount of privacy. Because it has a door that opens to the hall, it can also serve as a guest bathroom.

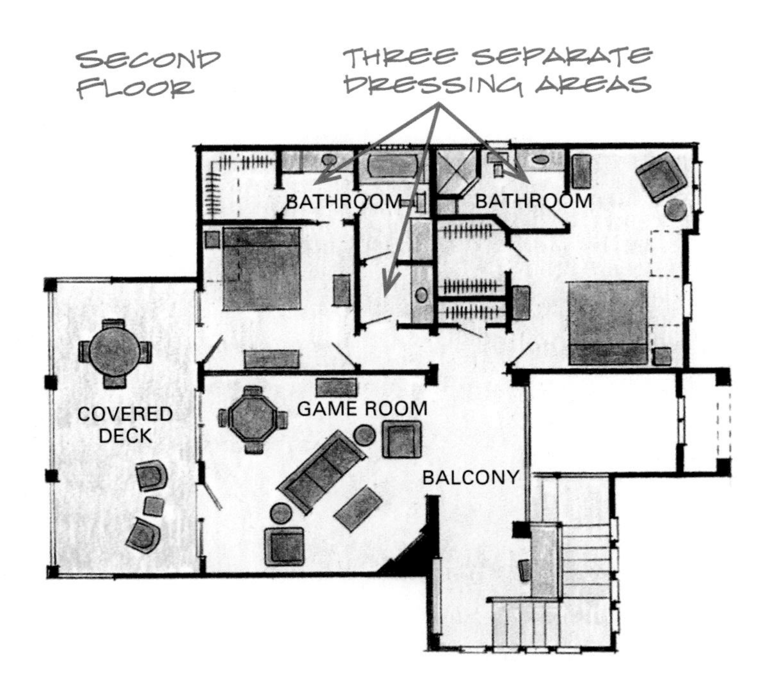

Build in privacy. Separate dressing areas, each with their own sink, provide much more privacy for everyone. If a bathroom is intended to be used by the house inhabitants at large, rather than being a bedroom's private bathroom, make sure it can be accessed from a public area, such as a hall, so that users are not forced to go through a bedroom.

If you want to have a swimming pool or to entertain in your backyard, give careful thought to the location of a half bath. You certainly won't want dripping-wet children or guests with muddy shoes having to travel through your family room to the powder room in the foyer! If the budget allows, you might consider locating a half bath near the rear entry *and* a powder room toward the foyer. Or you might want to locate a complete bathroom adjacent to your swimming pool.

Whatever you decide, secondary bathrooms for children or guests deserve some careful thought. Ideally each bedroom will have a private bath. However, most budgets simply don't allow such a luxury. A bathroom with a door between the dressing area (sinks) and the tub/toilet room is the next-best solution. This arrangement allows at least two people to use the bath simultaneously. At least in theory it does!

In reality the number of people using the bath depends on exactly whom we're talking about. Your teenage daughter and son will probably *not* use such a facility at the same time. However, two or three boys will usually have no such hesitancy.

Your guests might not be comfortable with a shared bath arrangement. Of course, you may not want them to be *too* comfortable! A more flexible, and slightly more expensive, arrangement involves completely separate dressing areas that share a common tub and toilet. This design provides a great deal more perceived privacy.

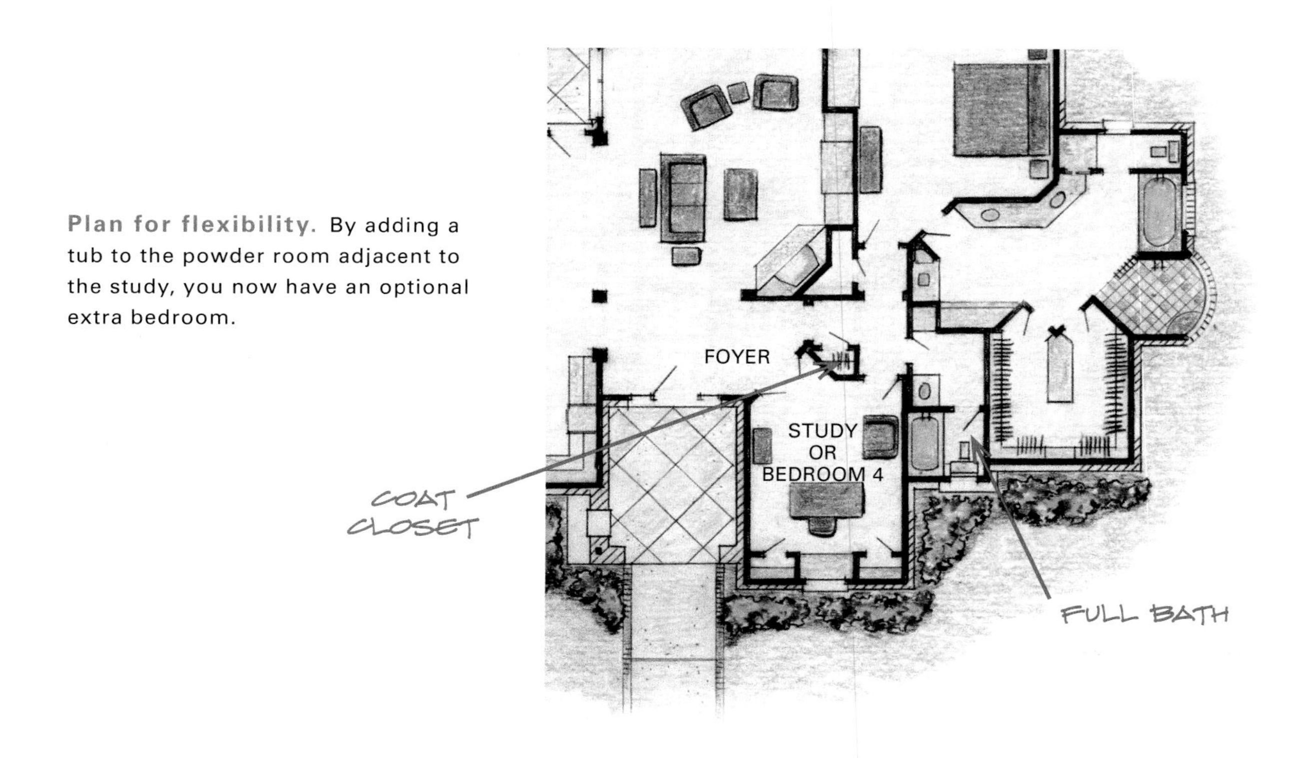

Plan for flexibility. By adding a tub to the powder room adjacent to the study, you now have an optional extra bedroom.

Once again, costs and budget will ultimately determine the exact number and design of your secondary bathrooms. Keep several ideas in mind:

- Two sinks are not much more expensive than one; the only extra cost is essentially just that of the extra sink fixture.
- Some people think that by installing a shower instead of a tub they'll save money. Actually, it's just the opposite. Even the least expensive one-piece shower with a glass door will be more costly than a tub with a shower curtain.
- Placing two secondary baths side by side will offer some savings of plumbing labor and materials. Obviously, the fixtures cost the same regardless of their location.
- If you have a powder room located adjacent to a study, you might consider adding a shower or tub. The costs will be minimal and the study then has the flexibility of being used as an extra bedroom with its own convenient bathroom.

Before you make any final decisions on your secondary baths, consider your objectives. Who exactly will be using these facilities? Consider both the near-term and long-range use. For example, if your children are almost grown, they may soon be returning to visit with their own families. Although there are no definite right or wrong answers here, remember that inadequate bathrooms are one of the top reasons many people either remodel or build a new home. It might be wiser to plan ahead now, even if it means you must conserve elsewhere.

13

Hardworking Rooms

As a youngster, I recall my mother's excitement when we moved into a house that had the clothes washer in an attached garage. It was several years later when she reluctantly accepted my father's offer to purchase a dryer. For years she continued to hang the wash on the clothesline in our backyard. Although this observation obviously proves my age, it also points out how far we've come with the design of laundry rooms.

Utility Rooms

Often the term *utility room* is used interchangeably with *laundry room*. But a laundry room technically contains only what's needed for cleaning clothes. Most new home designs include a multiuse area called a utility room that includes not only a washer and dryer but space enough to serve as a storage room, mudroom, pantry, sewing nook, computer alcove, and more. In the past the basement was traditionally the location for utility space. In areas without basements, the garage normally housed the washer and dryer. Neither of these locations is especially convenient.

Before you select the best location for your utility room, consider the various appliances you plan to place in it and all the tasks you hope to perform there. Typically the utility room is located adjacent to the kitchen, under the assumption that laundry will be processed simultaneously with kitchen activities. However, the realization that most soiled laundry generates from the bedrooms and baths has caused many people to rethink the location. Perhaps someplace closer to the source of the dirty clothes makes more sense.

You may want to consider a second-floor laundry room if all your bedrooms are located there. Some designs now feature a compact second-floor laundry in addition to one on the first floor. A laundry chute on the second level can at least expedite the transfer of dirty clothes directly to the laundry room below.

HEALTHY EXAMPLES

Convenient laundry areas

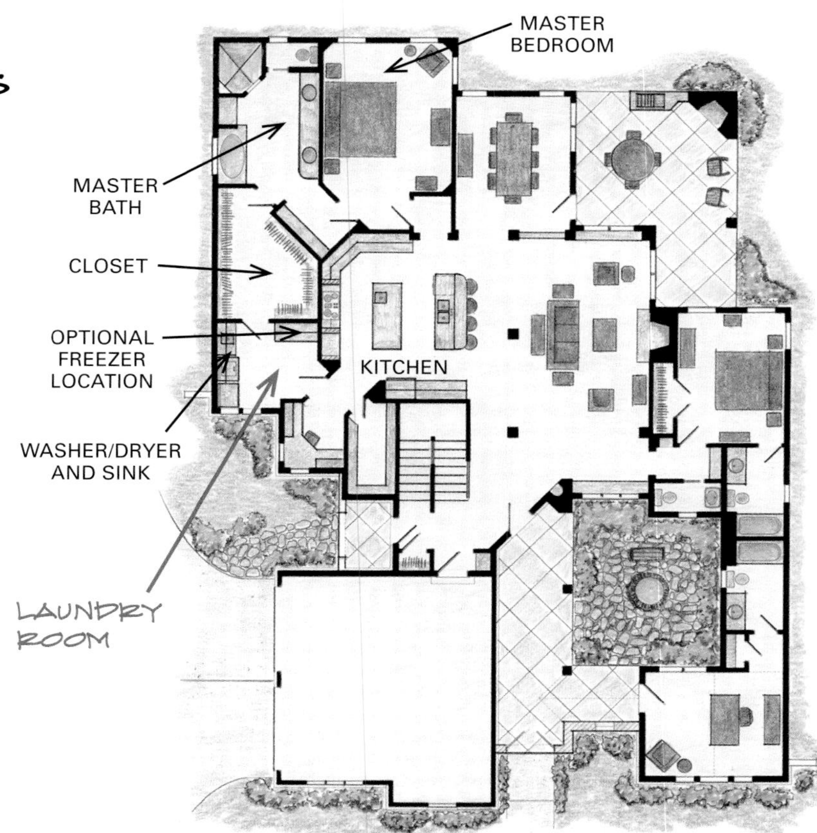

Example 1

Direct access. A door from the master closet directly into the laundry area can save a number of steps each day. This design also provides convenient access to the kitchen from the utility room. A freezer could easily be placed in the utility room.

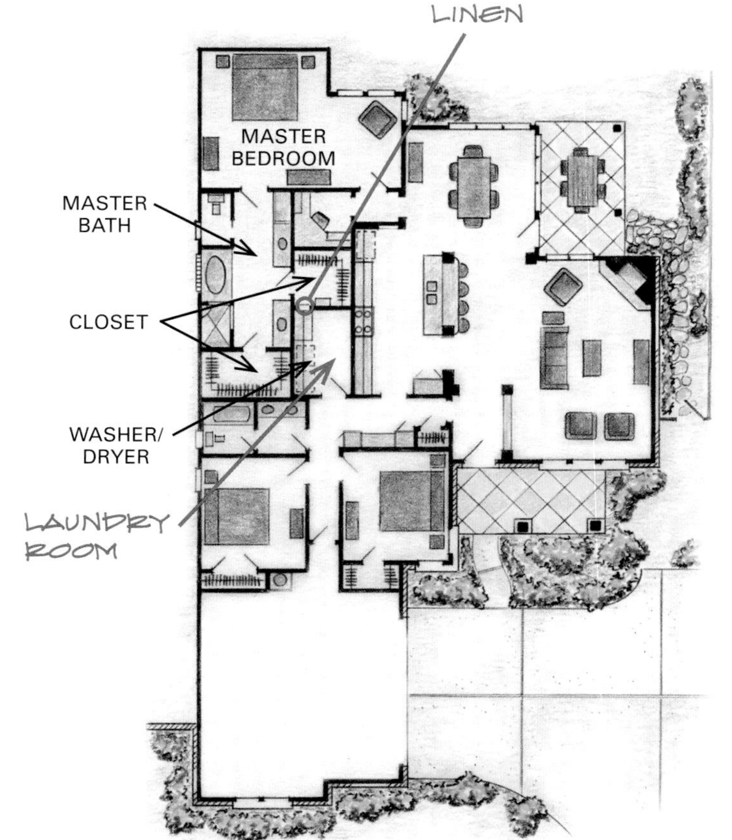

Example 2

Pass-through hamper. An alternative to placing a door between the master closet and laundry area is to add a two-way cabinet. This allows soiled and clean laundry to be exchanged between the two areas without compromising the privacy of the master bathroom. This location is also convenient to the secondary bedrooms and bath.

A word of caution here: to avoid injury of small children, be sure to place a safety latch on all laundry chutes. As an added precaution, have your builder align the chute so that it has a slight slope rather than a straight drop.

Some homeowners request a laundry room adjacent to the master bath, since a great deal of the laundry and linens originate from the master suite. A door from the master closet or bath that connects to the laundry can save a number of steps each day, especially if only adults occupy the house. However, with children still at home, this not only may prove to be inconvenient but also might become a privacy issue. Young children may particularly enjoy using this "secret passage" to their parents' bathroom!

Remember that the dryer will need an exhaust vent to the outside. This can be achieved by passing a vent up into the ceiling and then outside. However, if at all possible, locating the dryer on an outside wall will allow for much more efficient and safe ventilation. Although many of the newer appliances have been designed to operate with very little noise, noise still can be an issue. Therefore, avoid having the washer and dryer located on a wall that backs up to a bedroom or the family area.

In addition to a storage area for soiled clothes, you may want the utility room to include a place for sorting dirty laundry and folding clean laundry. This might involve

Design Diagnosis

An organized utility room

An efficiently designed utility room provides organization for cleaning supplies and plenty of counter space for laundry chores. Soiled laundry is easily sorted with the stack of bins next to the washer. Placing a window above the sink will allow for ventilation and natural light.

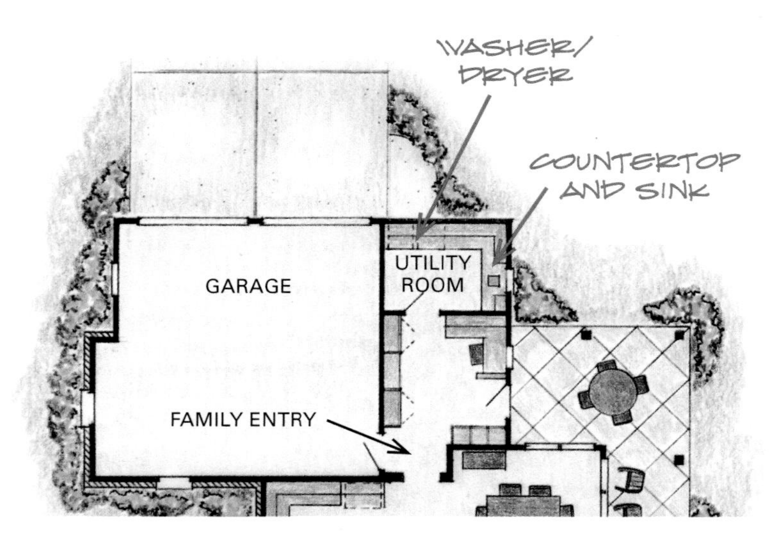

a stack of wire baskets or bins and a countertop. You may also want a sink for soaking clothes — or bathing the family pet — as well as storage spaces for the vacuum cleaner, brooms, mops, dustpans, and whatever other cleaning supplies you use.

Also consider an ironing board. While a fold-out board built into the wall offers convenient use, many people also want an old standby folding board that they can set up and use in the family room while watching television or observing the children at play.

Another logical location for ironing is near the clothing storage, so make sure you place an electrical outlet in your walk-in closet for use with the ironing board.

Quite often the utility room has enough space for a freezer. If so, a location close to the kitchen makes perfect sense. Depending on the size of your kitchen pantry, a small closet or tall cabinet in the utility room might come in handy as extra storage. The area may also double as a hobby area, sewing center, or computer alcove.

Avoid placing the utility room so that it becomes your entrance from the back door. Sure, utility rooms often double as mudrooms. However, we all know that family and friends often enter our homes through this back entrance. Save everyone the unpleasant experience of walking around the dirty laundry. *(See* Family Entry *on page 135.)*

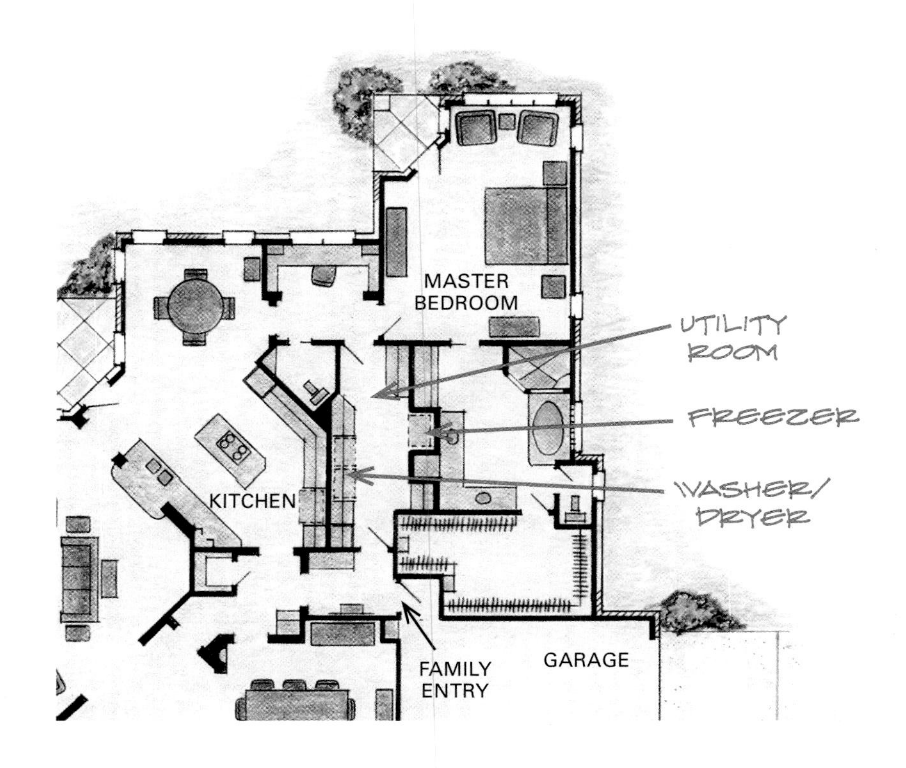

Pantry and laundry in one room. A utility room located next to the kitchen allows the option of placing a freezer and additional pantry storage in the same room with laundry facilities. With the room's two entrances, the master bedroom and garage are both convenient.

The Resource Center

While some utility rooms allow for a desk and computer, consider creating another dedicated area for these activities: a resource center. The demands of managing a household, raising children, and dealing with the requirements of our jobs create challenges for us all.

Probably the most stressful aspect of our busy lives relates directly to the lack of time available for organizing our daily affairs. A dedicated area for organizing our numerous obligations and tasks is a welcome addition to any home.

Usually located next to the kitchen and family area, a resource center not only provides a convenient location for a computer but also serves as a multifunctional place to plan daily activities, pay bills, and work on school projects. You might call it "command central." While such an area should provide enough room for a computer, telephone, and desk, it's much more than just a small home office. With file drawers, storage space for craft materials, bookshelves, mail sorting, and a corkboard for posting everything from the latest family photos and artwork to notices about upcoming events, it really is a family resource center. It can also be a place where children complete their homework while parents keep a watchful eye on their Web surfing.

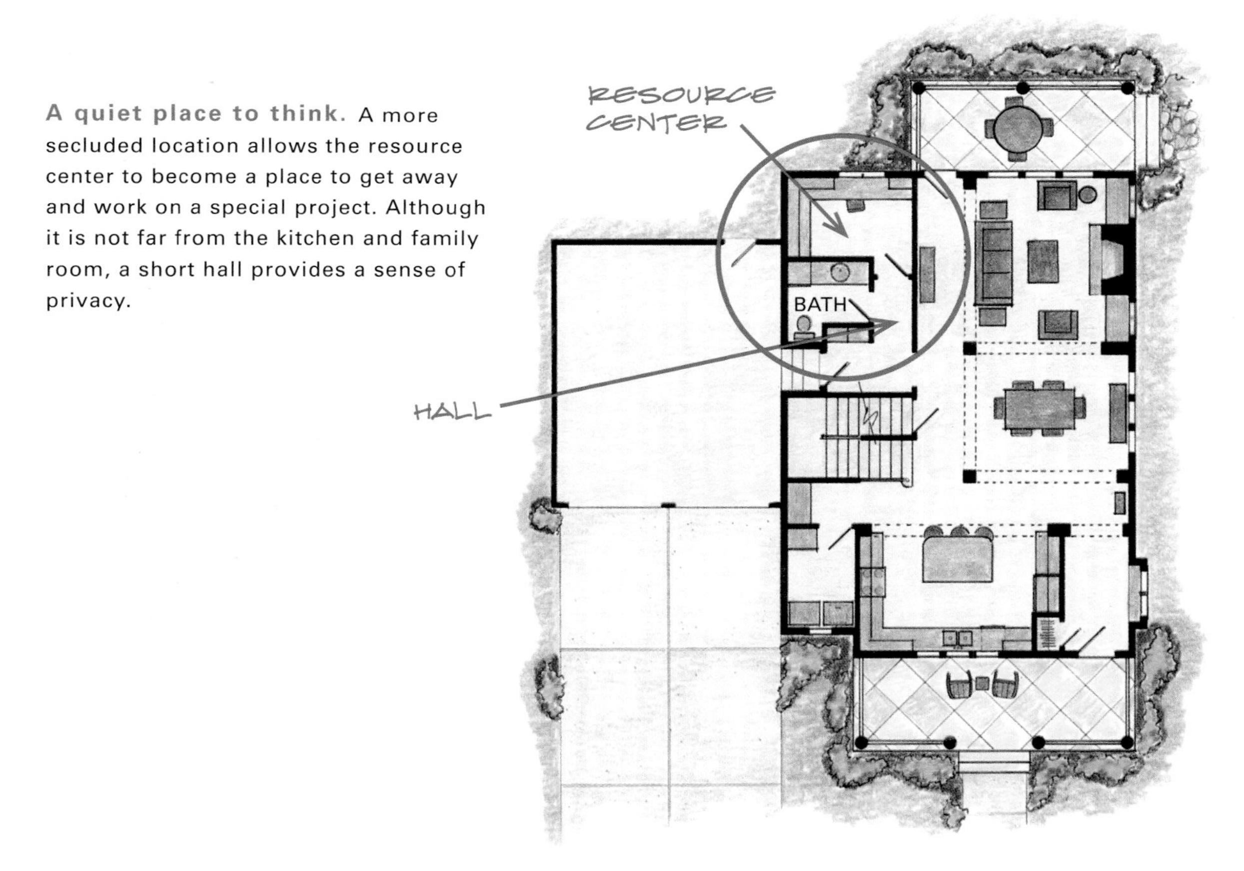

A quiet place to think. A more secluded location allows the resource center to become a place to get away and work on a special project. Although it is not far from the kitchen and family room, a short hall provides a sense of privacy.

Design Diagnosis

A convenient place to get organized

⊕ A computer and file drawers for organizing and paying bills are almost necessities these days. However, a resource center can also become an efficient and inspiring place to work on scrapbooks or other hobbies. Cabinets and drawers provide storage for supplies, while open shelves display photos, books, and other collectibles.

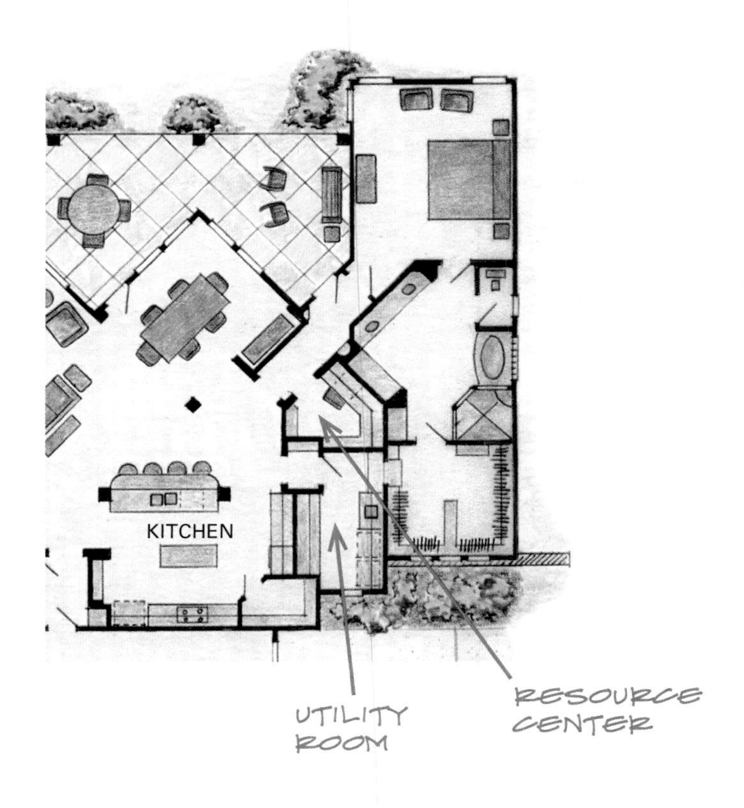

Thoughtful design and innovative cabinetry can conceal most of the clutter related to household administration:

- Install file drawers that can accommodate both letter- and legal-size folders, so that even oversize documents can be put away.
- Store printers, scanners, and other large electronic appliances on slide-out shelving to keep the desktop uncluttered.
- Use several mail slots to organize mail by category. Don't forget to leave room for a paper shredder and wastebasket for the junk mail.
- Although wireless technology seems to be rapidly replacing the need for wiring, have your builder go ahead and run all the necessary telephone and cable lines to the resource center. This will prevent future wiring clutter. It's even a good idea to run an open electrical PVC line (a plastic pipe used to hold electrical wiring) from the resource center to a mechanical room or attic just to allow for any future wiring requirements (your electrician can easily accomplish this for you).
- Designate an area for cell phones to be charged, including electrical outlets and space for the chargers.
- Install a cabinet for large poster boards and other arts and crafts supplies.
- Although open bookcases can be attractive, keep in mind that the resource center is primarily a working area. Shelves with cabinet doors will help keep clutter to a minimum.

Resource centers are just as essential in a 1,500-square-foot home as they are in a grand luxury home. Virtually all homeowners require a place to pay bills, sort mail, and organize daily tasks. Just think about the complexity of our lives and the massive amounts of confidential information we receive every day. Most people wouldn't want this information stacked on the kitchen counter.

At the risk of sounding less than objective, I urge you to give serious thought to any decision that eliminates the resource center. This is one feature that you will surely appreciate each and every day. If I'm wrong, you can always turn it into a storage closet! I've been including resource centers in the majority of my designs for the past several years. Most clients tell me this area has become one of the most appreciated features of their new home.

Design Diagnosis

Family entry into the resource center

⊕ Located next to the kitchen and utility room, this resource center is part of the family entry. A window and French door offer natural light and a view toward the rear yard. The large cork bulletin board provides space to display family photos and a calendar of upcoming events. Note the lockers adjacent to the French door, which could also be used to store craft supplies.

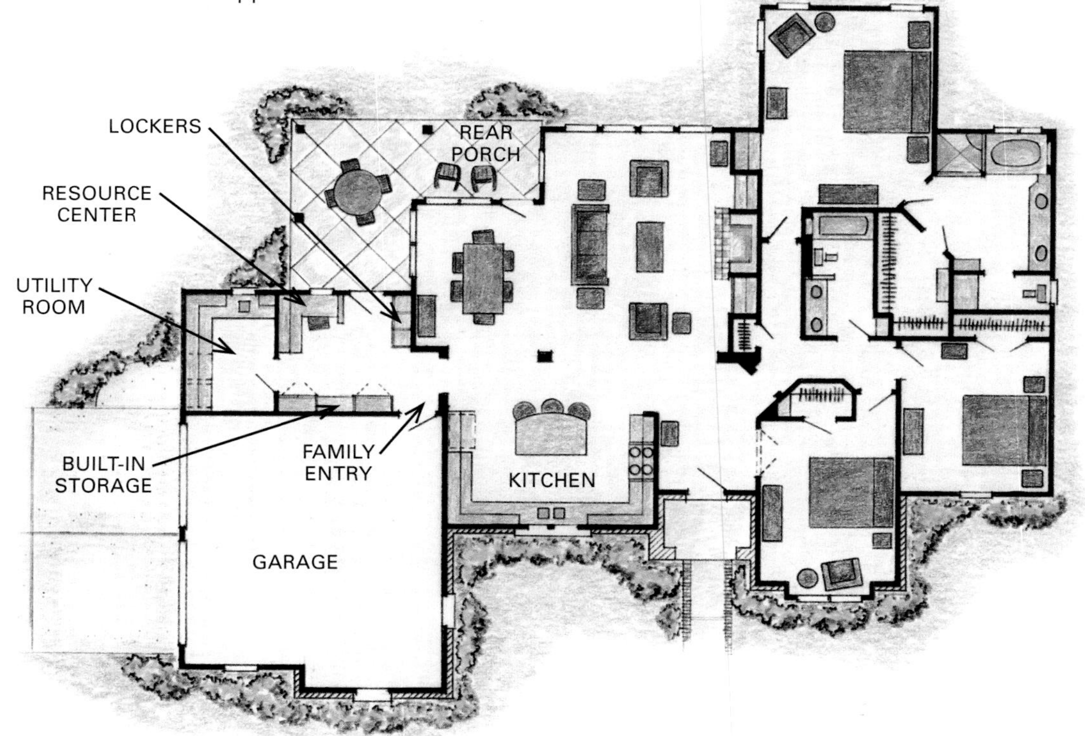

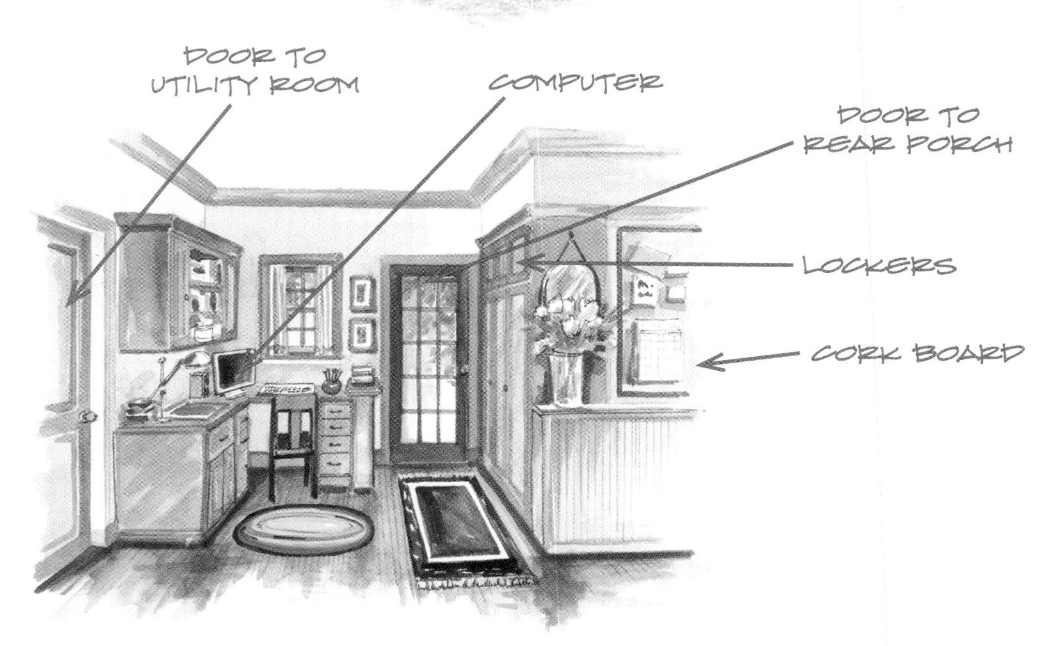

Design Diagnosis
Kitchen command center

⌖ A resource center quickly becomes the command center of the home. Conveniently located next to the kitchen, the area offers a place for a desk, computer, file drawers, and plenty of storage — everything you need to manage the household.

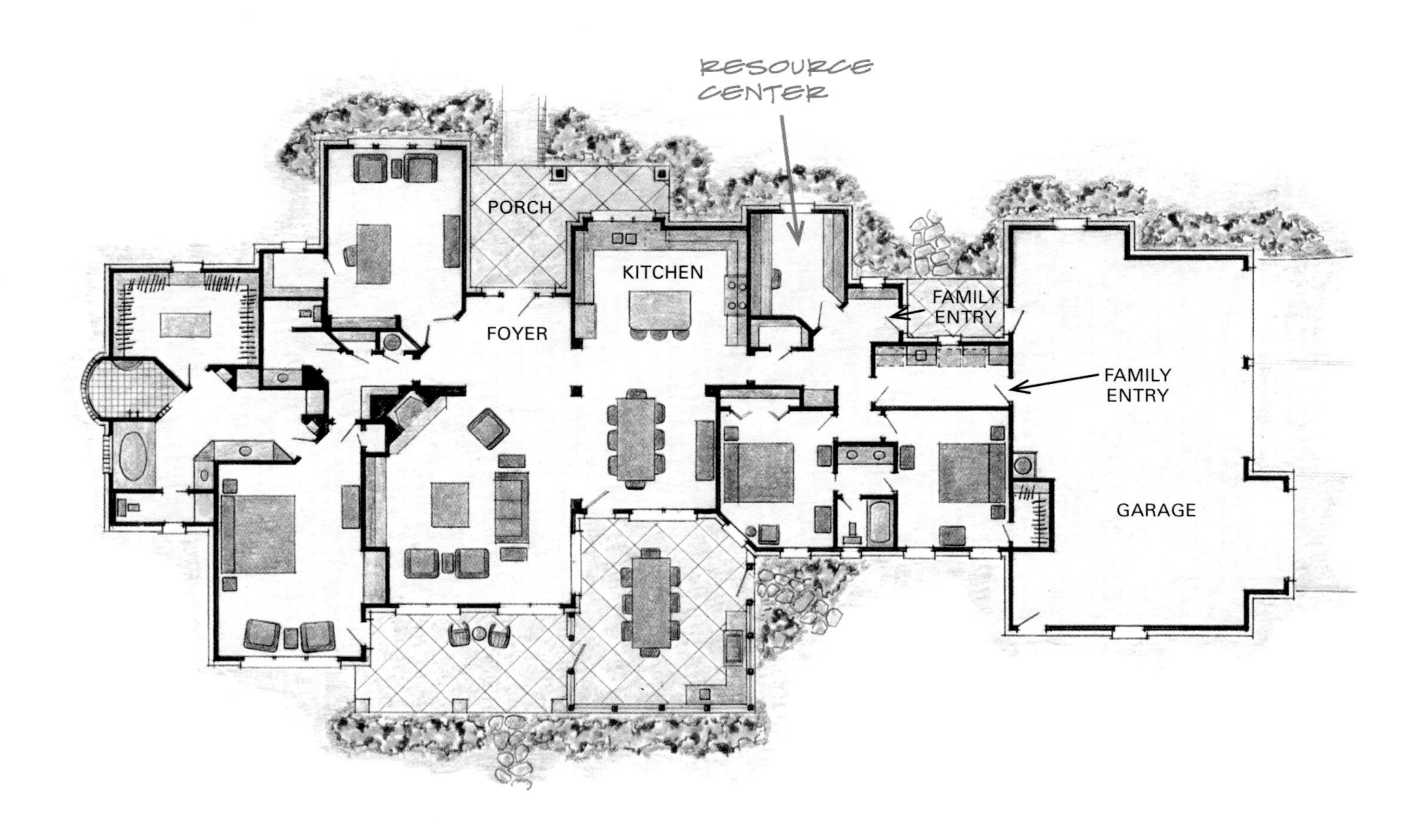

The Study

The study has been an integral part of many home plans for years. It is typically located near the foyer, and elaborate wood trim and built-in bookcases often make it one of the most impressive rooms in the home.

However, before you make an emotional choice based on how attractive the study might be, take into consideration exactly why you want this room and what activities will take place here.

For some, the study might simply be an elegant place to display books, paintings, and other works of art. If so, expensive credenzas and computer hutches will not get much use. Instead, make sure there's ample room for a couple of comfortable chairs or a small sofa. On the other hand, if you envision the study as an optional guest room, you'll need plenty of space for a pullout sofa bed and, most important, a full bath conveniently close by.

Many people plan to use their study as a retreat with a television or just a place to get away and read a book. Either way, some comfortable seating and adequate lighting will

Good light for reading. Natural light becomes a consideration for a study that will be used for reading or working at a desk. While a 10- foot vaulted ceiling such as this can emphasis the spaciousness of the room, exceptionally high ceilings may compromise the coziness.

be essential. While glass French doors add an attractive design element, you may want solid panel doors for more privacy. Double *pocket doors* that slide into the walls offer a space-saving option. If you've decided against a resource center for organizing household activities, the study will need the appropriate storage and workspace for these chores.

A growing number of people are finding the opportunity to work from their homes. Many companies, both large and small, have discovered the advantages of allowing employees to spend at least a few days of the week working at home. Most of these homebound workers rely on the Internet and overnight delivery services to accomplish their tasks.

For those who work at home, the study often becomes a home office. Although the traditional study might work fine as an office, first determine exactly what you'll need for a functional work environment. If you have clients or business associates visiting you, a location near the front door is desirable. This will allow people to enter and leave your office without intruding on the privacy of your family. The exact size of a study or office relates to its use. Any time you spend analyzing the furniture you will use can prevent major disappointments on move-in day. *(See page 110 for mapping room size and furniture placement.)*

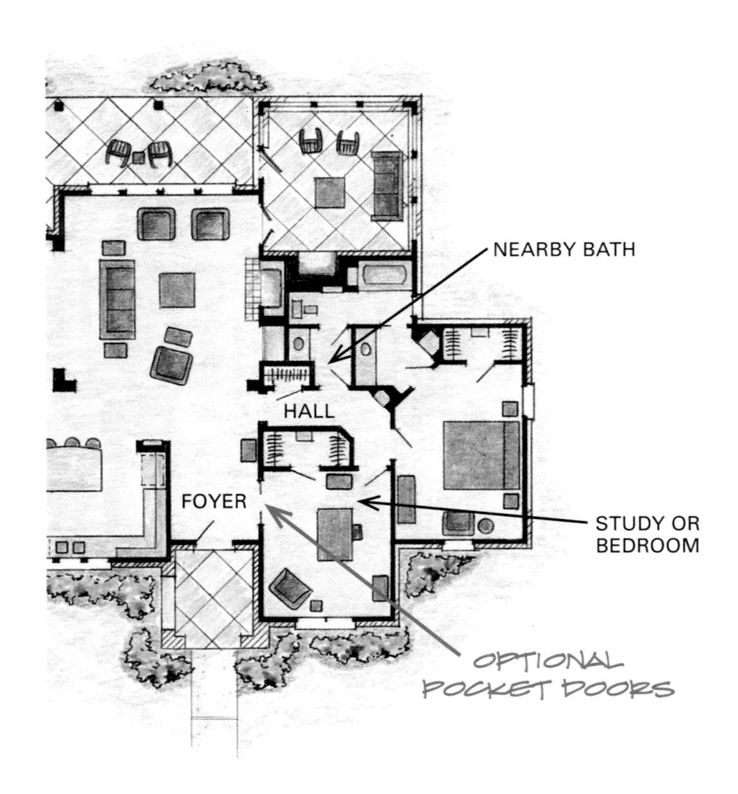

A study that doubles as a guest room. If you anticipate the study becoming an optional guest bedroom, make sure there's a full bathroom close by. In order to save space, consider using double pocket doors at the foyer entrance.

The Adaptable Casita

The original *casitas* (Spanish for "little houses") were small, crude shanties built for laborers in the Southwest. In recent years the term has been used to describe living quarters detached from the main home. These quarters tend to be flexible, adaptable spaces suitable for a wide range of uses, from a home office to guest quarters.

Locating your home office in a casita can resolve the issue of protecting your family's privacy when you interact with clients and coworkers. It can also help with the challenge of never being able to leave your work. For anyone who has ever worked at home, you know both the advantages and the disadvantages of having your office in the house. While the home office is always convenient for getting some work done, sometimes it's simply too difficult to leave work at the office when the office is in the next room.

The simple fact that a casita forces you to walk out the front door and down a covered walk to enter your office has a profound effect. The experience really becomes an act of "going to work." Another advantage is the privacy it provides.

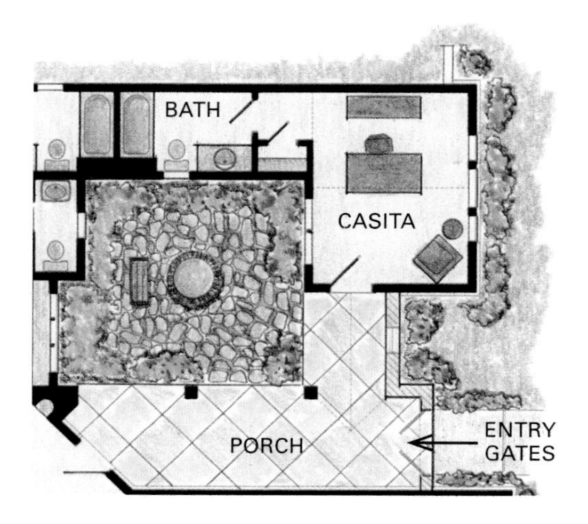

Office or hangout. A casita can be an ideal home office. It also can easily be transformed into a favorite hangout for your teenagers and their friends.

Even younger children will quickly understand the concept of a parent being unavailable when he or she is "at work" when "work" is in the next building.

Casitas have more recently been designed as often-luxurious accommodations for family members or guests. With a private bathroom and separate entrance, they maintain privacy for both the guest and the homeowner. In fact, be careful about how comfortable you make this area, or you may find that your guests overstay their welcome!

While casitas are ideal guest lodging for some homeowners, they also have diverse other uses. For a family with teenagers, the casita can serve as a game area that affords privacy for the teenagers and the parents. The teenagers will be thrilled to have the privacy of a separate building, but you'll still be able to easily monitor the situation because that building is right next to your house.

As the children eventually leave home, the casita can transform into that art studio you've always wanted, a secluded place to indulge your scrapbooking hobby, or, perhaps, a simple retreat from the house. If one of the children ends up back at home, everyone will be much happier with the privacy and seclusion the casita offers.

For many of us, the prospect of assuming the care of our parents is a real possibility. I've often had clients ask me to design living quarters over their garage for possible future use by a parent. I always remind them that, unfortunately, if one of their parents needs to live with them, he or she most likely will not be able to climb the stairs. It's hard for most of us to consider that when we're all young and healthy. The casita offers a perfect solution. With this use in mind, though, it makes sense to pay attention to universal design *(see page 131)* in the construction of the casita, making sure the doors are wide enough to accommodate a wheelchair and that the bathroom is spacious.

While casitas have traditionally been designed and built only with larger homes, you'll now find them included even in smaller-square-footage designs. The courtyard area created by these layouts offers a private outdoor living space. Unfortunately, people often ignore the importance of professional landscaping.

When adequate funds are reserved in the budget for plants, decking, and furniture, the courtyard area becomes one of the most desirable places in the home to relax and entertain.

Regardless of the purpose for which you intend to use the casita, be sure to address the question of air conditioning and heating with your builder. A zoned system that allows a separate thermostat for the casita is essential. This will allow whoever is occupying the casita to adjust the temperature as necessary there, and not be tied to the heating and cooling requirements of the larger house. In addition, when the casita is not occupied, you can reduce its heating and cooling requirements, thereby conserving energy and costs.

Privacy for family and guests. Casitas are uniquely flexible areas just waiting to respond to each homeowner's particular lifestyle. For some it's the ideal guest suite or housing for an older child returning home to stay for a while.

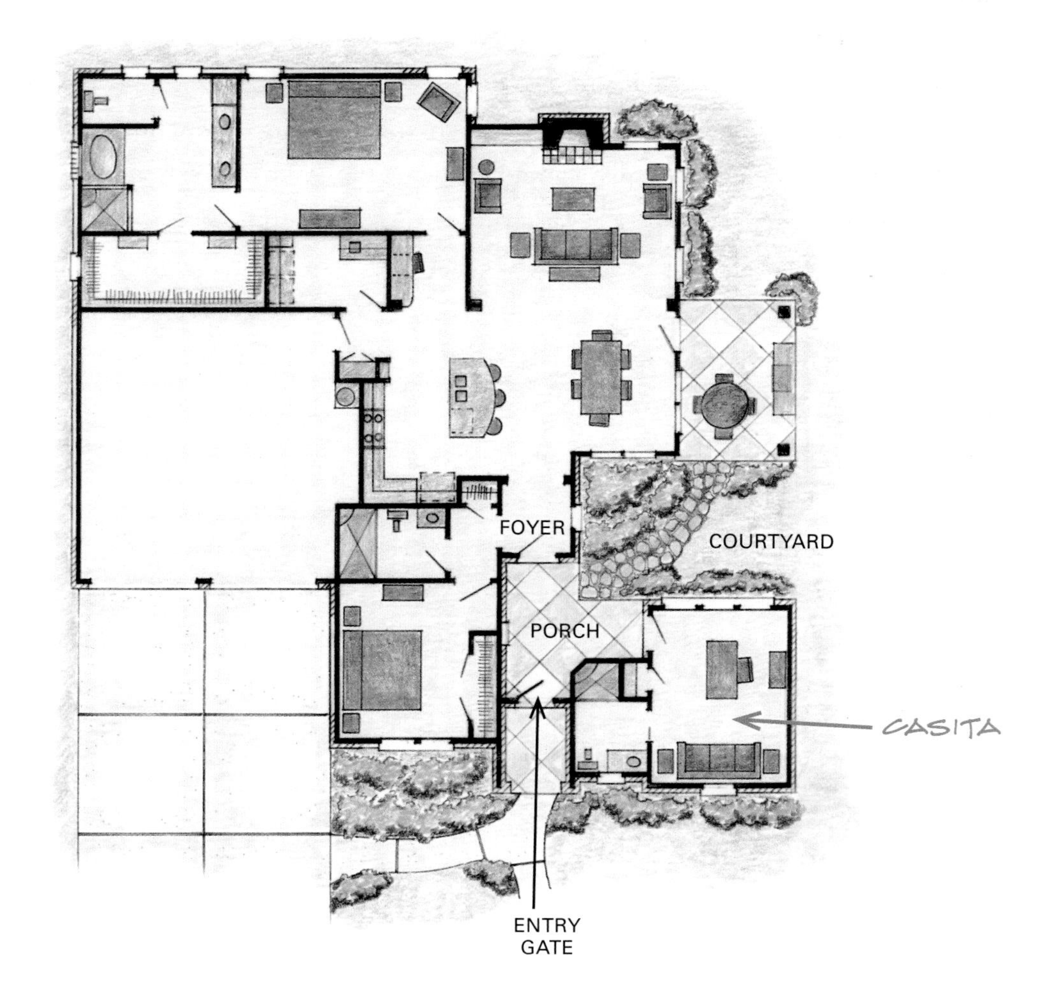

HEALTHY EXAMPLES

Casita options

Example 1

Walk to work. Since a casita-based home office is detached, clients and business associates can visit without actually entering your home. There's another benefit: you can leave your home each morning and walk to work. Even though the distance is short, the idea of leaving the office in the afternoon often makes working at home a more successful situation.

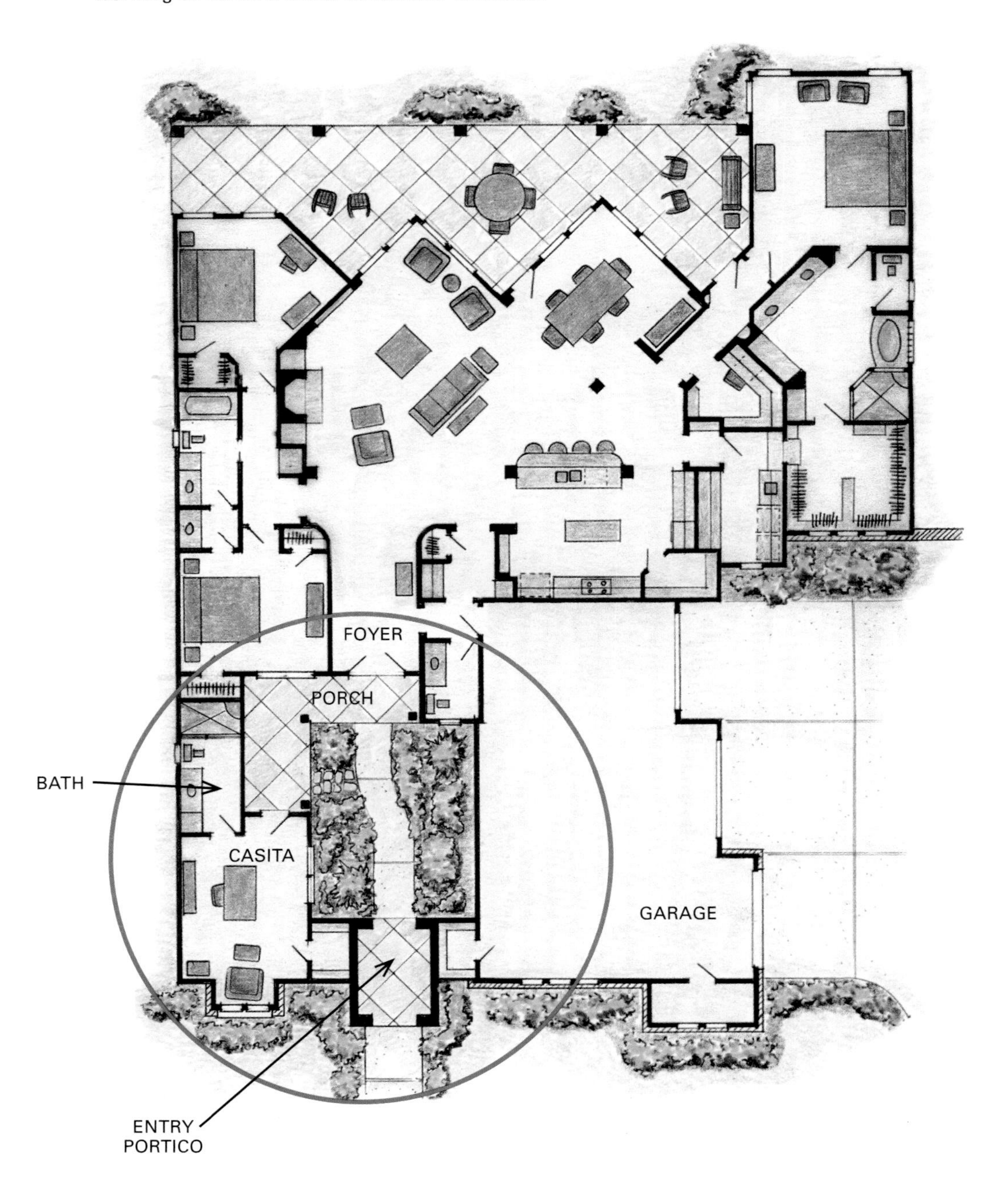

Example 2

⊕ **Accommodate elderly parents.** Even with smaller homes a casita can be a welcome flexible space. For elderly homeowners these private quarters might be used for a live-in caretaker. For other homeowners, these quarters might become home to elderly parents. For still others, the area is simply a secluded retreat overlooking a private courtyard.

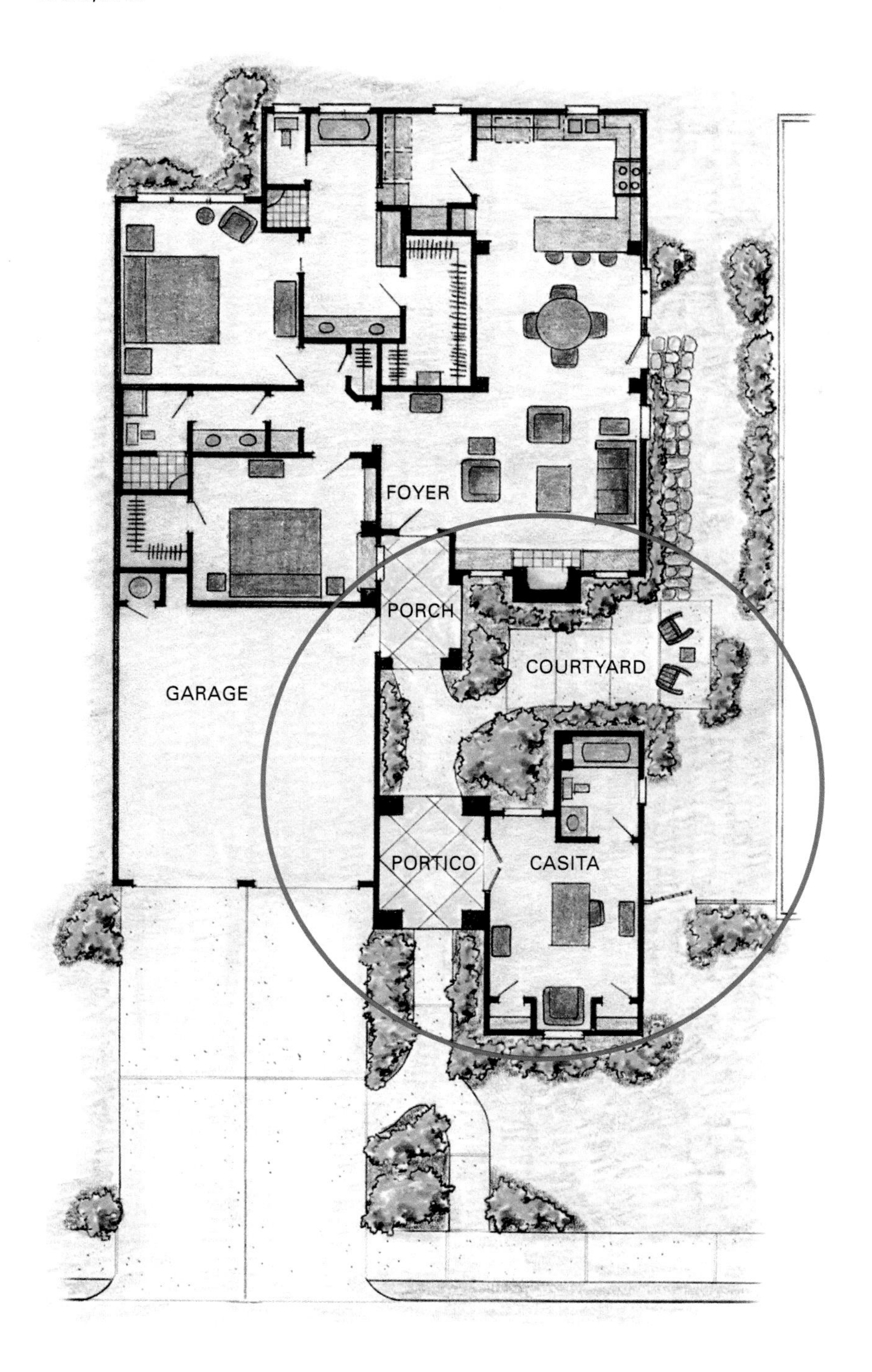

Appendix

This appendix contains two forms that you might find useful.

The **Design Criteria** form will allow you to organize the essential information you'll want to present to your designer or architect as you begin the process of creating a custom design. Even if you've decided to search for a pre-designed stock plan or a conceptual design, the exercise of answering these questions should prove valuable in helping you determine the specifics you want in your new home.

The **Stock Plan Customization Form** will help you determine and specify the various modifications you hope to make on a stock plan or conceptual design that you've already purchased. You might also find this form convenient for outlining the scope of a remodeling project.

Feel free to copy these forms or go online to www.homeplandoctor.com to download them.

Design Criteria

Family Information

Name ____________________

Spouse's name ____________________

Children's names & ages ____________________

____

Contact Information

Address ____________________

Telephone (home) ____________________

(office) ____________________

(cell) ____________________

(fax) ____________________

E-mail ____________________

Property Location

Address ____________________

____

About Our New Home

For the following questions, provide short answers or "yes" or "no."

Interior

Approximate square footage (living area): ______

____

1-story or 2-story: ____________________

Number of bedrooms (including master bedroom): ____________________

Master bedroom location (1st or 2nd floor): ______

____

Will one of the bedrooms be used as a guest room?

____

If so, does it need to be on the 1st floor?

____

Master bath:

Shower (size, doorless?): ____________________

Whirlpool tub (5' or 6'): ____________________

Closets (his-and-her walk-in closets?): ______

Secondary baths:

Full or half? ____________________

Accessible from the outside? ____________________

Typical ceiling height: ____________________

Universal design (barrier free) elements:

____

____

____

Rooms

Check all that apply and write a brief description of features, including special ceiling heights.

☐ Kitchen: ______________________________

____

☐ Formal dining room or ☐ One large dining area: ______________________________

____

☐ Breakfast room: ______________________________

____

☐ Family room: ______________________________

____

☐ Formal living room: ______________________________

____

☐ Study/library: ______________________________

____

☐ Media room/home theater: ______________________________

____

☐ Master bedroom: ______________________________

____

☐ Master bath: ______________________________

____

☐ Secondary bedrooms: ______________________________

____

☐ Secondary baths: ______________________________

____

☐ Utility/laundry room: ______________________________

____

☐ Family entry: ______________________________

____

☐ Resource center: ______________________________

____

☐ Game room: ______________________________

____

☐ Home office: ______________________________

____

☐ Garage: ___ Attached or ___ Detached   Number of cars: _____

Garage door sizes: ________________ Storage area (size): __________________

Work bench: ____

Exterior

Wall material (select one or more for combination):

☐ Brick

☐ Stone

☐ Stucco

☐ Siding

__ cement board

__ vinyl

__ cedar shake

__ other: ________________________________

Windows

☐ Vinyl

☐ Clad wood

Exterior wall framing

☐ 2×4

☐ 2×6

Roofing

☐ Composition

☐ Tile

☐ Metal

☐ Other

Foundation

☐ Concrete slab

☐ Crawl space

☐ Basement (full)

☐ Basement (walk-out)

Porches

☐ Front

☐ Rear

Comments: ____

____

____

____

____

____

____

____

____

____

____

Stock Plan Customization Form

Plan Number: ________________

Designer or Architect: ______________________________

Authorization to revise and/or redraw plans:

____ Enclosed

____ Attached to plans

____ I have already purchased this plan

____ I plan to purchase this plan

Existing square footage	Estimated revised square footage
Living area: ________ sq. ft.	________ sq. ft.
Garage: ________ sq. ft.	________ sq. ft.
Porches: ________ sq. ft.	________ sq. ft.

Interior

Requested modifications: check all that apply and write a brief description of changes

☐ Kitchen: ____________________

☐ Formal dining room: ____________________

☐ Informal dining (breakfast): ____________________

☐ Family room: ____________________

☐ Living room: ____________________

☐ Study: ____________________

☐ Media room: ____________________

☐ Family entry: ____________________

☐ Foyer: ____________________

☐ Master Bedroom: ____________________

☐ Bedroom 2: ____________________

☐ Bedroom 3: ____________________

☐ Bedroom 4: ____________________

☐ Resource center: ____________________

☐ Master bath: ____________________

☐ Bath 2: ____________________

☐ Bath 3: ____________________

☐ Half bath: ____________________

☐ Utility room: ____________________

- ☐ Game room: ______________________
____
- ☐ Home office: ______________________
____
- ☐ Garage (number of cars): ______________________
____
- ☐ Other: ______________________
____
- ☐ Other: ______________________
____
- ☐ Other: ______________________
____

Exterior

Wall material (select one or more for combination):

- ☐ Brick ☐ Stucco
- ☐ Stone ☐ Siding
  - __ cement board
  - __ vinyl
  - __ cedar shake
  - __ other: ______________________

Windows

Describe any specific changes: ______________________
____

Exterior wall framing

- ☐ 2×4 @ 16" oc
- ☐ 2×6 @ 16" oc

Ceiling heights ______________

Roofing

- ☐ Composition ☐ Metal
- ☐ Tile ☐ Other

Foundation

- ☐ Concrete slab
- ☐ Crawl space
- ☐ Basement (full)
- ☐ Basement (walk-out)

Porches

- ☐ Add front porch
- ☐ Change front porch
  Describe: ______________________
____
- ☐ Add rear porch
- ☐ Add rear screened porch

☐ Convert plan to universal (barrier-free) design

Comments: ______________________
____
____

Your name ______________________ Spouse's name ______________________

Children ______________________

Contact Information

Mailing address ______________________

City, State, Zip ______________________

Telephone: home ______________________ other ______________________

E-mail address ______________________

Location of building site ______________________

Resources

Helpful Organizations

American Institute of Building Design (AIBD)
www.aibd.org
For a list of qualified AIBD designers in your area

American Institute of Architects (AIA)
www.aia.org
For a list of registered architects

The Center for Universal Design
www.design.ncsu.edu/cud
For information regarding universal design

Congress of Residential Architecture (CORA)
www.corarchitecture.org
Dedicated to the improvement of residential architecture by promoting dialogue between homeowners, builders, and designers

The Design Linc
www.designlinc.com
Offers design tips and links to other related products for creating accessible environments

U.S. Green Building Council
www.usgbc.org
Works to transform the way buildings and communities are designed, built, and operated; envisions an environmentally responsible, healthy, and prosperous environment that improves the quality of life

Home Plan Sources

Garlinghouse Company
www.familyhomeplans.com
Design plans for many types of living spaces

HDA Inc.
www.houseplansandmore.com
Design plans for many types of architectural styles

Home Plan Doctor
www.homeplandoctor.com
Offers links to various stock plan sources, along with a selection of conceptual designs

Home Plans
Move Inc.
www.homeplans.com
Home plan customization services

Traditional Neighborhood Development

New Urbanism
www.newurbanism.org
Provides a history of New Urbanism and information regarding sustainable construction

Congress for the New Urbanism
www.cnu.org
Defines and discusses the essential qualities of urban places

Town Paper
www.tndtownpaper.com
A newspaper offering up-to-date information on Traditional Neighborhood Developments

TND Homes
www.tndhomes.com
Offers numerous links to relevant Web sites along with a selection of building/plans

Transit Oriented Development (TOD)
www.transitorienteddevelopment.org
Information on creating compact, walkable communities centered around high quality train systems, making it possible to live a higher quality life without complete dependence on a car for mobility and survival

Interior Design

Artist
Sandra LaMarche/McCarthy
www.sandralamarche.com
An award-winning graphic designer, artist, and webmaster

Acknowledgments

Several years ago, after my presentation to a group of young people about careers in architecture, a young man blurted out in amazement, "You mean you get *paid* to draw pictures of houses?" I simply smiled and replied, "Yes." After all, that *is* what I do.

My passion for drawing began at an early age when my mother patiently showed me how to sketch everything from animals to space ships. Although my ability was far from exceptional, she always provided the encouragement and praise that inspired me to refine my skills. I credit both of my parents for my initial interest in houses. I recall numerous Sunday afternoons spent touring new homes and listening to my mother point out the features of each plan.

While in college, I developed an interest in writing. Now, after almost thirty years of being paid to "draw pictures of houses," I find myself also being paid to write about them! Certainly, thanks are in order.

First thanks go to my wife, Debbie, who has offered her unconditional support throughout my career. If not for her patience and understanding during my many late-night writing sessions, this book would never have materialized.

I must also thank two young men who worked in my office for several years. Steve and Gary Iltis have always inspired me with their talent and work ethic. Many of the ideas in this book are a direct result of our conversations about home design.

Thanks also go to a truly talented artist, Sandra LaMarche/McCarthy, for her wonderful watercolor illustrations of home interiors found in this book.

Special thanks must be given to the editors and staff at Storey Publishing for their careful guidance and enthusiasm; to Deborah Balmuth, for her initial interest in the project; to Pam Art, who believed in this book enough to move forward; to Mary Velgos for her talent and insight in creating the page design and layout; to Jayme Hummer, for publicizing the book; and to Jessica Richard for keeping me informed throughout the process. Finally, to Nancy Wood, I offer my sincere thanks for her never-ending patience with a rookie author. Even more important, her critical analysis of the content has resulted in a book that far surpasses my original manuscript.

Conceptual Plan Index

To obtain the full conceptual plans for the examples illustrated in this book, please go to www.homeplandoctor.com and request the appropriate plan number, using the following list as a guide.

For the illustration on page	Request plan number
6	LWG-2113-CP
8 (top)	LWG-3750-CP
8 (bottom)	LWG-3245-CP
10	LWG-1402-CP
39 (top)	LWG-2425-CP
39 (bottom)	LWG-2405-CP
40	LWG-2405-CP
43	LWG-2550-CP
44	LWG-2113-CP
46	LWG-2975-CP
47 (top)	LWG-1765-CP
47 (bottom)	LWG-1660-CP
51	LWG-2425-CP
53	LWG-2113-CP
54	LWG-3369-CP
55	LWG-3370-CP
56	LWG-2630-CP
58	LWG-1600-CP
59 (top)	LWG-1960-CP
59 (bottom)	LWG-2160-CP
61	LWG-2405-CP
62	LWG-1830-CP
63	LWG-1538-CP
71 (top)	LWG-1995-CP
71 (bottom)	LWG-2505-CP
73 (top)	LWG-2750-CP
73 (bottom)	LWG-2885-CP
75 (top)	LWG-1430-CP
75 (bottom)	LWG-1790-CP
79	LWG-2550-CP
81	LWG-2830-CP
82	LWG-1362-CP
83	LWG-2630-CP
87	LWG-1600-CP
88	LWG-2630-CP
92	LWG-1885-CP
93 (top)	LWG-1996-CP
93 (bottom)	LWG-2471-B-CP
95	LWG-1362-CP
96	LWG-3160-CP
97	LWG-2160-CP
98	LWG-2425-CP
99	LWG-2997-CP
103	LWG-3160-CP
104	LWG-1402-CP
106	LWG-2630-CP
107	LWG-2471-B-CP
108 (top)	LWG-2997-CP
108 (bottom)	LWG-1886-CP
121 (top)	LWG-2471-B-CP
121 (bottom)	LWG-2160-CP
122	LWG-2630-CP
124 (left)	LWG-3750-CP
124 (right)	LWG-2113-CP
125	LWG-2070-CP
126	LWG-3370-CP
127	LWG-2405-CP
129	LWG-2215-CP
132	LWG-1830-CP
137	LWG-3160-CP
138 (top)	LWG-2405-CP
138 (bottom)	LWG-2997-CP
139	LWG-2160-CP
140	LWG-2630-CP
141	LWG-2113-CP
143 (top)	LWG-2471-CP
143 (bottom)	LWG-3160-CP
145	LWG-3160-CP
147	LWG-2471-CP
148	LWG-2630-CP
152	LWG-2405-CP
153 (top)	LWG-2630-CP
153 (bottom)	LWG-3160-CP
154	LWG-2425-CP
156 (top)	LWG-2630-CP
156 (bottom)	LWG-1402-CP
158 (top)	LWG-1362-CP
158 (bottom)	LWG-2405-CP
159	LWG-1960-CP
160	LWG-3160-CP
165	LWG-2471-CP
166	LWG-2723-CP
167	LWG-2997-CP
169	LWG-2405-CP
170	LWG-2070-CP
171	LWG-2185-CP
172	LWG-2750-CP
175 (top)	LWG-2750-CP
175 (bottom)	LWG-2975-CP
176	LWG-3370-CP
177	LWG-2630-CP
178	LWG-3160-CP
180	LWG-2975-CP
181	LWG-1996-CP
182	LWG-4090-CP
183	LWG-2750-CP
185 (top)	LWG-2997-CP
185 (bottom)	LWG-2160-CP
186	LWG-2113-CP
187	LWG-3369-CP
188	LWG-2405-CP
189	LWG-2630-CP
191	LWG-2113-CP
192	LWG-3160-CP
194	LWG-2425-CP
195	LWG-2997-CP
197	LWG-2005-CP
198	LWG-2885-CP
199	LWG-1660-CP

General Index

Page numbers in *italics* indicate illustrations.

T

U

V

W

Z

Other Storey Titles You Will Enjoy

Be Your Own House Contractor, by Carl Heldmann.
The book to help you save 25 percent on building your own home — without lifting a hammer!
176 pages. Paper. ISBN 978-1-58017-840-2.

Build a Classic Timber-Framed House, by Jack A. Sobon.
Complete instructions and plans for building a hall-and-parlor home.
208 pages. Paper. ISBN 978-0-88266-841-3.

Build Your Own Low-Cost Log Home, by Roger Hard.
Instructions, illustrations, photographs, tables, and charts to create the house of your dreams.
200 pages. Paper. ISBN 978-0-88266-399-9.

The Classic Hewn-Log House, by Charles McRaven.
From hewing the first log to laying the last chimney stone, this covers every aspect of hewn-log construction and restoration.
208 pages. Paper. ISBN 978-1-58017-590-6.

The Outdoor Shower, by Ethan Fierro.
Designs and material inspirations for a variety of outdoor showers, from the simple to the elaborate.
144 pages. Paper. ISBN 978-1-58017-552-4.

Step-by-Step Outdoor Stonework, edited by Mike Lawrence.
More than 20 easy-to-build projects, illustrated with drawings and color photographs.
96 pages. Paper. ISBN 978-0-88266-891-8.

Stone Primer, by Charles McRaven.
The essential guide for homeowners who want to add the elegance of stone, inside and out.
272 pages. Paper. ISBN 978-1-58017-670-5.
Hardcover with jacket. ISBN 978-1-58017-666-9.